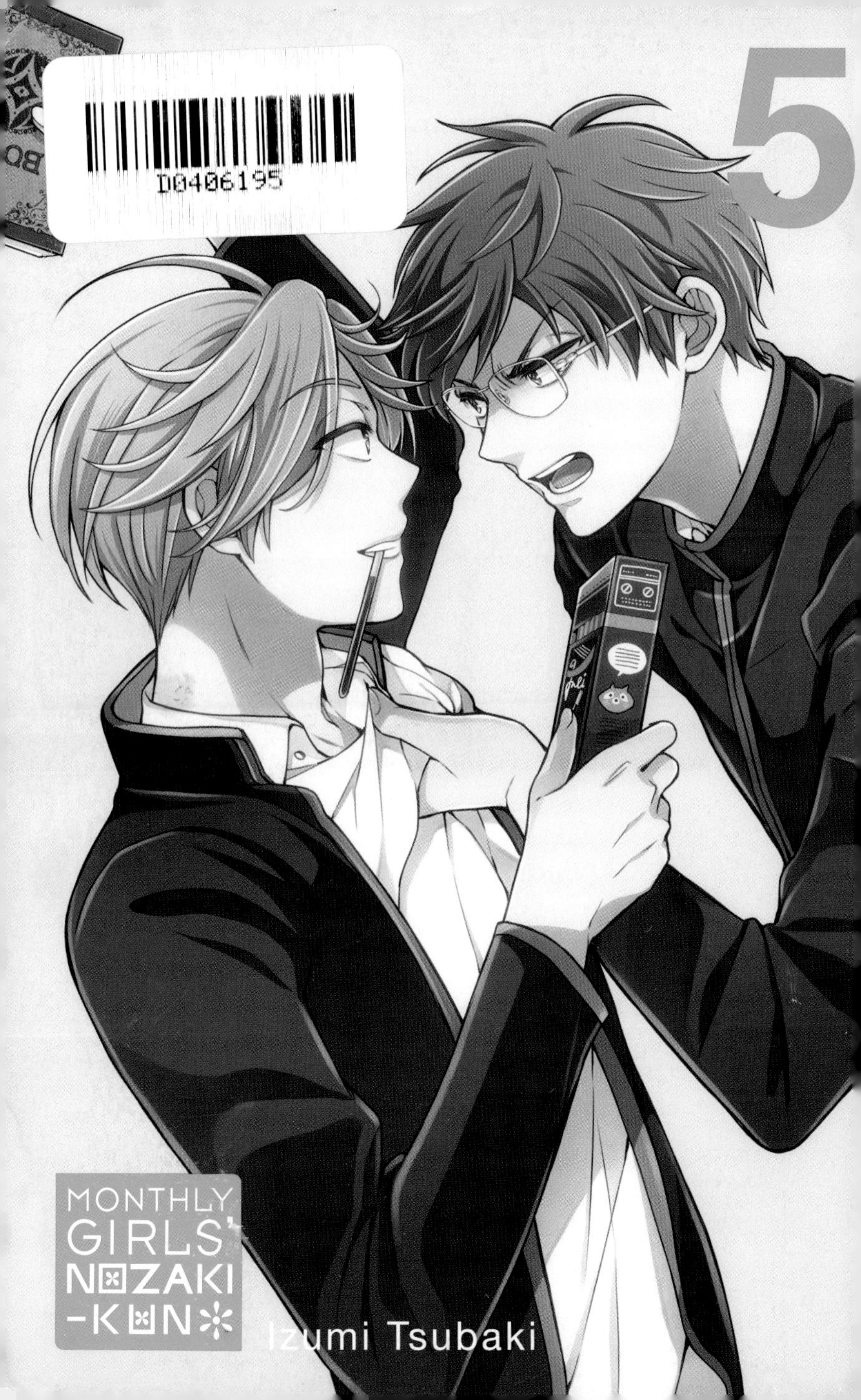

5

MONTHLY GIRLS' NOZAKI-KUN

Izumi Tsubaki

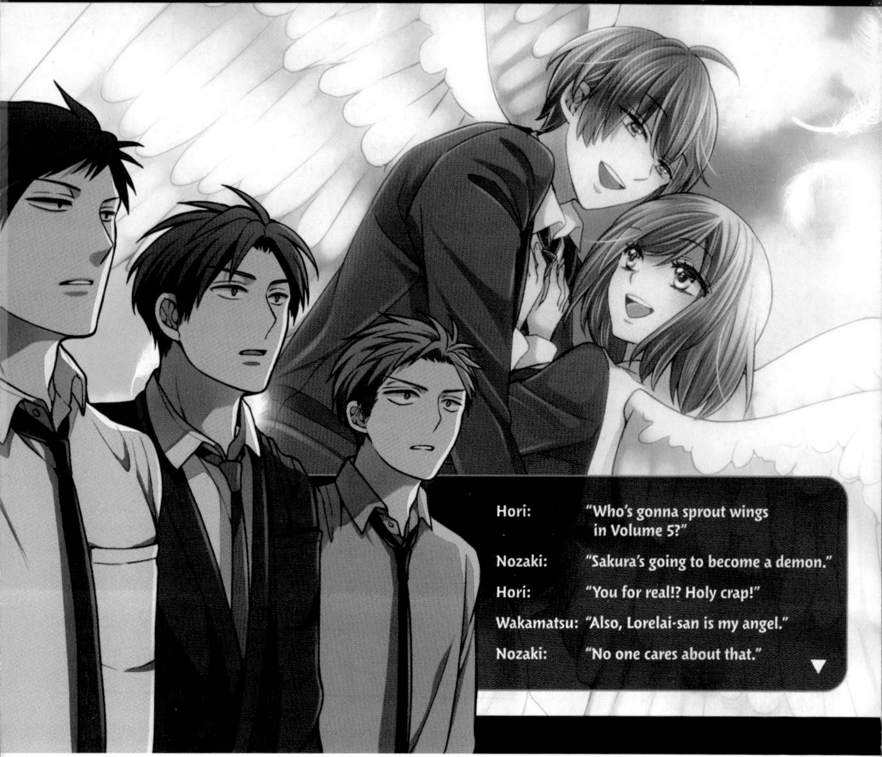
Hori: "Who's gonna sprout wings in Volume 5?"
Nozaki: "Sakura's going to become a demon."
Hori: "You for real!? Holy crap!"
Wakamatsu: "Also, Lorelai-san is my angel."
Nozaki: "No one cares about that."

MONTHLY GIRLS' NOZAKI-KUN 5

contents

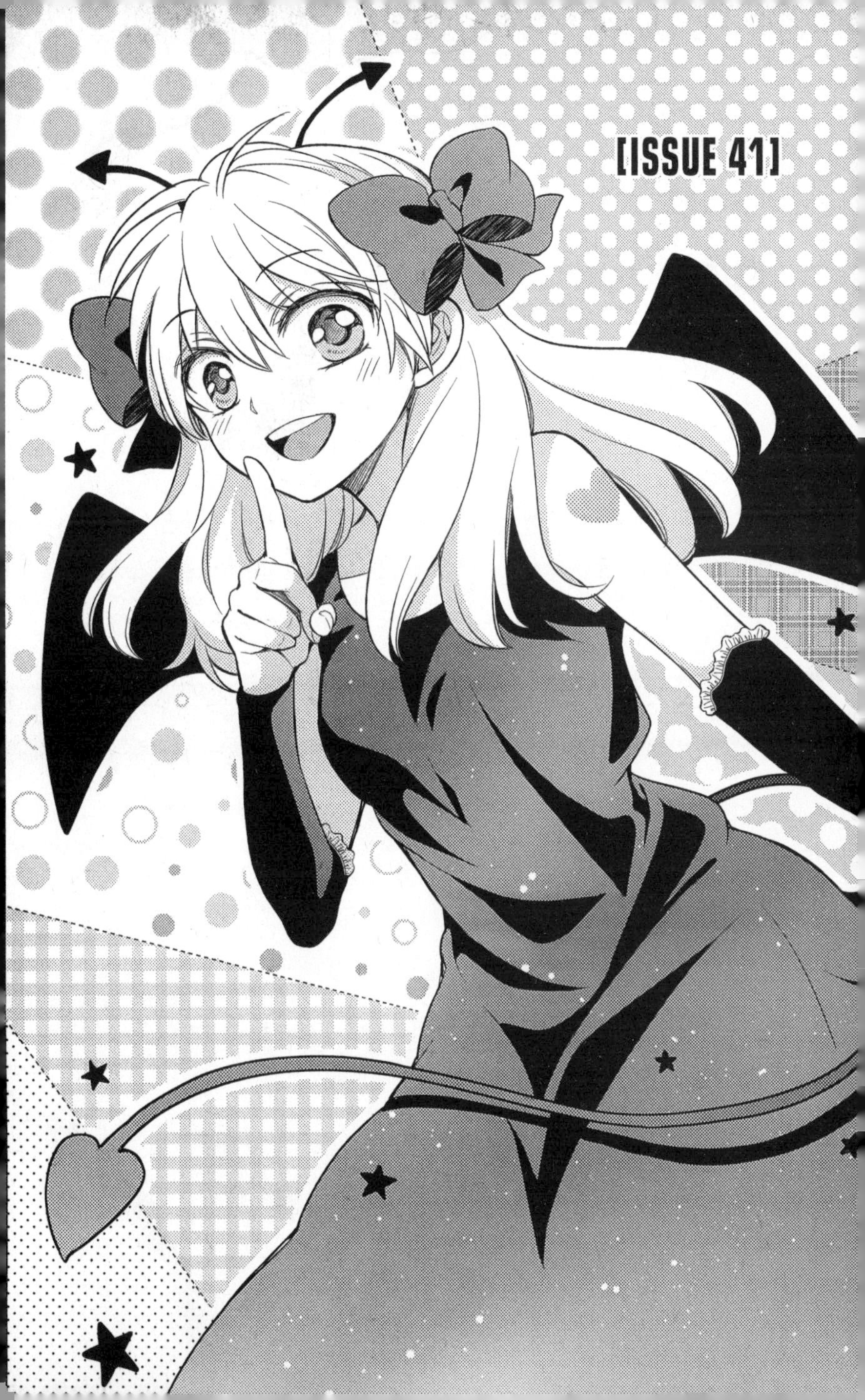
[ISSUE 41]

BECAUSE SHE'S DILIGENT

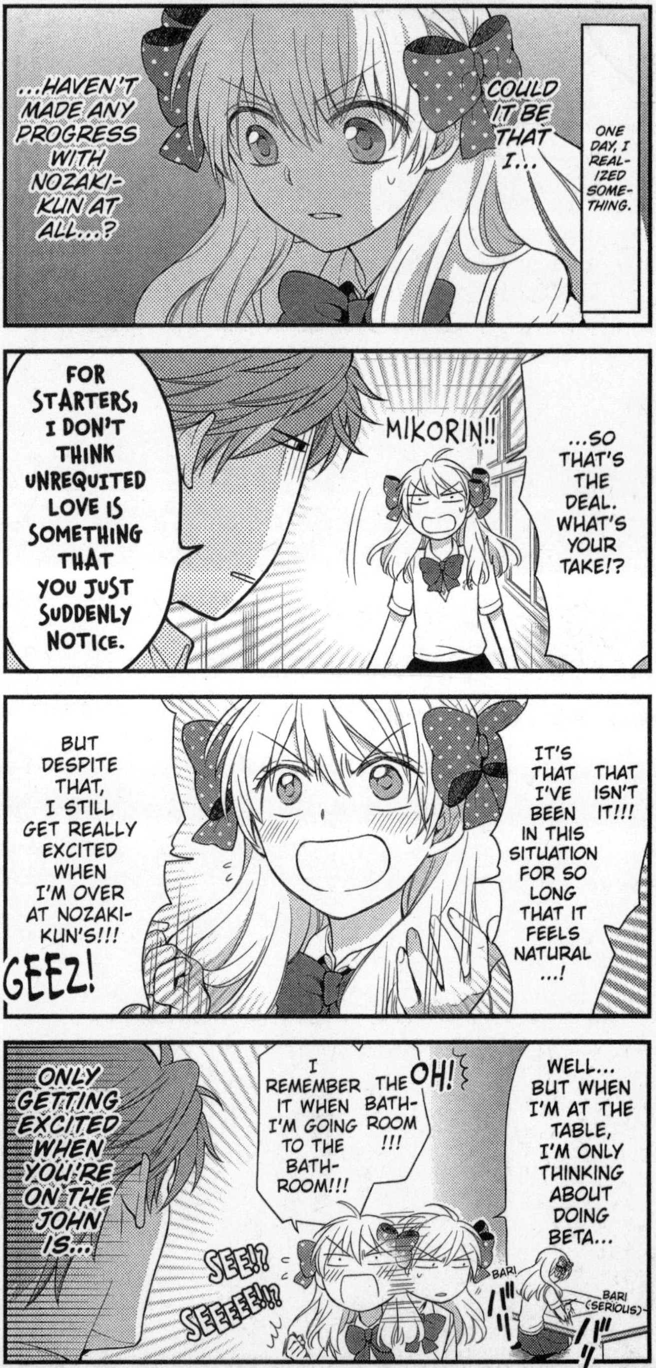
ONE DAY, I REALIZED SOMETHING.
COULD IT BE THAT I...
...HAVEN'T MADE ANY PROGRESS WITH NOZAKI-KUN AT ALL...?
...SO THAT'S THE DEAL. WHAT'S YOUR TAKE!?
MIKORIN!!
FOR STARTERS, I DON'T THINK UNREQUITED LOVE IS SOMETHING THAT YOU JUST SUDDENLY NOTICE.
THAT ISN'T IT!!!
IT'S THAT I'VE BEEN IN THIS SITUATION FOR SO LONG THAT IT FEELS NATURAL...!
BUT DESPITE THAT, I STILL GET REALLY EXCITED WHEN I'M OVER AT NOZAKI-KUN'S!!!
GEEZ!
WELL... BUT WHEN I'M AT THE TABLE, I'M ONLY THINKING ABOUT DOING BETA...
BARI
BARI (SERIOUS)
OH!
THE BATHROOM!!!
I REMEMBER IT WHEN I'M GOING TO THE BATHROOM!!!
SEE!?
SEEEEE!!?
ONLY GETTING EXCITED WHEN YOU'RE ON THE JOHN IS...!

BECAUSE THEY'VE GOTTEN CLOSE

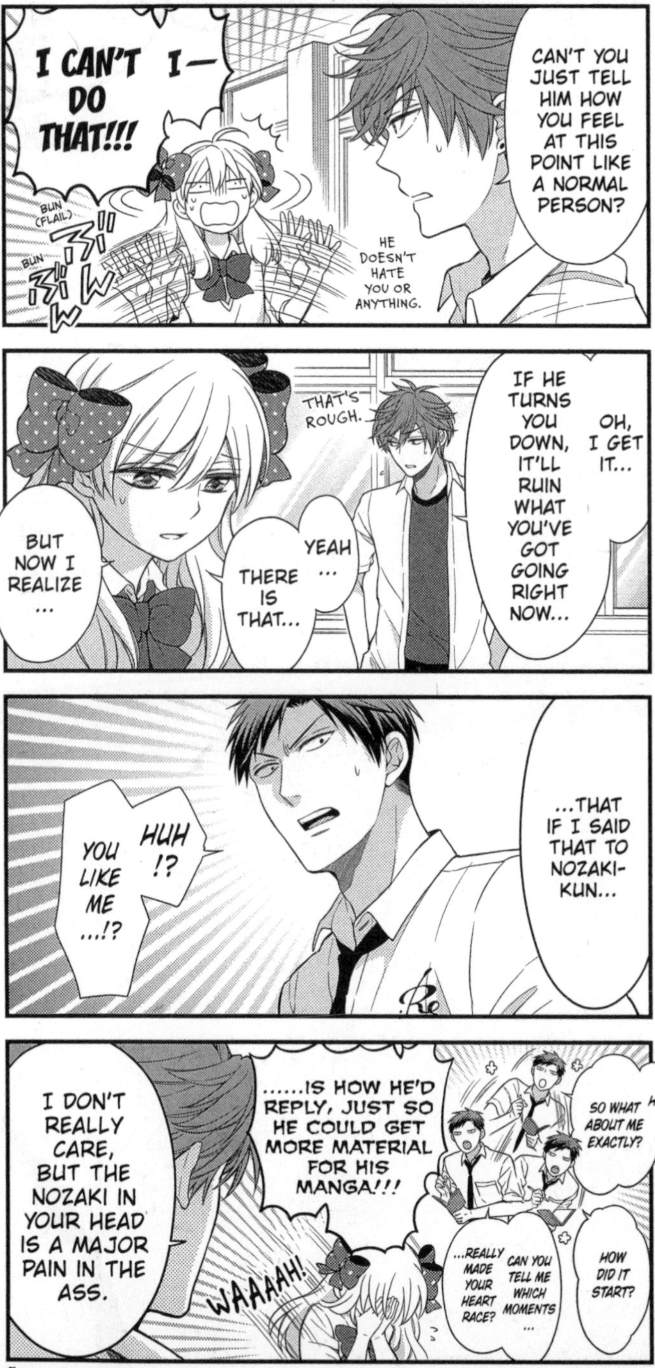
CAN'T YOU JUST TELL HIM HOW YOU FEEL AT THIS POINT LIKE A NORMAL PERSON?
HE DOESN'T HATE YOU OR ANYTHING.
I— I CAN'T DO THAT!!!
BUN (FLAIL)
BUN
IF HE TURNS YOU DOWN, IT'LL RUIN WHAT YOU'VE GOT GOING RIGHT NOW...
OH, I GET IT...
THAT'S ROUGH.
YEAH ...
THERE IS THAT...
BUT NOW I REALIZE ...
...THAT IF I SAID THAT TO NOZAKI-KUN...
HUH !?
YOU LIKE ME ...!?
HUH!?
SO WHAT ABOUT ME EXACTLY?
HOW DID IT START?
CAN YOU TELL ME WHICH MOMENTS ...
...REALLY MADE YOUR HEART RACE?
......IS HOW HE'D REPLY, JUST SO HE COULD GET MORE MATERIAL FOR HIS MANGA!!!
I DON'T REALLY CARE, BUT THE NOZAKI IN YOUR HEAD IS A MAJOR PAIN IN THE ASS.
WAAAAH!

TRYING TO BE HIS TYPE

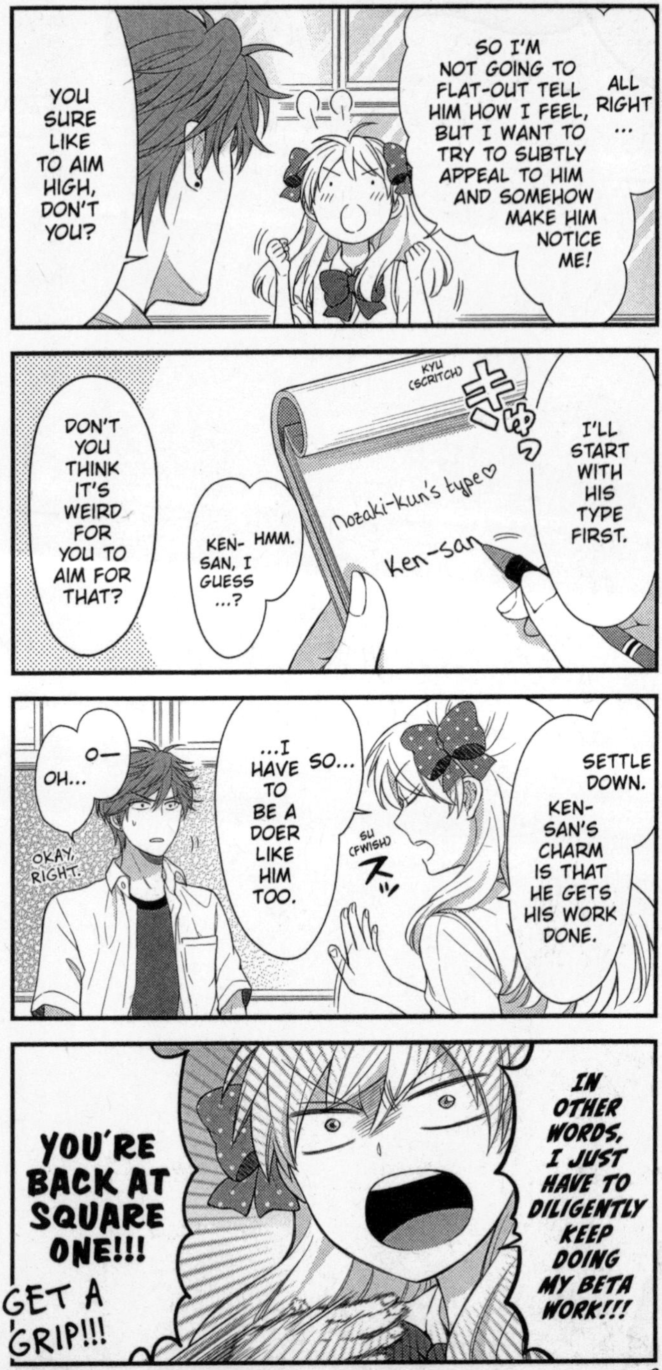
ALL RIGHT ...
SO I'M NOT GOING TO FLAT-OUT TELL HIM HOW I FEEL, BUT I WANT TO TRY TO SUBTLY APPEAL TO HIM AND SOMEHOW MAKE HIM NOTICE ME!
YOU SURE LIKE TO AIM HIGH, DON'T YOU?
I'LL START WITH HIS TYPE FIRST.
きゅっ
KYU (SCRITCH)
Nozaki-kun's type♡
Ken-san
HMM.
KEN-SAN, I GUESS ...?
DON'T YOU THINK IT'S WEIRD FOR YOU TO AIM FOR THAT?
SETTLE DOWN.
KEN-SAN'S CHARM IS THAT HE GETS HIS WORK DONE.
スッ
SU (FWISH)
SO...
...I HAVE TO BE A DOER LIKE HIM TOO.
O— OH...
OKAY, RIGHT.
IN OTHER WORDS, I JUST HAVE TO DILIGENTLY KEEP DOING MY BETA WORK!!!
YOU'RE BACK AT SQUARE ONE!!!
GET A GRIP!!!

SIMULATION

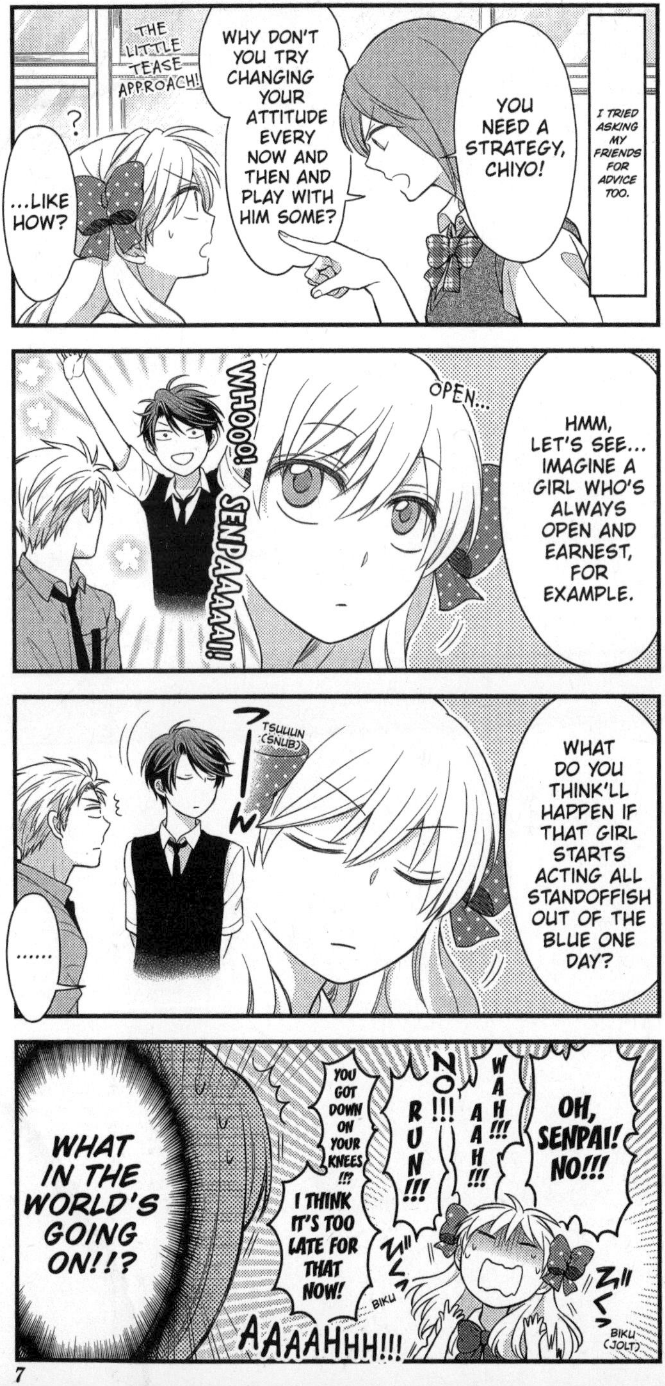
I TRIED ASKING MY FRIENDS FOR ADVICE TOO.
YOU NEED A STRATEGY, CHIYO!
WHY DON'T YOU TRY CHANGING YOUR ATTITUDE EVERY NOW AND THEN AND PLAY WITH HIM SOME?
THE LITTLE TEASE APPROACH!
?
...LIKE HOW?
HMM, LET'S SEE... IMAGINE A GIRL WHO'S ALWAYS OPEN AND EARNEST, FOR EXAMPLE.
OPEN...
WHOOO! SENPAAAAAI!
WHAT DO YOU THINK'LL HAPPEN IF THAT GIRL STARTS ACTING ALL STANDOFFISH OUT OF THE BLUE ONE DAY?
TSUUUN (SNUB)
......
OH, SENPAI! NO!!!
WAH!!! AAH!!!
NO!!! RUN!!!
YOU GOT DOWN ON YOUR KNEES!!?
I THINK IT'S TOO LATE FOR THAT NOW!
BIKU (JOLT)
BIKU
AAAAHHH!!!
WHAT IN THE WORLD'S GOING ON!!?

A CALCULATED STRATEGY

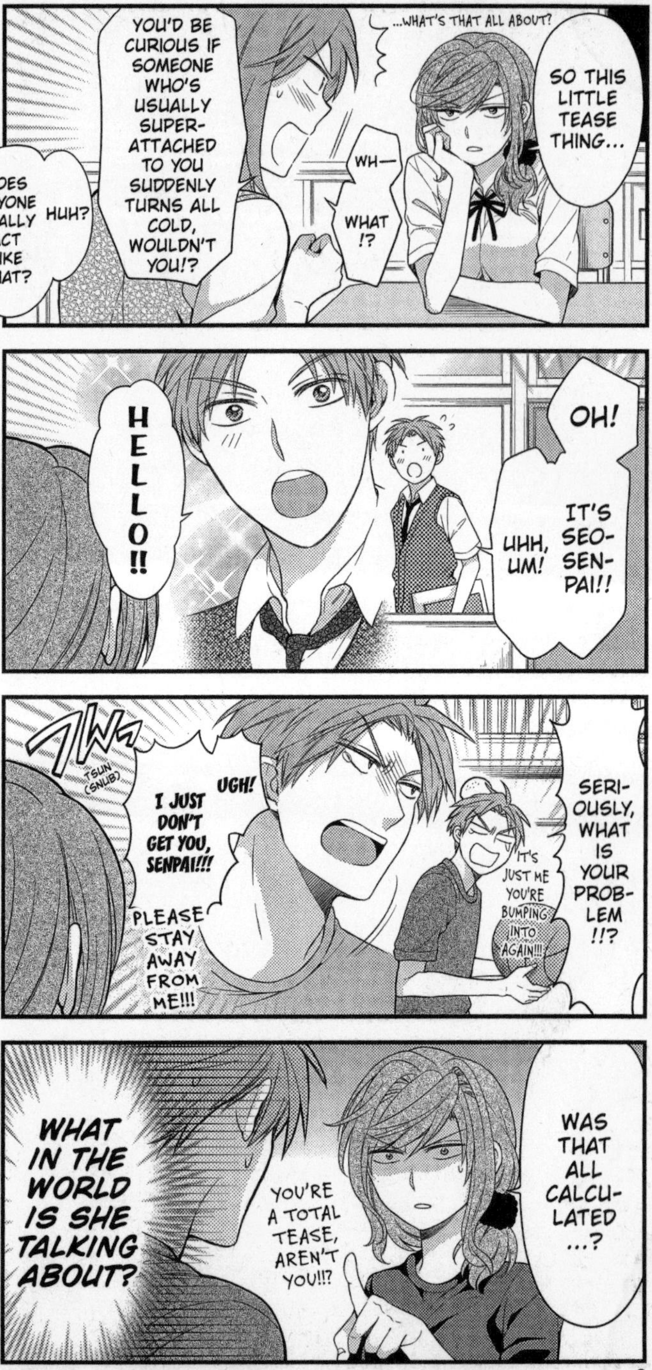
SO THIS LITTLE TEASE THING...
...WHAT'S THAT ALL ABOUT?
WH— WHAT!?
YOU'D BE CURIOUS IF SOMEONE WHO'S USUALLY SUPER-ATTACHED TO YOU SUDDENLY TURNS ALL COLD, WOULDN'T YOU!?
HUH?
DOES ANYONE REALLY ACT LIKE THAT?
OH!
IT'S SEO-SENPAI!!
UHH, UM!
HELLO!!
SERIOUSLY, WHAT IS YOUR PROBLEM!!?
IT'S JUST ME YOU'RE BUMPING INTO AGAIN!!!
UGH!
I JUST DON'T GET YOU, SENPAI!!!
TSUN (SNUB)
PLEASE STAY AWAY FROM ME!!!
WAS THAT ALL CALCULATED...?
YOU'RE A TOTAL TEASE, AREN'T YOU!!?
WHAT IN THE WORLD IS SHE TALKING ABOUT?

LITTLE TEASE

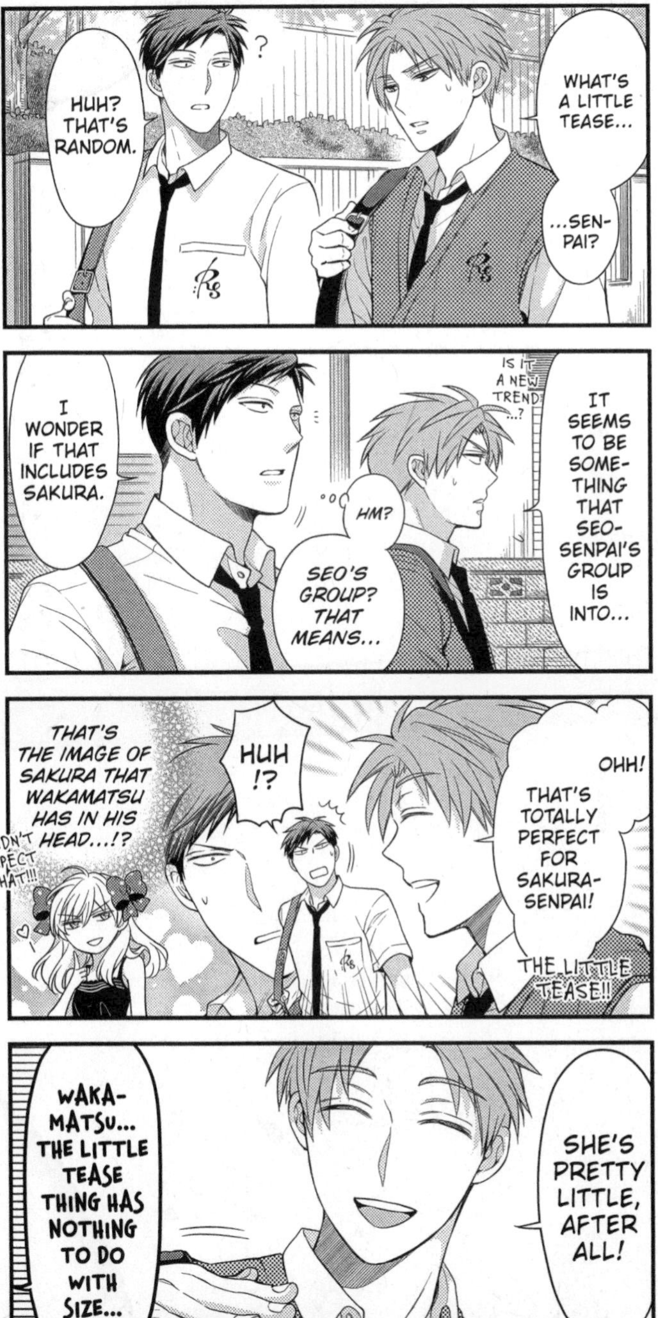
WHAT'S A LITTLE TEASE...
...SEN-PAI?
?
HUH? THAT'S RANDOM.
IS IT A NEW TREND...?
IT SEEMS TO BE SOME-THING THAT SEO-SENPAI'S GROUP IS INTO...
HM?
SEO'S GROUP? THAT MEANS...
I WONDER IF THAT INCLUDES SAKURA.
OHH!
THAT'S TOTALLY PERFECT FOR SAKURA-SENPAI!
THE LITTLE TEASE!!
HUH!?
THAT'S THE IMAGE OF SAKURA THAT WAKAMATSU HAS IN HIS HEAD...!?
I DIDN'T EXPECT THAT!!!
SHE'S PRETTY LITTLE, AFTER ALL!
WAKA-MATSU... THE LITTLE TEASE THING HAS NOTHING TO DO WITH SIZE...

THE DEFINITION OF A LITTLE TEASE

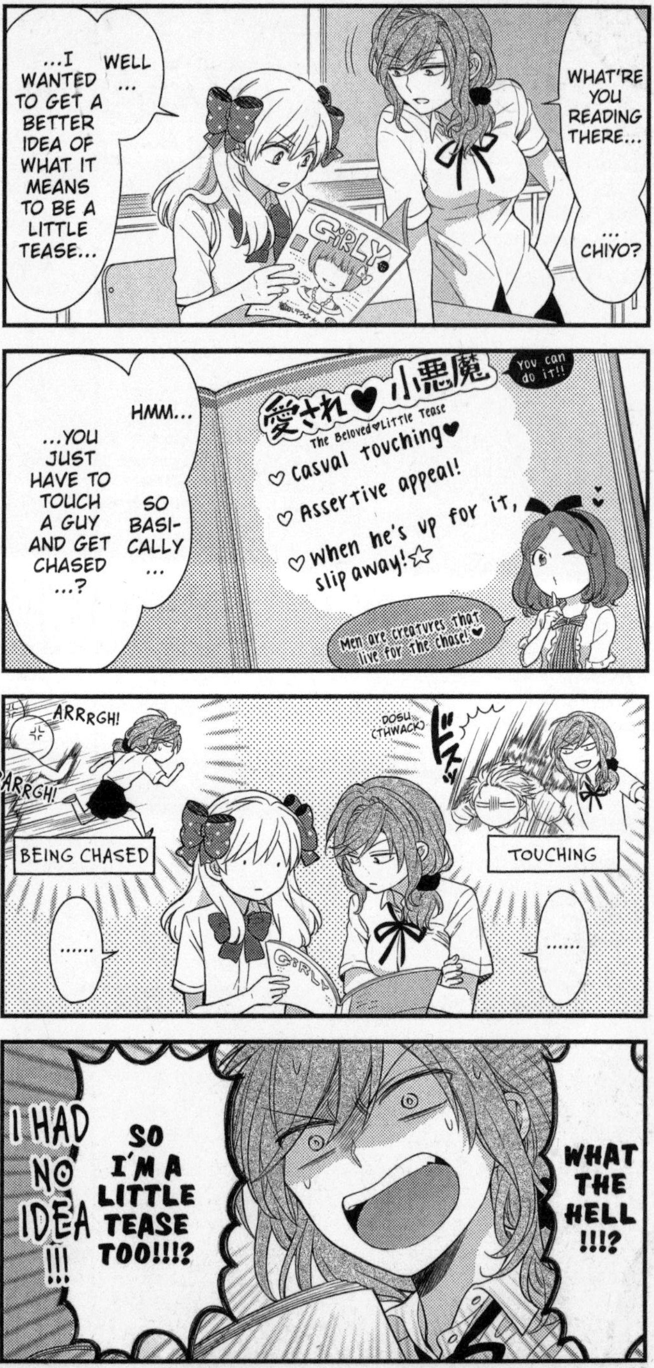
WHAT'RE YOU READING THERE... ...CHIYO?
WELL ...
...I WANTED TO GET A BETTER IDEA OF WHAT IT MEANS TO BE A LITTLE TEASE...
You can do it!!
愛され♥小悪魔
The Beloved♥Little Tease
Casual touching♥
Assertive appeal!
When he's up for it, slip away!☆
Men are creatures that live for the chase!♥
HMM...
SO BASICALLY ...
...YOU JUST HAVE TO TOUCH A GUY AND GET CHASED ...?
DOSU (THWACK)
ドスッ
TOUCHING
ARRRGH!
RARRGH!
BEING CHASED
......
......
WHAT THE HELL !!!?
SO I'M A LITTLE TEASE TOO!!!?
I HAD NO IDEA !!!

PUTTING THE LITTLE TEASE INTO PRACTICE

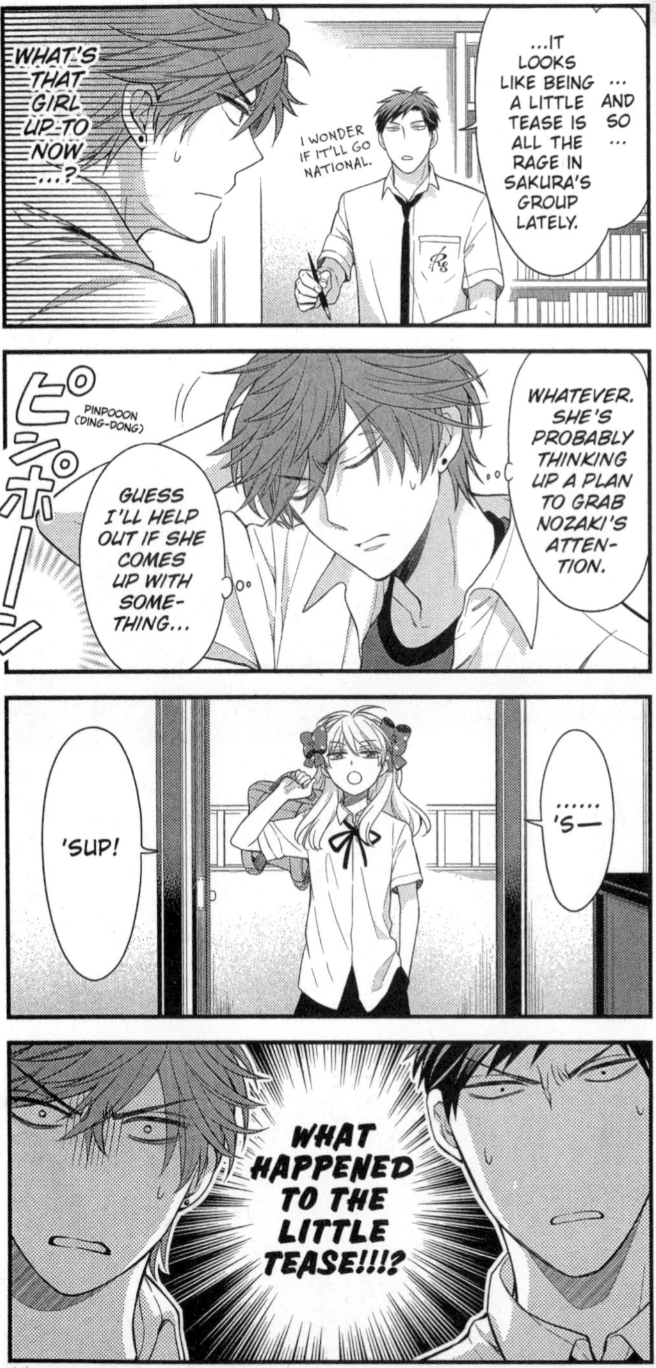
...IT LOOKS LIKE BEING A LITTLE TEASE IS ALL THE RAGE IN SAKURA'S GROUP LATELY.
...AND SO...
I WONDER IF IT'LL GO NATIONAL.
WHAT'S THAT GIRL UP TO NOW...?
WHATEVER. SHE'S PROBABLY THINKING UP A PLAN TO GRAB NOZAKI'S ATTENTION.
GUESS I'LL HELP OUT IF SHE COMES UP WITH SOMETHING...
ピンポーン
PINPOOON (DING-DONG)
......'S—
'SUP!
WHAT HAPPENED TO THE LITTLE TEASE!!!?

WHAT REALLY CATCHES HIS EYE

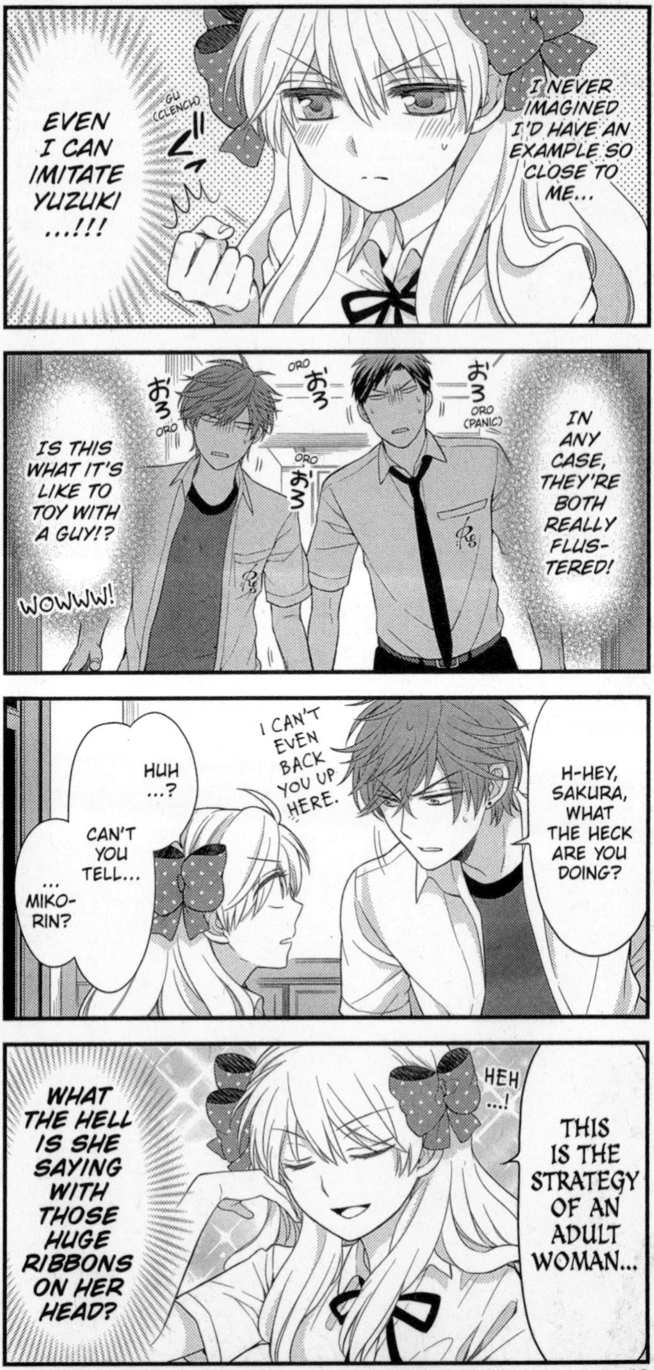
I NEVER IMAGINED I'D HAVE AN EXAMPLE SO CLOSE TO ME...
GU (CLENCH)
EVEN I CAN IMITATE YUZUKI ...!!!
IN ANY CASE, THEY'RE BOTH REALLY FLUS-TERED!
おろ ORO (PANIC)
おろ ORO
おろ ORO
おろ ORO
IS THIS WHAT IT'S LIKE TO TOY WITH A GUY!?
WOWWW!
H-HEY, SAKURA, WHAT THE HECK ARE YOU DOING?
I CAN'T EVEN BACK YOU UP HERE.
HUH ...?
CAN'T YOU TELL... ...MIKO-RIN?
THIS IS THE STRATEGY OF AN ADULT WOMAN...
HEH ...!
WHAT THE HELL IS SHE SAYING WITH THOSE HUGE RIBBONS ON HER HEAD?

A CHANGE IN THEIR RELATIONSHIP?

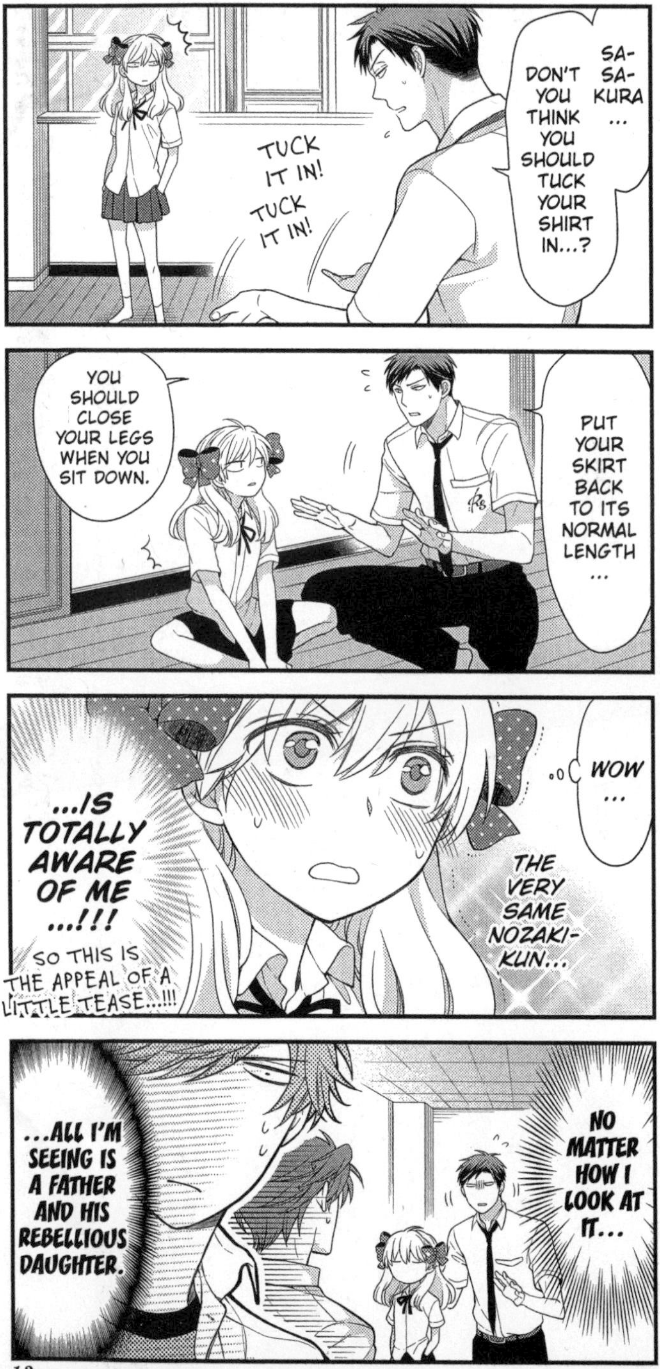
SASAKURA... DON'T YOU THINK YOU SHOULD TUCK YOUR SHIRT IN...?
TUCK IT IN! TUCK IT IN!
PUT YOUR SKIRT BACK TO ITS NORMAL LENGTH...
YOU SHOULD CLOSE YOUR LEGS WHEN YOU SIT DOWN.
WOW...
THE VERY SAME NOZAKI-KUN...
...IS TOTALLY AWARE OF ME...!!!
SO THIS IS THE APPEAL OF A LITTLE TEASE...!!!
NO MATTER HOW I LOOK AT IT...
...ALL I'M SEEING IS A FATHER AND HIS REBELLIOUS DAUGHTER.

BECAUSE SHE'S DILIGENT

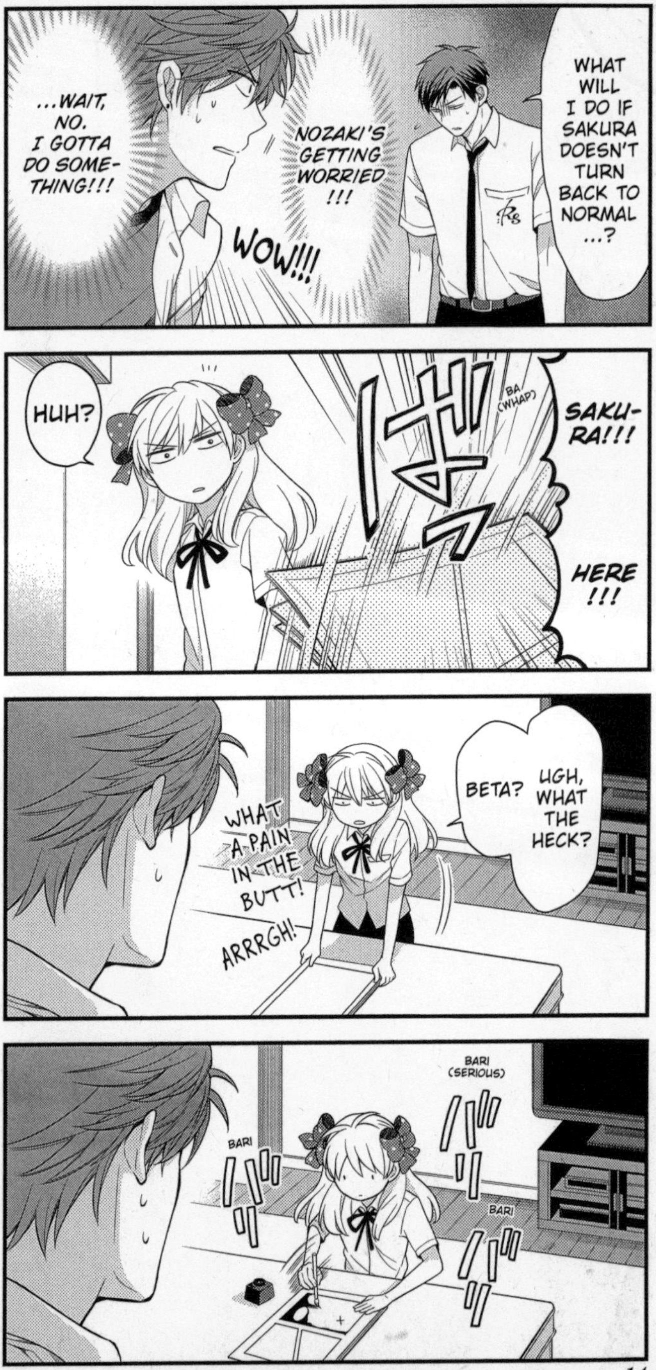
WHAT WILL I DO IF SAKURA DOESN'T TURN BACK TO NORMAL ...?
NOZAKI'S GETTING WORRIED !!!
WOW!!!
...WAIT, NO. I GOTTA DO SOME-THING!!!
SAKU-RA!!!
HERE !!!
BA (WHAP)
HUH?
BETA? UGH, WHAT THE HECK?
WHAT A PAIN IN THE BUTT!
ARRRGH!
BARI (SERIOUS)
BARI
BARI

A LITTLE TEASE, IN THE END

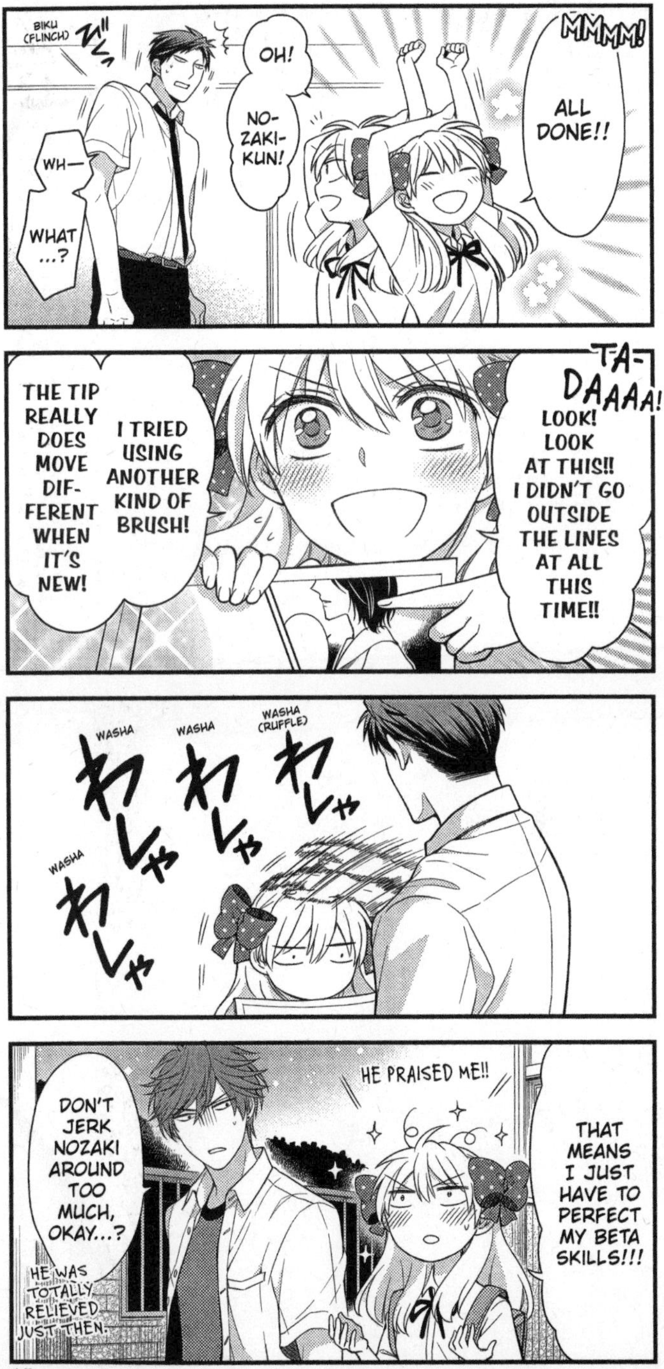
MMMM!
ALL DONE!!
OH!
NO-ZAKI-KUN!
BIKU (FLINCH)
ビクッ
WH—
WHAT ...?
TA-DAAAAA!
LOOK! LOOK AT THIS!! I DIDN'T GO OUTSIDE THE LINES AT ALL THIS TIME!!
I TRIED USING ANOTHER KIND OF BRUSH!
THE TIP REALLY DOES MOVE DIF-FERENT WHEN IT'S NEW!
WASHA (RUFFLE)
わしゃ
WASHA
わしゃ
WASHA
わしゃ
WASHA
わしゃ
THAT MEANS I JUST HAVE TO PERFECT MY BETA SKILLS!!!
HE PRAISED ME!!
DON'T JERK NOZAKI AROUND TOO MUCH, OKAY...?
HE WAS TOTALLY RELIEVED JUST THEN.

"WAIT"

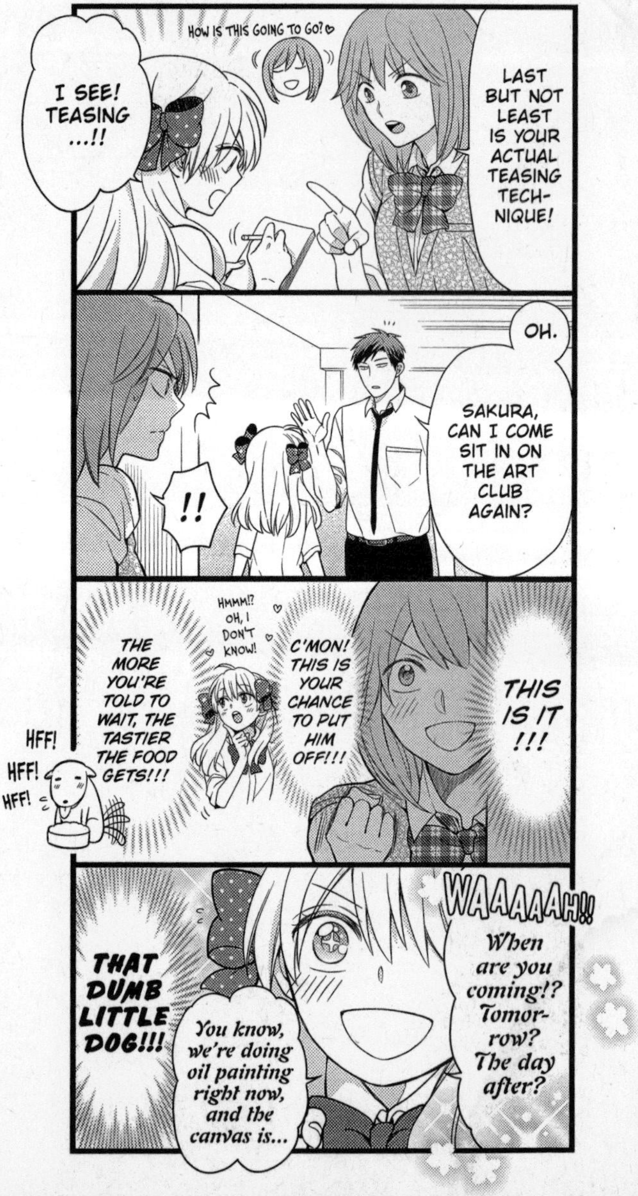
LAST BUT NOT LEAST IS YOUR ACTUAL TEASING TECH-NIQUE!
HOW IS THIS GOING TO GO?♡
I SEE! TEASING ...!!
OH.
SAKURA, CAN I COME SIT IN ON THE ART CLUB AGAIN?
!!
THIS IS IT!!!
C'MON! THIS IS YOUR CHANCE TO PUT HIM OFF!!!
HMMM!? OH, I DON'T KNOW!
THE MORE YOU'RE TOLD TO WAIT, THE TASTIER THE FOOD GETS!!!
HFF! HFF! HFF!
WAAAAAH!!
When are you coming!? Tomor-row? The day after?
You know, we're doing oil painting right now, and the canvas is...
THAT DUMB LITTLE DOG!!!

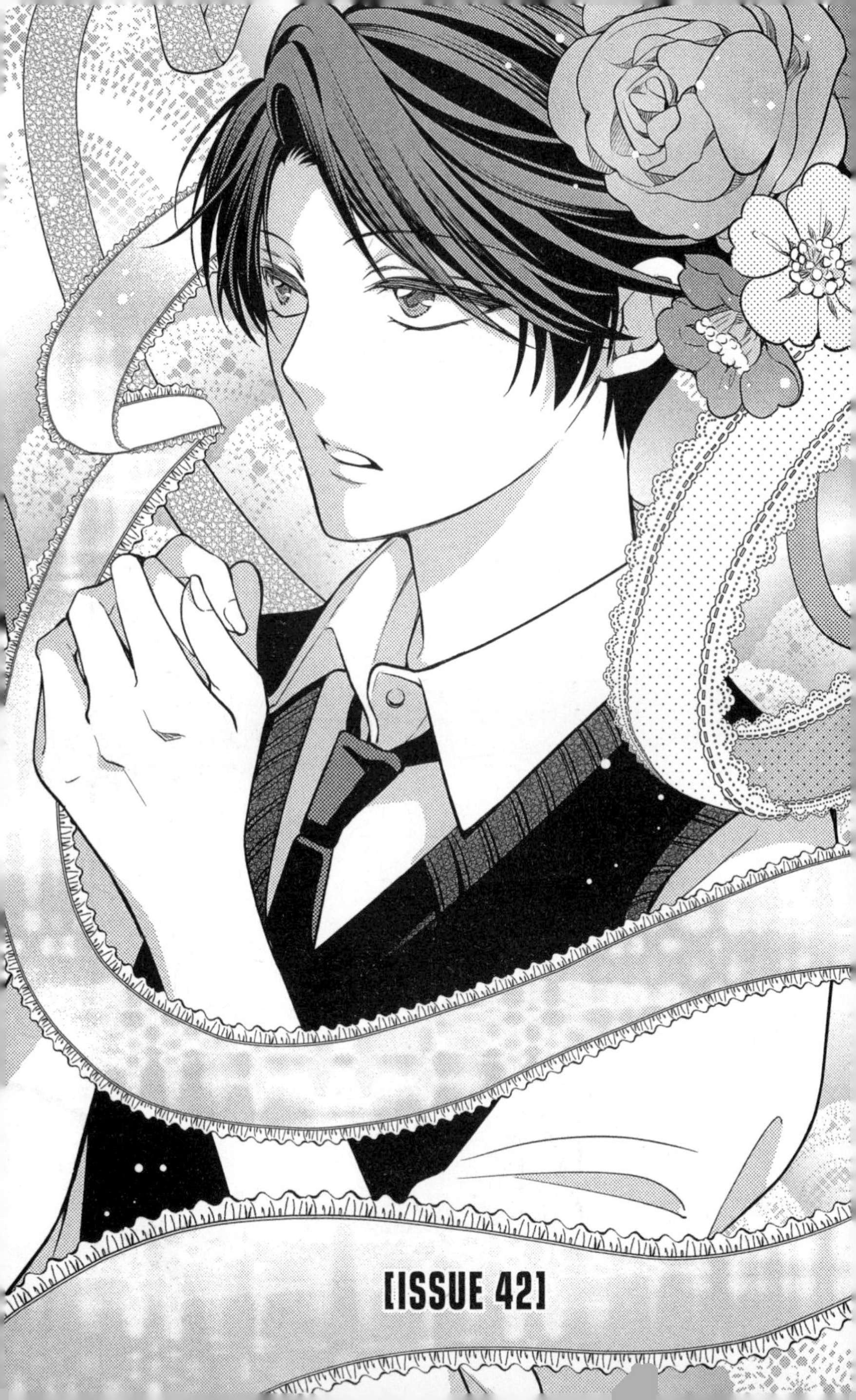
[ISSUE 42]

HEART-POUNDING☆SHORTCUT SETTINGS

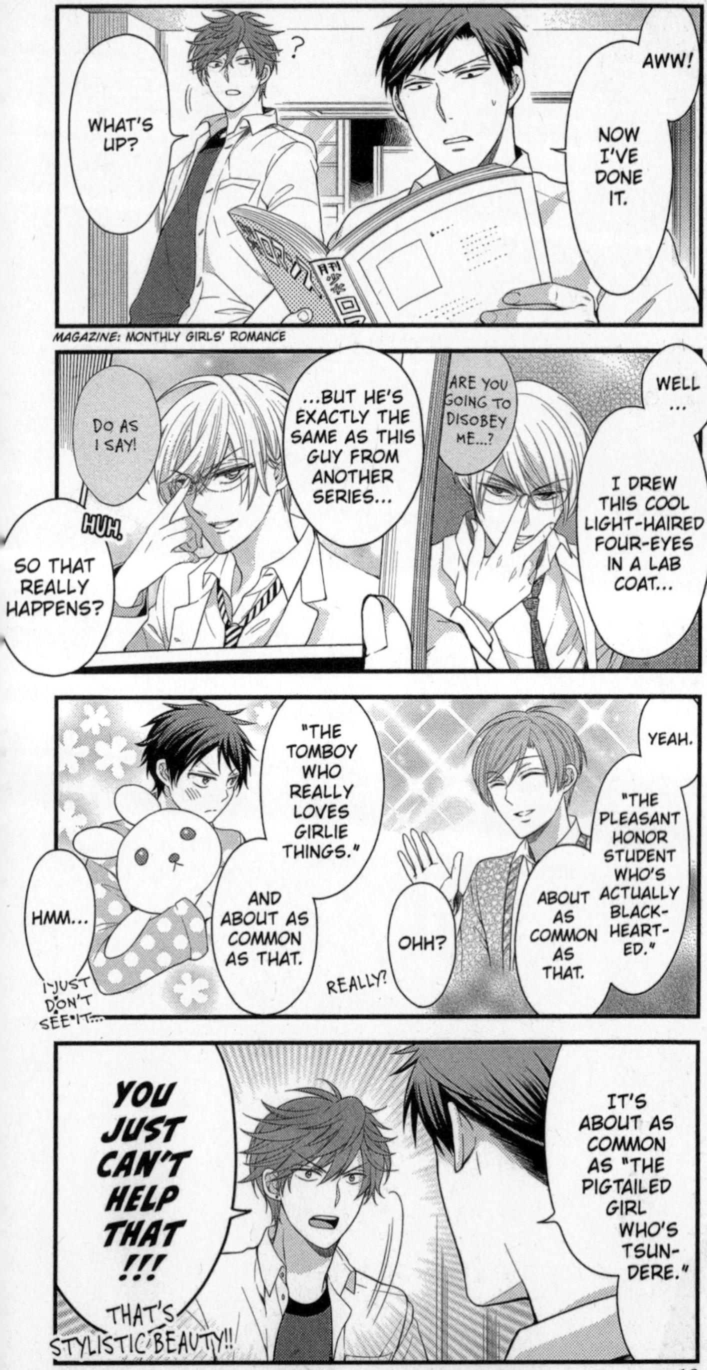
AWW!
NOW I'VE DONE IT.
?
WHAT'S UP?
MAGAZINE: MONTHLY GIRLS' ROMANCE
WELL...
I DREW THIS COOL LIGHT-HAIRED FOUR-EYES IN A LAB COAT...
ARE YOU GOING TO DISOBEY ME...?
...BUT HE'S EXACTLY THE SAME AS THIS GUY FROM ANOTHER SERIES...
DO AS I SAY!
HUH.
SO THAT REALLY HAPPENS?
YEAH.
"THE PLEASANT HONOR STUDENT WHO'S ACTUALLY BLACK-HEARTED."
ABOUT AS COMMON AS THAT.
OHH?
REALLY?
"THE TOMBOY WHO REALLY LOVES GIRLIE THINGS."
AND ABOUT AS COMMON AS THAT.
HMM...
I JUST DON'T SEE IT...
IT'S ABOUT AS COMMON AS "THE PIGTAILED GIRL WHO'S TSUNDERE."
YOU JUST CAN'T HELP THAT!!!
THAT'S STYLISTIC BEAUTY!!

THE HEART OF A WISTFUL WOMAN

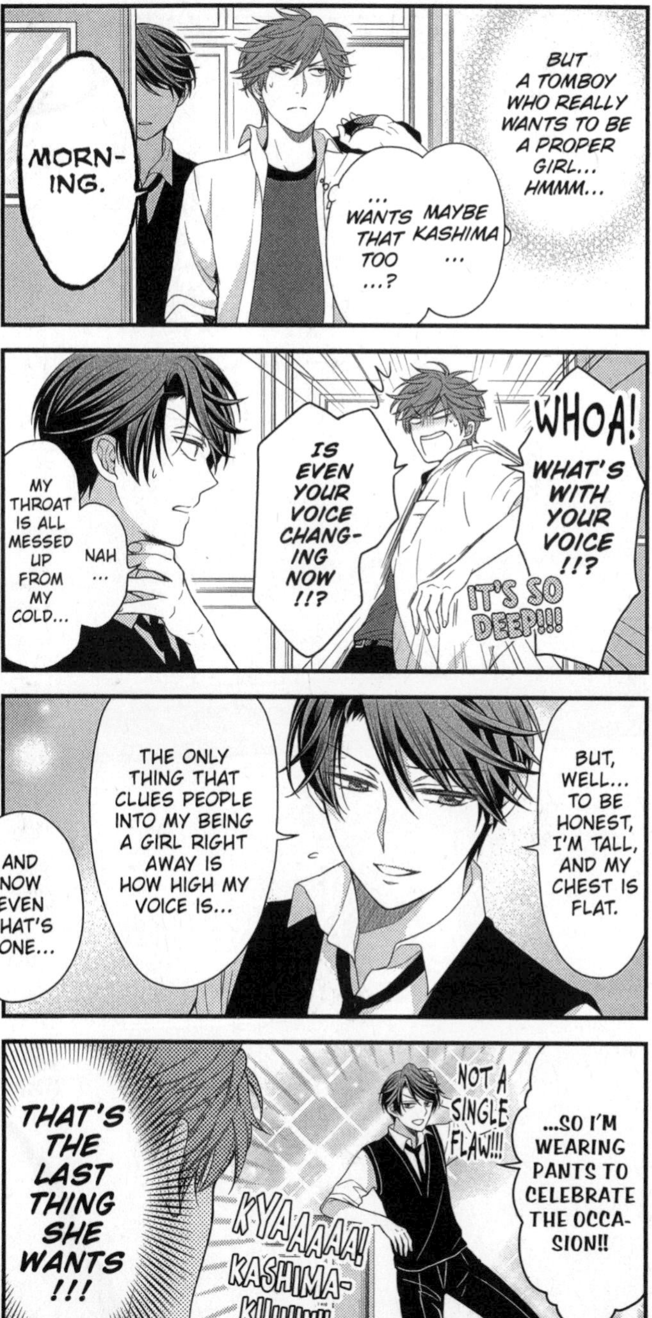
BUT A TOMBOY WHO REALLY WANTS TO BE A PROPER GIRL... HMMM...
MAYBE KASHIMA...
...WANTS THAT TOO...?
MORNING.
WHOA! WHAT'S WITH YOUR VOICE!!?
IT'S SO DEEP!!!
IS EVEN YOUR VOICE CHANGING NOW!!?
NAH...
MY THROAT IS ALL MESSED UP FROM MY COLD...
BUT, WELL... TO BE HONEST, I'M TALL, AND MY CHEST IS FLAT.
THE ONLY THING THAT CLUES PEOPLE INTO MY BEING A GIRL RIGHT AWAY IS HOW HIGH MY VOICE IS...
AND NOW EVEN THAT'S GONE...
...SO I'M WEARING PANTS TO CELEBRATE THE OCCASION!!
NOT A SINGLE FLAW!!!
KYAAAAA! KASHIMA-KUUUN!!
THAT'S THE LAST THING SHE WANTS!!!

A FAMILIAR FEELING

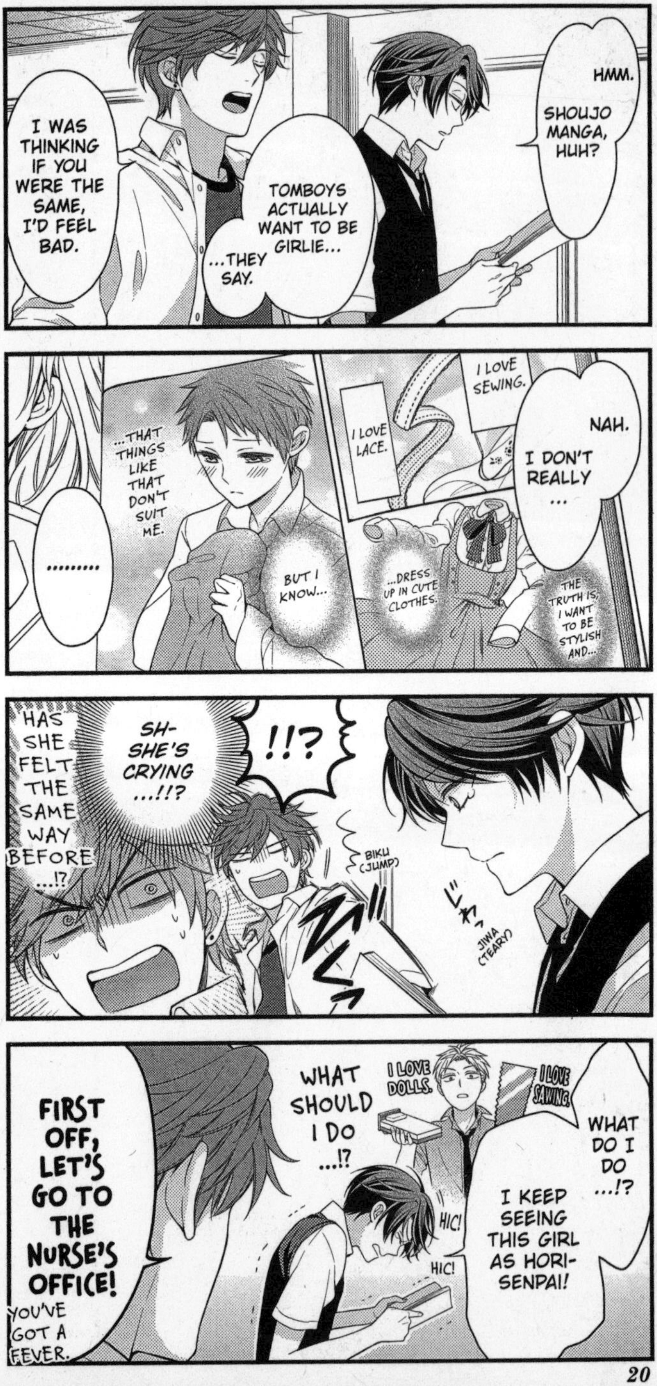
HMM.
SHOUJO MANGA, HUH?
TOMBOYS ACTUALLY WANT TO BE GIRLIE...
...THEY SAY.
I WAS THINKING IF YOU WERE THE SAME, I'D FEEL BAD.
NAH.
I DON'T REALLY ...
I LOVE SEWING.
I LOVE LACE.
THE TRUTH IS, I WANT TO BE STYLISH AND...
...DRESS UP IN CUTE CLOTHES.
BUT I KNOW...
...THAT THINGS LIKE THAT DON'T SUIT ME.
....
JIWA (TEARY)
BIKU (JUMP)
!!?
SH-SHE'S CRYING ...!!?
HAS SHE FELT THE SAME WAY BEFORE ...!?
WHAT DO I DO ...!?
I LOVE SAWING.
I KEEP SEEING THIS GIRL AS HORI-SENPAI!
I LOVE DOLLS.
HIC!
HIC!
WHAT SHOULD I DO ...!?
FIRST OFF, LET'S GO TO THE NURSE'S OFFICE!
YOU'VE GOT A FEVER.

ROLE REVERSAL

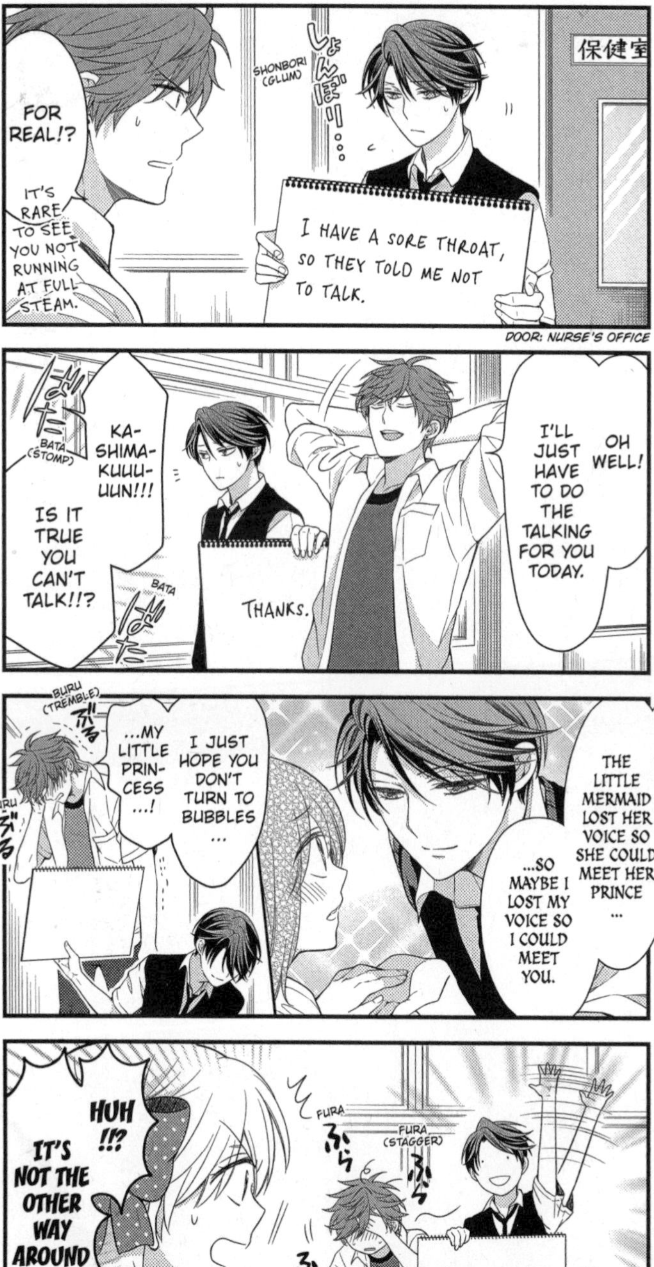
SHONBORI (GLUM)
I HAVE A SORE THROAT, SO THEY TOLD ME NOT TO TALK.
FOR REAL!?
IT'S RARE TO SEE YOU NOT RUNNING AT FULL STEAM.
DOOR: NURSE'S OFFICE
OH WELL!
I'LL JUST HAVE TO DO THE TALKING FOR YOU TODAY.
THANKS.
BATA
KA-SHIMA-KUUUU-UUN!!!
IS IT TRUE YOU CAN'T TALK!!?
BATA (STOMP)
DON'T CRY.
THE LITTLE MERMAID LOST HER VOICE SO SHE COULD MEET HER PRINCE...
...SO MAYBE I LOST MY VOICE SO I COULD MEET YOU.
I JUST HOPE YOU DON'T TURN TO BUBBLES...
...MY LITTLE PRINCESS...!
BURU (TREMBLE)
BURU
I HAVE A COOOLD!
FURA (STAGGER)
FURA
FURA
HUH!!?
IT'S NOT THE OTHER WAY AROUND!!?

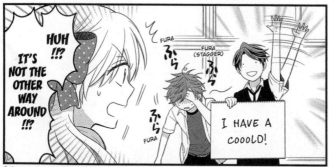

STRAIGHTFORWARD PEOPLE

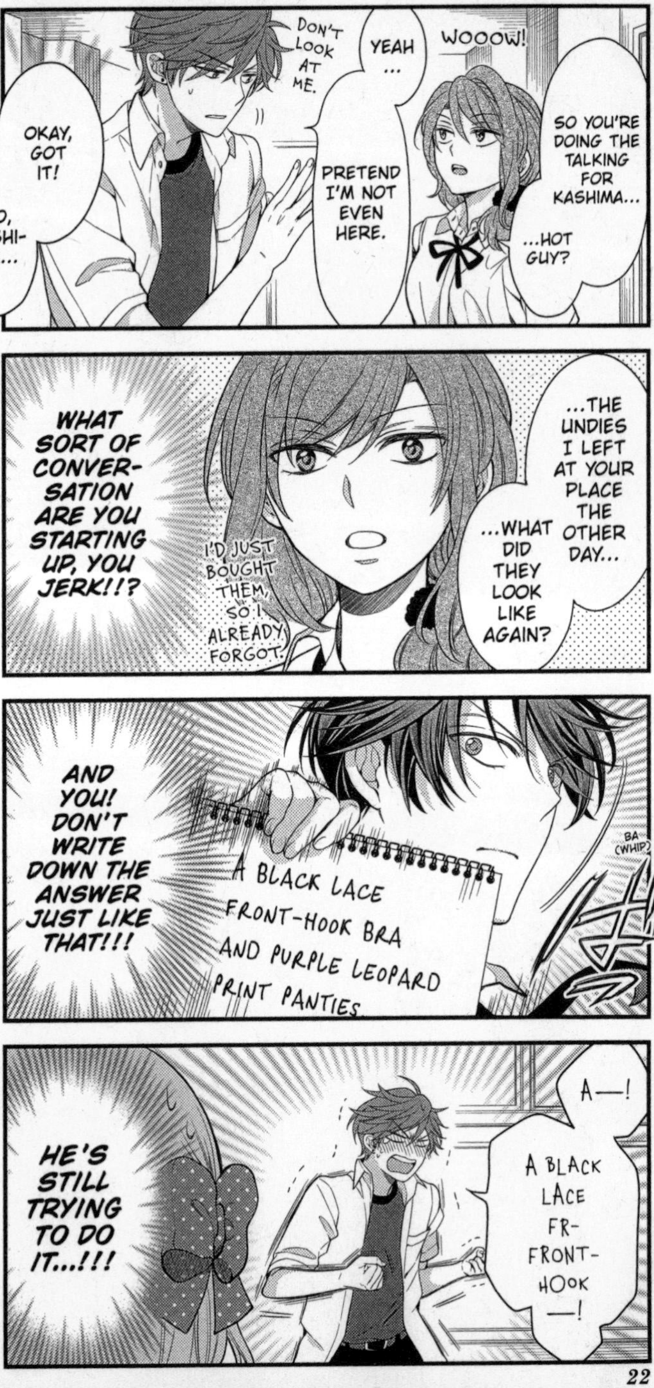
WOOOW!
SO YOU'RE DOING THE TALKING FOR KASHIMA...
...HOT GUY?
YEAH...
PRETEND I'M NOT EVEN HERE.
DON'T LOOK AT ME.
OKAY, GOT IT!
SO, KASHIMA...
...THE UNDIES I LEFT AT YOUR PLACE THE OTHER DAY...
...WHAT DID THEY LOOK LIKE AGAIN?
I'D JUST BOUGHT THEM, SO I ALREADY FORGOT.
WHAT SORT OF CONVERSATION ARE YOU STARTING UP, YOU JERK!!?
BA (WHIP)
A BLACK LACE FRONT-HOOK BRA AND PURPLE LEOPARD PRINT PANTIES
AND YOU! DON'T WRITE DOWN THE ANSWER JUST LIKE THAT!!!
A—!
A BLACK LACE FR-FRONT-HOOK—!
HE'S STILL TRYING TO DO IT...!!!

WHAT SHE WANTS TO TELL SENPAI

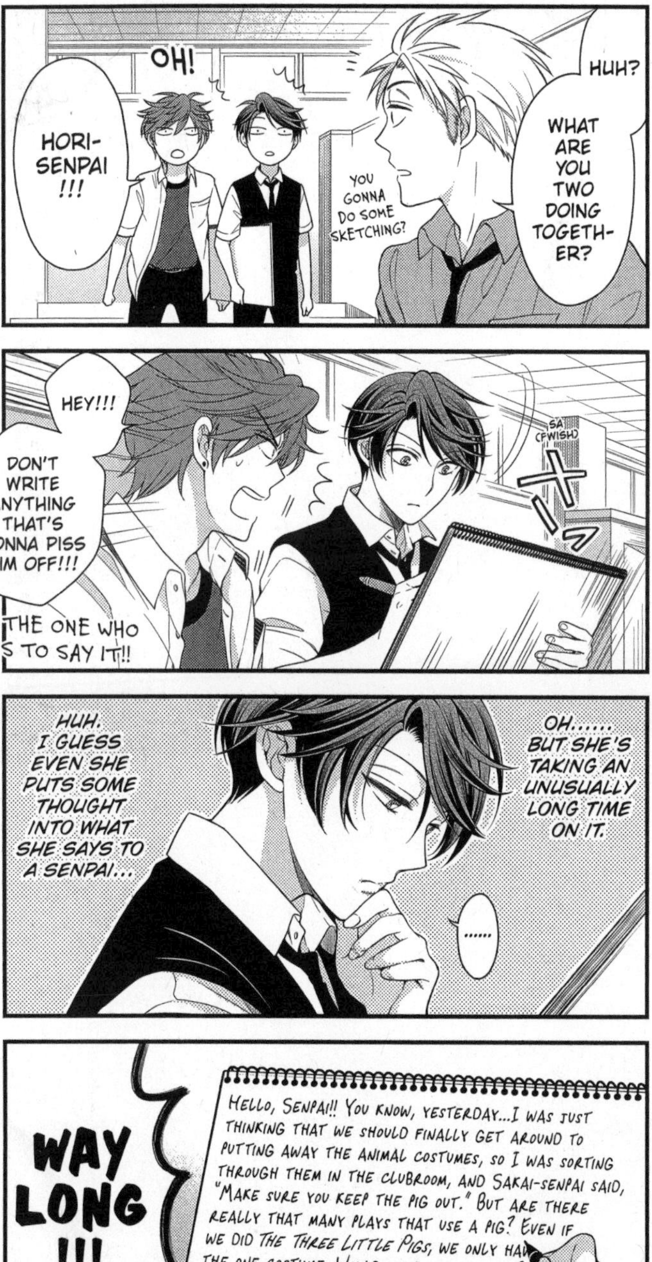
HUH?
WHAT ARE YOU TWO DOING TOGETHER?
YOU GONNA DO SOME SKETCHING?
OH!
HORI-SENPAI!!!
SA (FWISH)
HEY!!!
DON'T WRITE ANYTHING THAT'S GONNA PISS HIM OFF!!!
I'M THE ONE WHO HAS TO SAY IT!!
OH...... BUT SHE'S TAKING AN UNUSUALLY LONG TIME ON IT.
HUH. I GUESS EVEN SHE PUTS SOME THOUGHT INTO WHAT SHE SAYS TO A SENPAI...
......
HELLO, SENPAI!! YOU KNOW, YESTERDAY...I WAS JUST THINKING THAT WE SHOULD FINALLY GET AROUND TO PUTTING AWAY THE ANIMAL COSTUMES, SO I WAS SORTING THROUGH THEM IN THE CLUBROOM, AND SAKAI-SENPAI SAID, "MAKE SURE YOU KEEP THE PIG OUT." BUT ARE THERE REALLY THAT MANY PLAYS THAT USE A PIG? EVEN IF WE DID THE THREE LITTLE PIGS, WE ONLY HAVE THE ONE COSTUME. WOULD WE BUY TWO MORE? OR JUST HAVE ONE PERSON WORK HARD AT PLAYING THREE PARTS? SANDA SAID, "HE REALLY LIKES MAKING GIRLS WEAR THAT ONE," BUT IT'S SKIN-COLORED SO
WAY LONG!!!

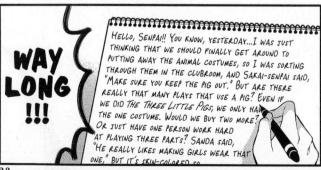

NO NEED FOR WORDS

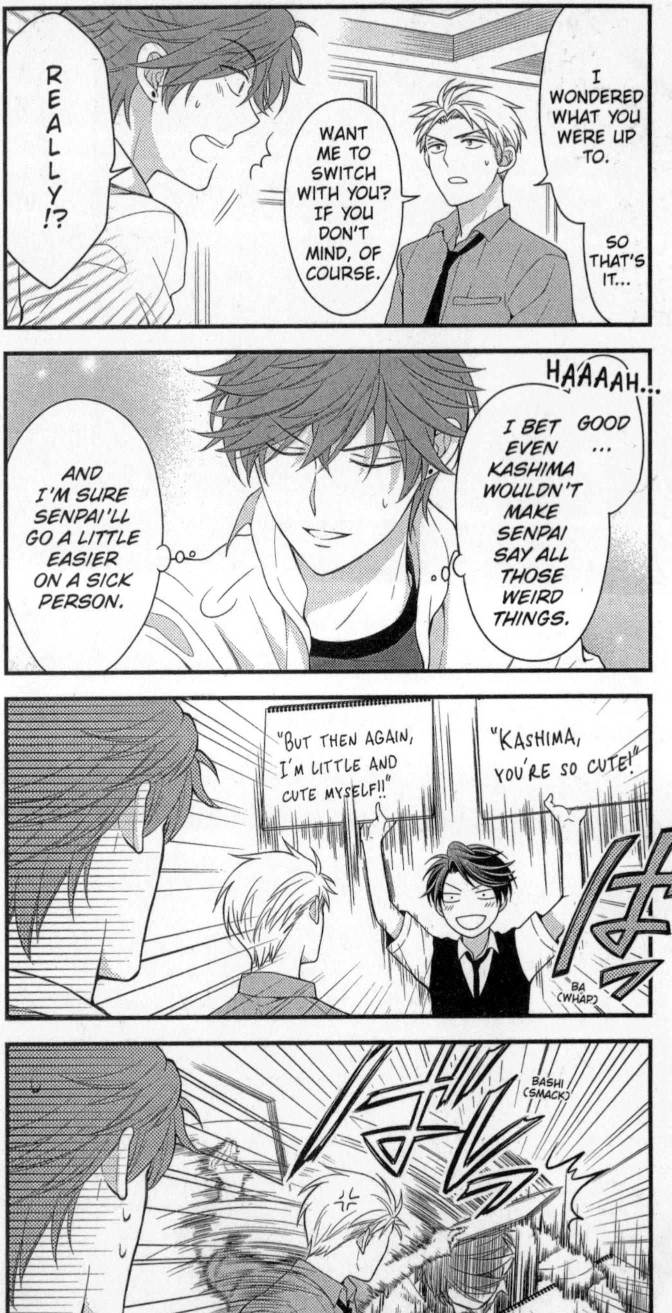
I WONDERED WHAT YOU WERE UP TO.
SO THAT'S IT...
WANT ME TO SWITCH WITH YOU? IF YOU DON'T MIND, OF COURSE.
REALLY!?
HAAAAH...
GOOD...
I BET EVEN KASHIMA WOULDN'T MAKE SENPAI SAY ALL THOSE WEIRD THINGS.
AND I'M SURE SENPAI'LL GO A LITTLE EASIER ON A SICK PERSON.
BA (WHAP)
"KASHIMA, YOU'RE SO CUTE!"
"BUT THEN AGAIN, I'M LITTLE AND CUTE MYSELF!!"
BASHI (SMACK)

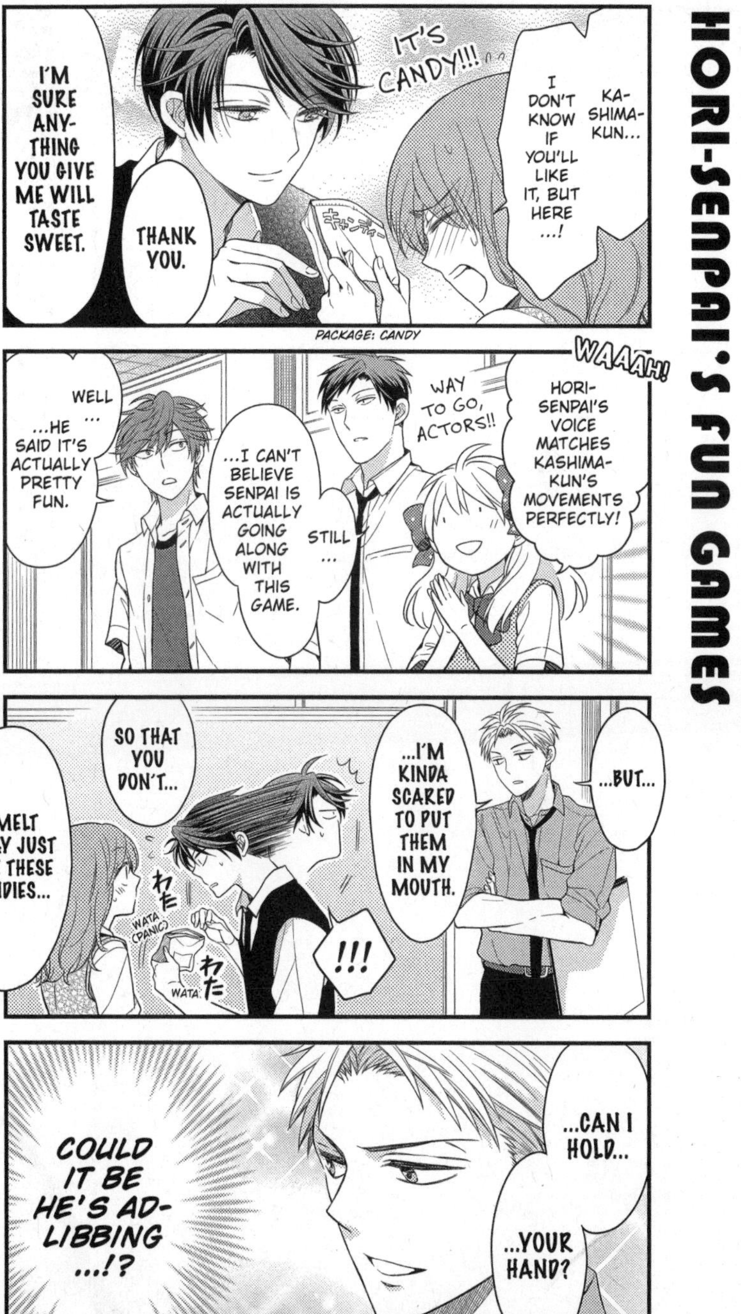
HORI-SENPAI'S FUN GAMES
KA-SHIMA-KUN...
I DON'T KNOW IF YOU'LL LIKE IT, BUT HERE ...!
IT'S CANDY!!!
キャンディー
THANK YOU.
I'M SURE ANYTHING YOU GIVE ME WILL TASTE SWEET.
PACKAGE: CANDY
WAAAH!
HORI-SENPAI'S VOICE MATCHES KASHIMA-KUN'S MOVEMENTS PERFECTLY!
WAY TO GO, ACTORS!!
STILL...
...I CAN'T BELIEVE SENPAI IS ACTUALLY GOING ALONG WITH THIS GAME.
WELL...
...HE SAID IT'S ACTUALLY PRETTY FUN.
...BUT...
...I'M KINDA SCARED TO PUT THEM IN MY MOUTH.
!!!
SO THAT YOU DON'T...
...MELT AWAY JUST LIKE THESE CANDIES...
わた
WATA (PANIC)
わた
WATA
...CAN I HOLD...
...YOUR HAND?
COULD IT BE HE'S AD-LIBBING...!?

READ THIS!

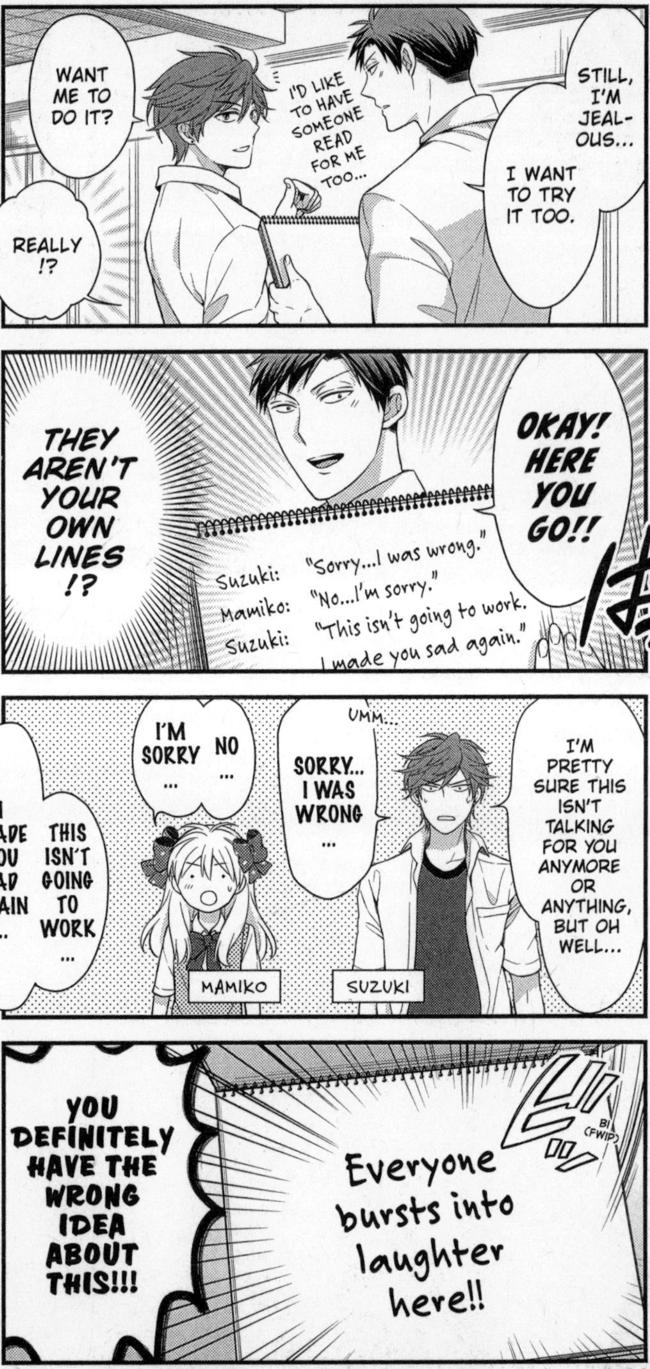
STILL, I'M JEAL-OUS...
I WANT TO TRY IT TOO.
I'D LIKE TO HAVE SOMEONE READ FOR ME TOO...
WANT ME TO DO IT?
REALLY!?
OKAY! HERE YOU GO!!
BA (WHAP)
Suzuki: "Sorry...I was wrong."
Mamiko: "No...I'm sorry."
Suzuki: "This isn't going to work. I made you sad again."
THEY AREN'T YOUR OWN LINES!?
I'M PRETTY SURE THIS ISN'T TALKING FOR YOU ANYMORE OR ANYTHING, BUT OH WELL...
UMM...
SORRY... I WAS WRONG...
NO...
I'M SORRY...
THIS ISN'T GOING TO WORK...
I MADE YOU SAD AGAIN...
SUZUKI
MAMIKO
BI (FWIP)
Everyone bursts into laughter here!!
YOU DEFINITELY HAVE THE WRONG IDEA ABOUT THIS!!!

EXPRESSIONS OF HAPPINESS

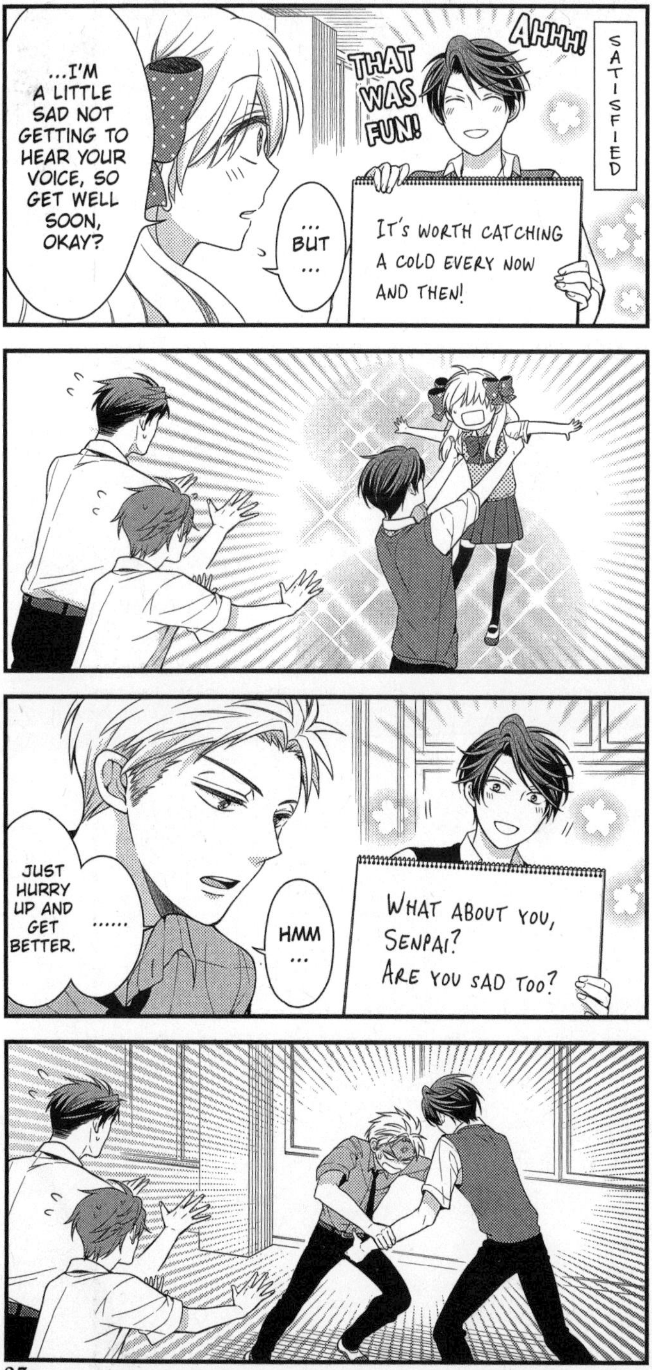
SATISFIED
AHHH!
THAT WAS FUN!
IT'S WORTH CATCHING A COLD EVERY NOW AND THEN!
...BUT...
...I'M A LITTLE SAD NOT GETTING TO HEAR YOUR VOICE, SO GET WELL SOON, OKAY?
WHAT ABOUT YOU, SENPAI? ARE YOU SAD TOO?
HMM...
......
JUST HURRY UP AND GET BETTER.

I'LL READ ANYTHING!

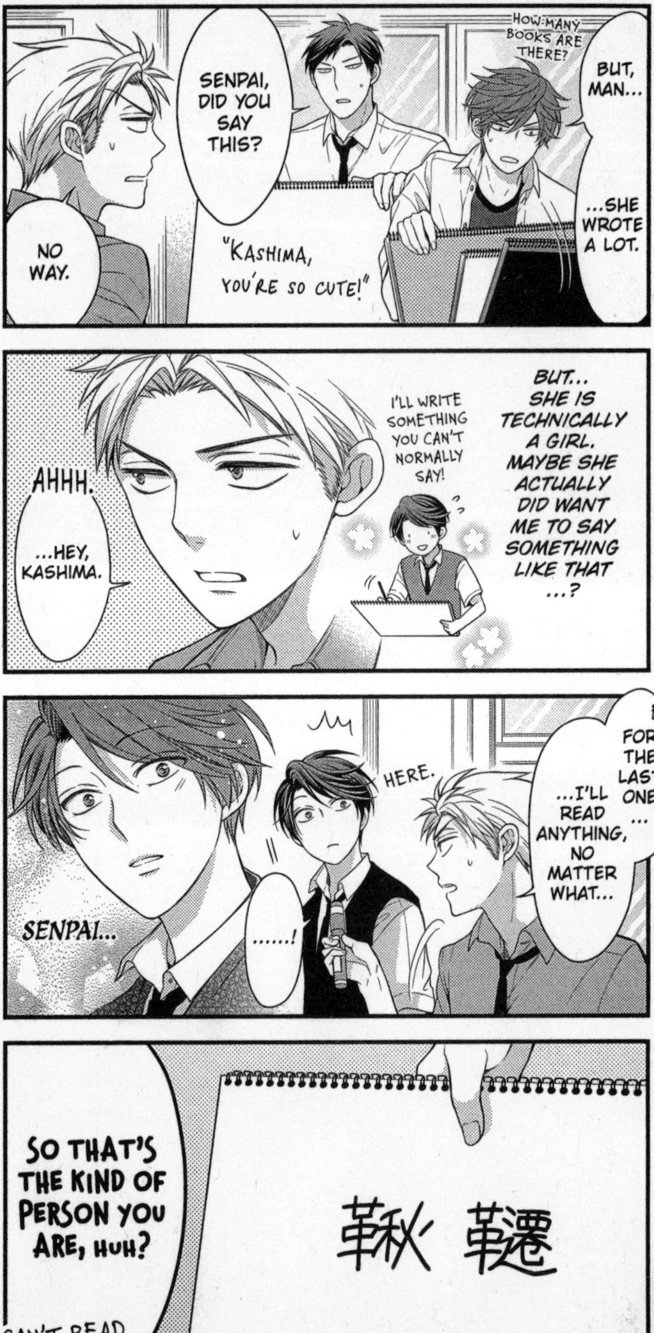
HOW MANY BOOKS ARE THERE?
BUT, MAN...
...SHE WROTE A LOT.
SENPAI, DID YOU SAY THIS?
"KASHIMA, YOU'RE SO CUTE!"
NO WAY.
BUT... SHE IS TECHNICALLY A GIRL. MAYBE SHE ACTUALLY DID WANT ME TO SAY SOMETHING LIKE THAT...?
I'LL WRITE SOMETHING YOU CAN'T NORMALLY SAY!
AHHH.
...HEY, KASHIMA.
ER... FOR THE LAST ONE...
...I'LL READ ANYTHING, NO MATTER WHAT...
HERE.
......!
SENPAI...
鞦韆
SO THAT'S THE KIND OF PERSON YOU ARE, HUH?
I CAN'T READ THAT!

※THE WORD KASHIMA WRITES HERE IS BURANKO, OR "SWING," AS IN THE PLAYGROUND EQUIPMENT. IN JAPANESE, THIS WORD IS RARELY WRITTEN IN KANJI, HENCE HORI'S RETORT.

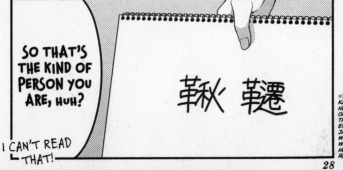

DROP THE ARCHETYPICAL CHARACTERISTICS

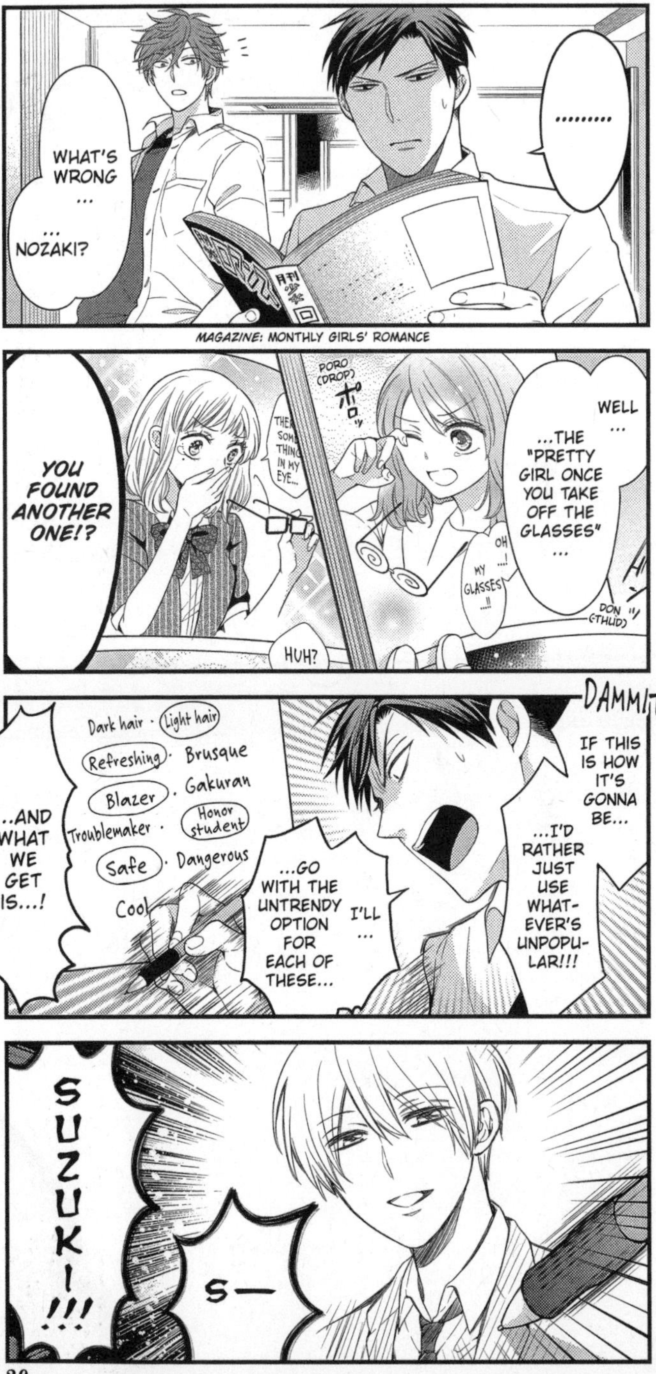
....
WHAT'S WRONG ... ... NOZAKI?
MAGAZINE: MONTHLY GIRLS' ROMANCE
WELL ...
...THE "PRETTY GIRL ONCE YOU TAKE OFF THE GLASSES" ...
DON (THUD)
OH ...! MY GLASSES ...!!
PORO (DROP)
THER SOME THING IN MY EYE...
YOU FOUND ANOTHER ONE!?
HUH?
DAMMIT!
IF THIS IS HOW IT'S GONNA BE...
...I'D RATHER JUST USE WHAT-EVER'S UNPOPU-LAR!!!
I'LL ...
...GO WITH THE UNTRENDY OPTION FOR EACH OF THESE...
Dark hair · Light hair
Refreshing · Brusque
Blazer · Gakuran
Troublemaker · Honor student
Safe · Dangerous
Cool
...AND WHAT WE GET IS...!
S—
SUZUKI!!!

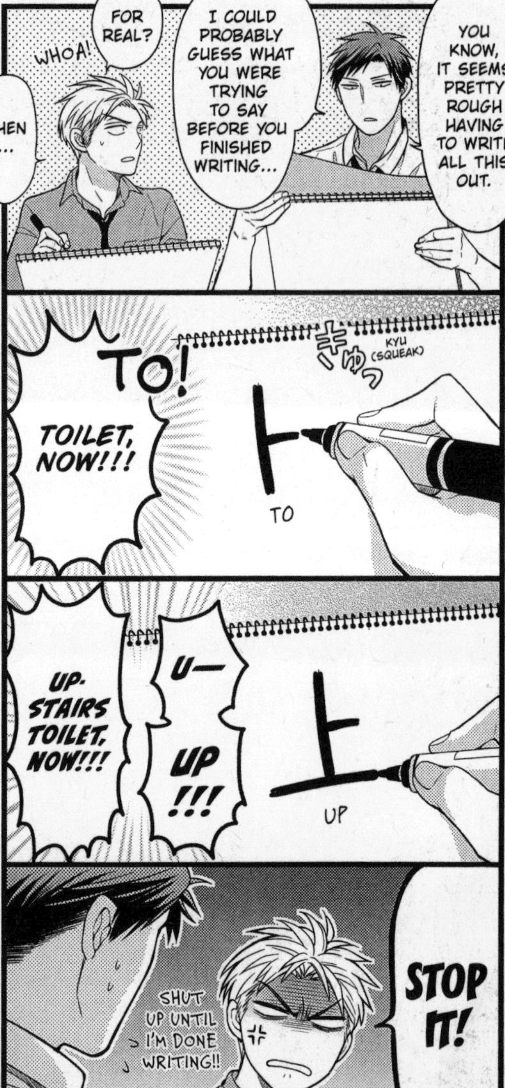
YOU KNOW, IT SEEMS PRETTY ROUGH HAVING TO WRITE ALL THIS OUT.
I COULD PROBABLY GUESS WHAT YOU WERE TRYING TO SAY BEFORE YOU FINISHED WRITING...
FOR REAL?
WHOA!
THEN ...
きゅっ
KYU (SQUEAK)
ト
TO
TO!
TOILET, NOW!!!
上
UP
U—
UP !!!
UP-STAIRS TOILET, NOW!!!
STOP IT!
SHUT UP UNTIL I'M DONE WRITING!!

※THE FIRST TWO STROKES OF THE KANJI FOR "UP" LOOK LIKE THE KATAKANA TO. SO NOZAKI'S JUST GUESSING WILDLY.

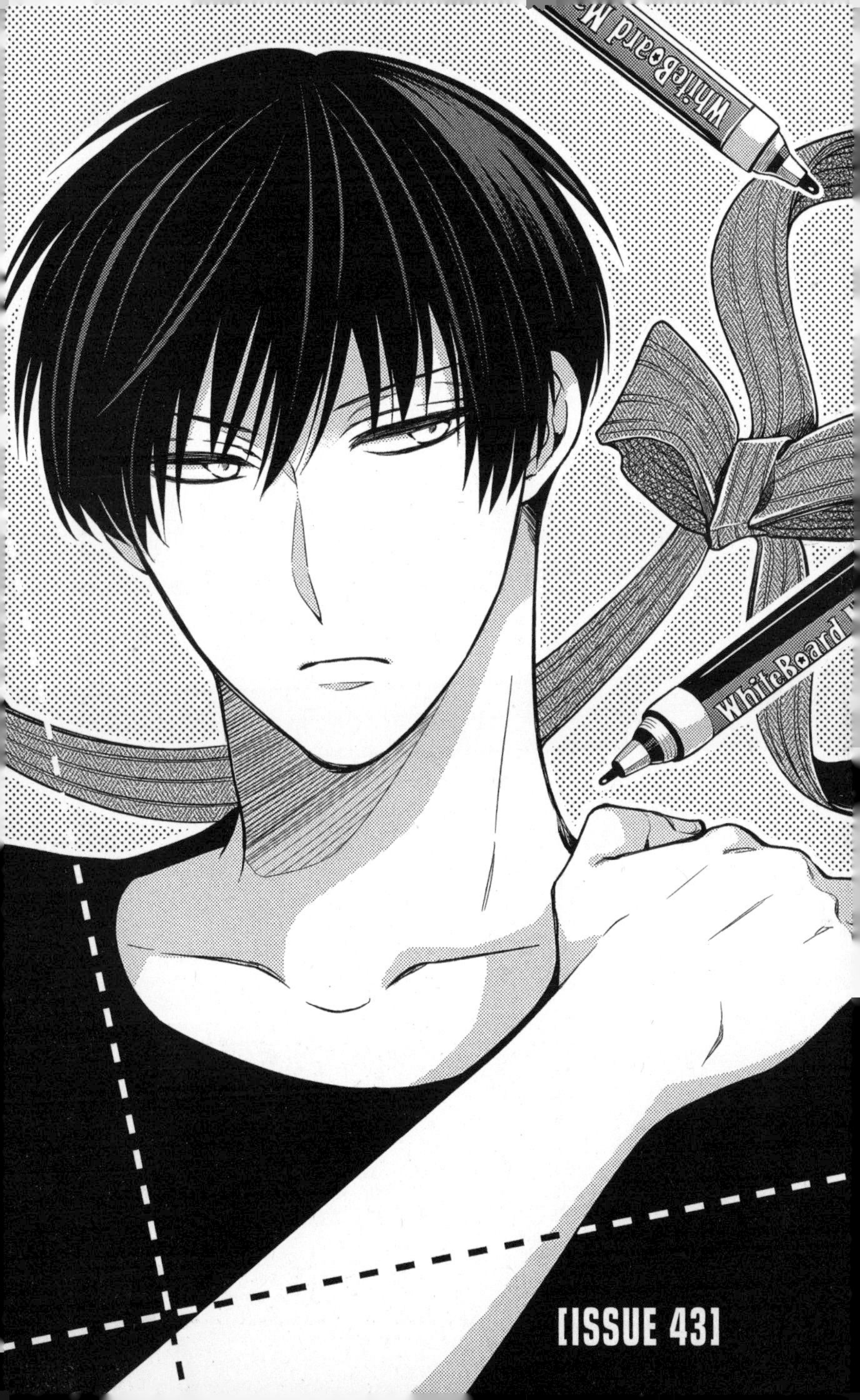
WhiteBoard
WhiteBoard
[ISSUE 43]

DELUXE BACKGROUND CHARACTERS

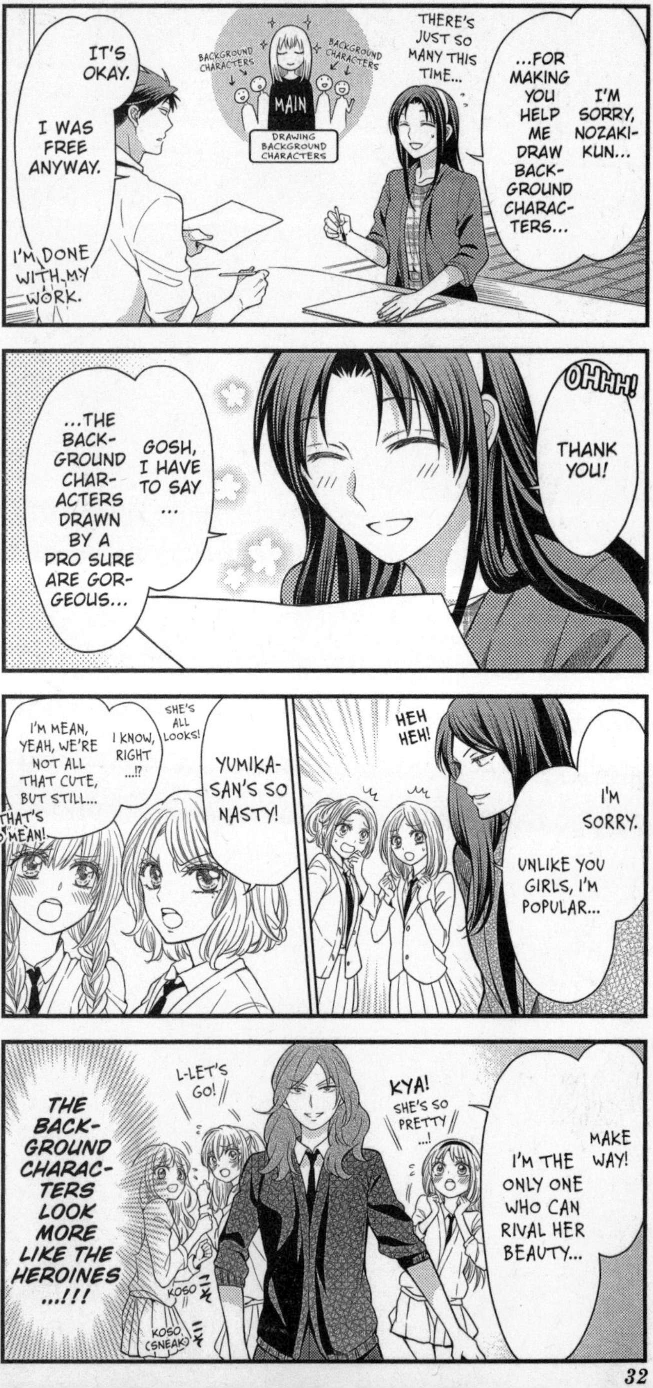
I'M SORRY, NOZAKI-KUN...
...FOR MAKING YOU HELP ME DRAW BACK-GROUND CHARAC-TERS...
THERE'S JUST SO MANY THIS TIME...
BACKGROUND CHARACTERS
MAIN
BACKGROUND CHARACTERS
DRAWING BACKGROUND CHARACTERS
IT'S OKAY.
I WAS FREE ANYWAY.
I'M DONE WITH MY WORK.
OHHH!
THANK YOU!
GOSH, I HAVE TO SAY...
...THE BACK-GROUND CHAR-ACTERS DRAWN BY A PRO SURE ARE GOR-GEOUS...
I'M SORRY.
UNLIKE YOU GIRLS, I'M POPULAR...
HEH HEH!
YUMIKA-SAN'S SO NASTY!
SHE'S ALL LOOKS!
I KNOW, RIGHT...!?
I'M MEAN, YEAH, WE'RE NOT ALL THAT CUTE, BUT STILL...
...THAT'S SO MEAN!
MAKE WAY!
I'M THE ONLY ONE WHO CAN RIVAL HER BEAUTY...
KYA! SHE'S SO PRETTY...!
L-LET'S GO!
KOSO
KOSO (SNEAK)
THE BACK-GROUND CHARAC-TERS LOOK MORE LIKE THE HEROINES...!!!

THE REAL THING AND THE FAKE

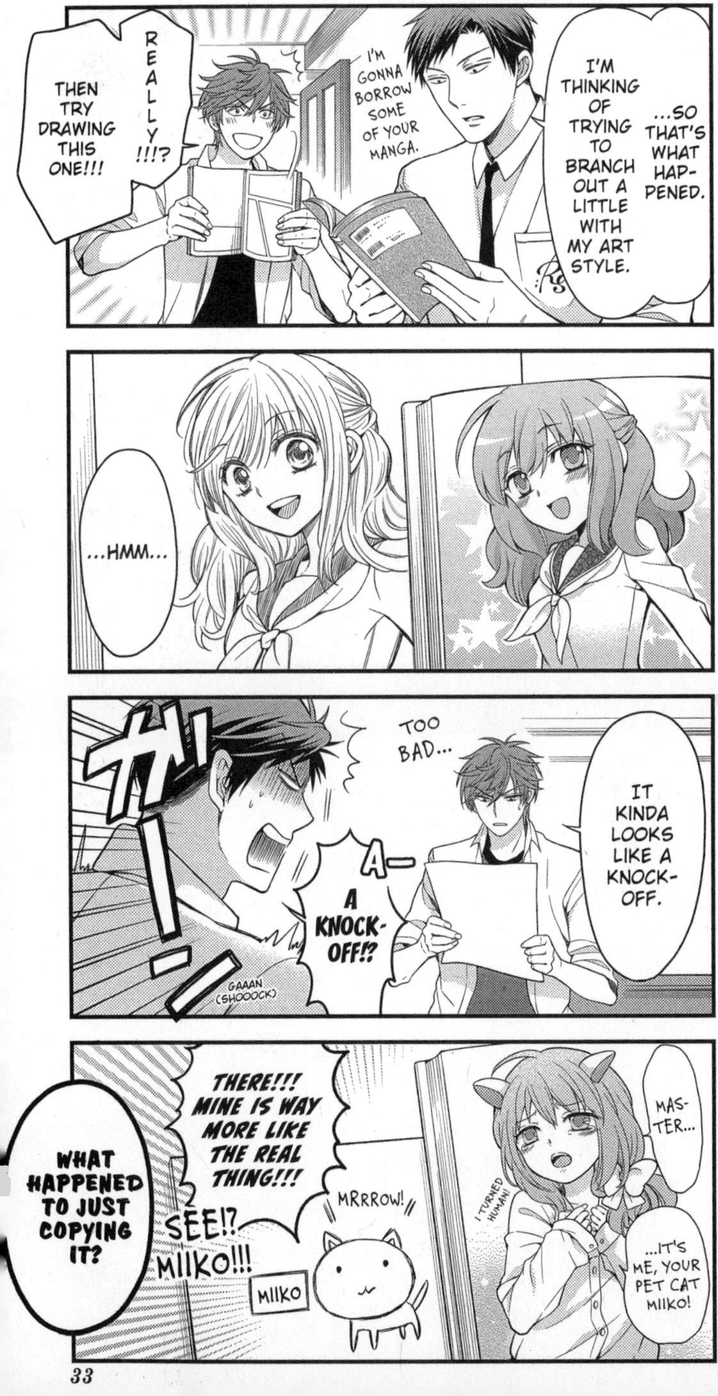
...SO THAT'S WHAT HAPPENED.
I'M THINKING OF TRYING TO BRANCH OUT A LITTLE WITH MY ART STYLE.
I'M GONNA BORROW SOME OF YOUR MANGA.
REALLY!!!?
THEN TRY DRAWING THIS ONE!!!
...HMM...
IT KINDA LOOKS LIKE A KNOCK-OFF.
TOO BAD...
A— A KNOCK-OFF!?
GAAAN (SHOOOCK)
MAS-TER...
...IT'S ME, YOUR PET CAT MIIKO!
I TURNED HUMAN!
MRRROW!
THERE!!! MINE IS WAY MORE LIKE THE REAL THING!!!
SEE!? MIIKO!!!
MIIKO
WHAT HAPPENED TO JUST COPYING IT?

COPYING

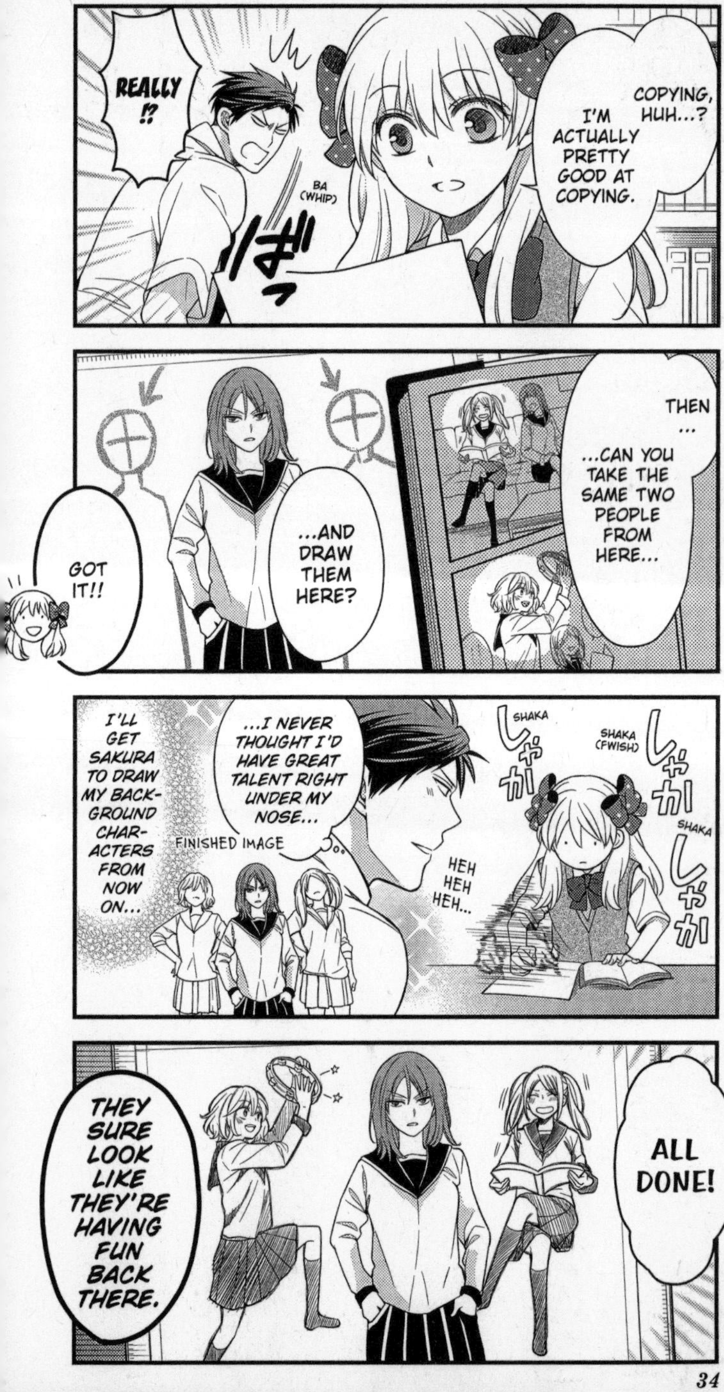

COPYING, HUH...?
I'M ACTUALLY PRETTY GOOD AT COPYING.
BA (WHIP)
REALLY!?
THEN ...
...CAN YOU TAKE THE SAME TWO PEOPLE FROM HERE...
...AND DRAW THEM HERE?
GOT IT!!
SHAKA
SHAKA (FWISH)
SHAKA
HEH HEH HEH...
...I NEVER THOUGHT I'D HAVE GREAT TALENT RIGHT UNDER MY NOSE...
FINISHED IMAGE
I'LL GET SAKURA TO DRAW MY BACKGROUND CHARACTERS FROM NOW ON...
ALL DONE!
THEY SURE LOOK LIKE THEY'RE HAVING FUN BACK THERE.

A BIG BROTHER'S EXPECTATIONS

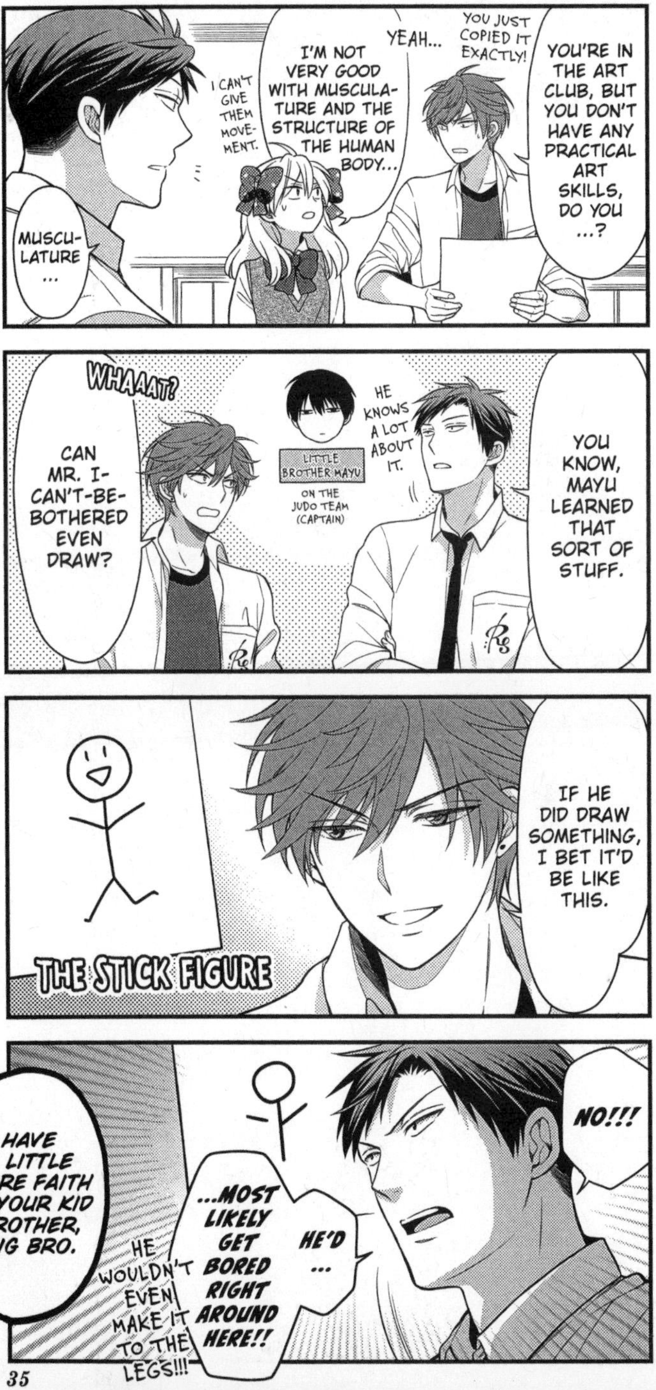
YOU'RE IN THE ART CLUB, BUT YOU DON'T HAVE ANY PRACTICAL ART SKILLS, DO YOU ...?
YOU JUST COPIED IT EXACTLY!
YEAH...
I'M NOT VERY GOOD WITH MUSCULA-TURE AND THE STRUCTURE OF THE HUMAN BODY...
I CAN'T GIVE THEM MOVE-MENT.
MUSCU-LATURE ...
YOU KNOW, MAYU LEARNED THAT SORT OF STUFF.
HE KNOWS A LOT ABOUT IT.
LITTLE BROTHER MAYU
ON THE JUDO TEAM (CAPTAIN)
WHAAAT?
CAN MR. I-CAN'T-BE-BOTHERED EVEN DRAW?
IF HE DID DRAW SOMETHING, I BET IT'D BE LIKE THIS.
THE STICK FIGURE
NO!!!
HE'D ...
...MOST LIKELY GET BORED RIGHT AROUND HERE!!
HE WOULDN'T EVEN MAKE IT TO THE LEGS!!!
HAVE A LITTLE MORE FAITH IN YOUR KID BROTHER, BIG BRO.

DAILY ENERGY DISTRIBUTION

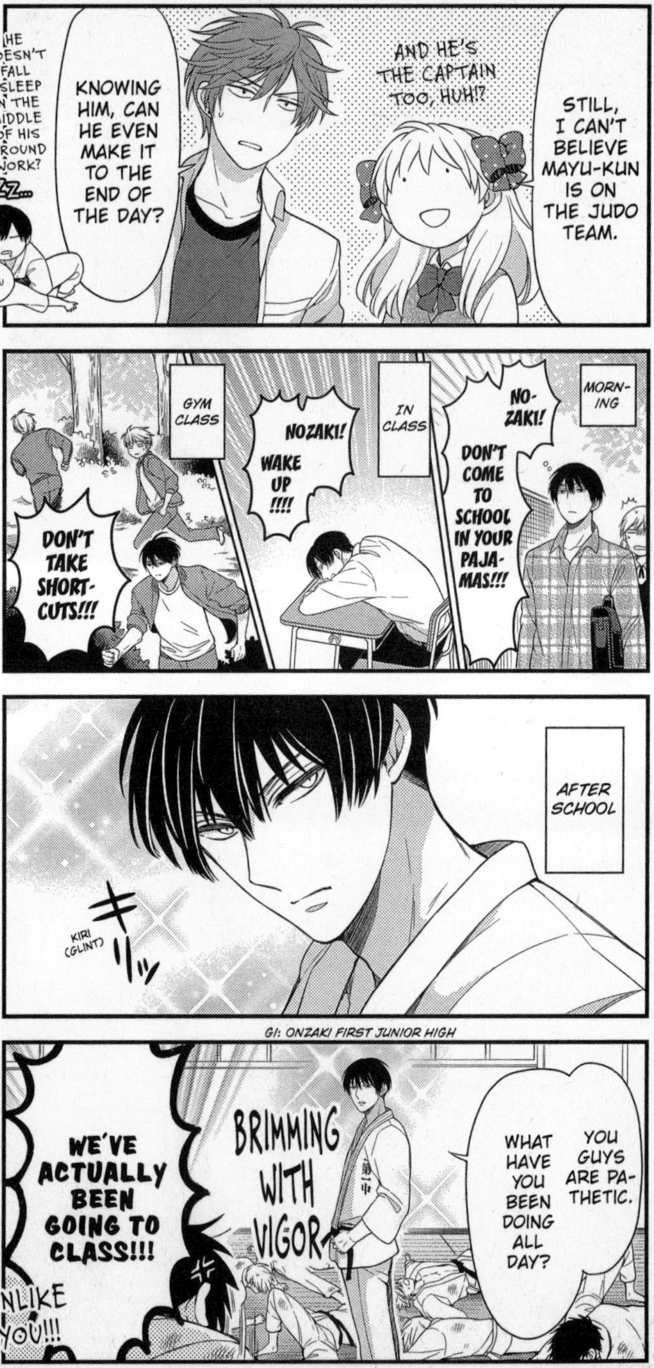
STILL, I CAN'T BELIEVE MAYU-KUN IS ON THE JUDO TEAM.
AND HE'S THE CAPTAIN TOO, HUH!?
KNOWING HIM, CAN HE EVEN MAKE IT TO THE END OF THE DAY?
HE DOESN'T FALL ASLEEP IN THE MIDDLE OF HIS GROUND WORK?
ZZZ...
MORNING
NO-ZAKI! DON'T COME TO SCHOOL IN YOUR PAJA-MAS!!!
IN CLASS
NOZAKI! WAKE UP!!!!
GYM CLASS
DON'T TAKE SHORT-CUTS!!!
AFTER SCHOOL
KIRI (GLINT)
YOU GUYS ARE PA-THETIC.
WHAT HAVE YOU BEEN DOING ALL DAY?
BRIMMING WITH VIGOR
WE'VE ACTUALLY BEEN GOING TO CLASS!!!
UNLIKE YOU!!!
GI: ONZAKI FIRST JUNIOR HIGH

ALARMING EXPERIMENTAL RESULTS

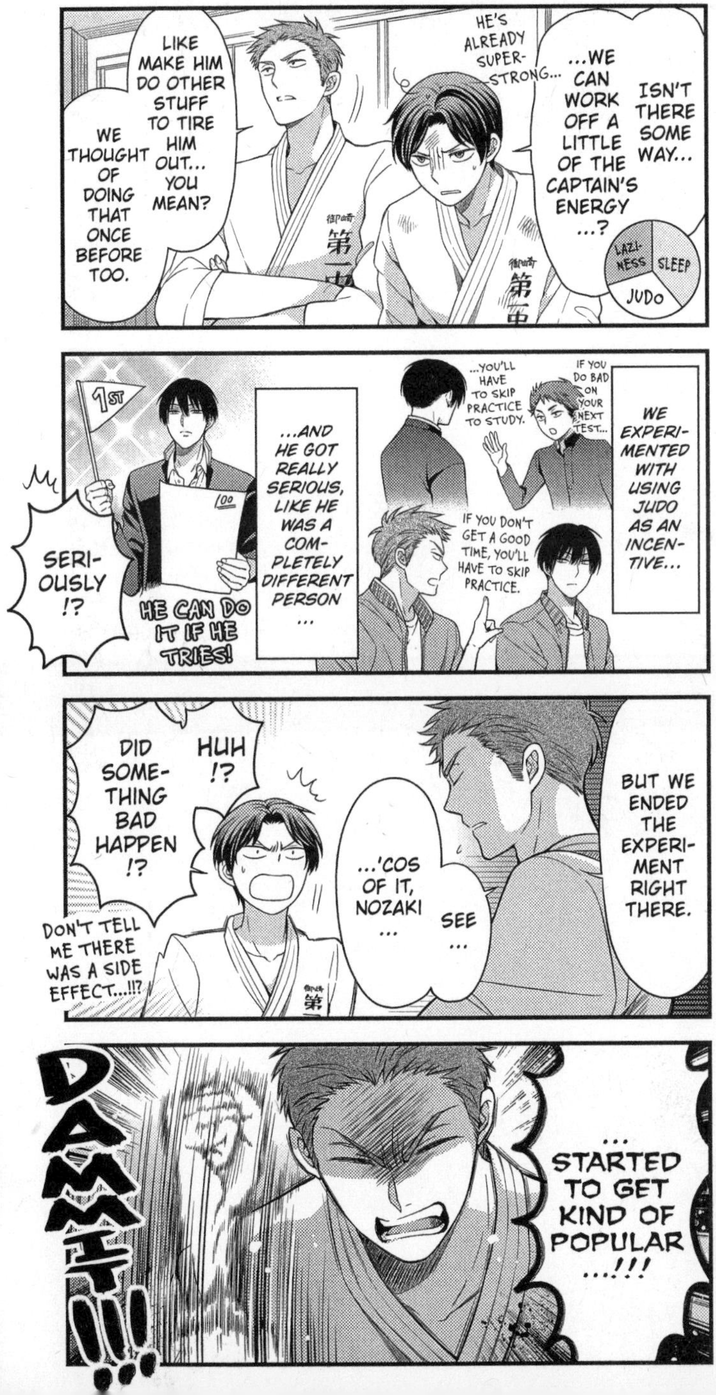
ISN'T THERE SOME WAY...
...WE CAN WORK OFF A LITTLE OF THE CAPTAIN'S ENERGY ...?
HE'S ALREADY SUPER-STRONG...
SLEEP
LAZI-NESS
JUDO
LIKE MAKE HIM DO OTHER STUFF TO TIRE HIM OUT... YOU MEAN?
WE THOUGHT OF DOING THAT ONCE BEFORE TOO.
WE EXPERIMENTED WITH USING JUDO AS AN INCENTIVE...
IF YOU DO BAD ON YOUR NEXT TEST...
...YOU'LL HAVE TO SKIP PRACTICE TO STUDY.
IF YOU DON'T GET A GOOD TIME, YOU'LL HAVE TO SKIP PRACTICE.
...AND HE GOT REALLY SERIOUS, LIKE HE WAS A COMPLETELY DIFFERENT PERSON ...
1ST
100
HE CAN DO IT IF HE TRIES!
SERIOUSLY !?
BUT WE ENDED THE EXPERIMENT RIGHT THERE.
SEE ...
...'COS OF IT, NOZAKI ...
HUH !?
DID SOMETHING BAD HAPPEN !?
DON'T TELL ME THERE WAS A SIDE EFFECT...!!?
... STARTED TO GET KIND OF POPULAR ...!!!
DAMMIT!!!

BIG NOZAKI QUALITY

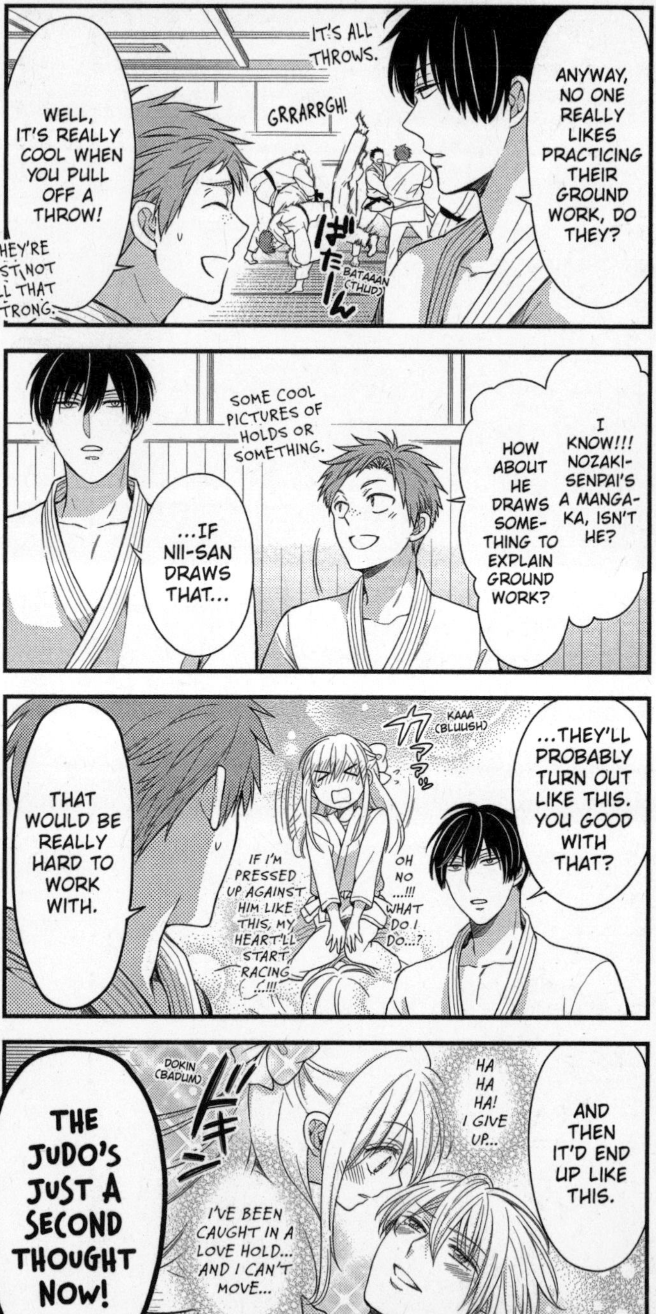

ANYWAY, NO ONE REALLY LIKES PRACTICING THEIR GROUND WORK, DO THEY?
IT'S ALL THROWS.
GRRARRGH!
ばたーん
BATAAAN (THUD)
WELL, IT'S REALLY COOL WHEN YOU PULL OFF A THROW!
THEY'RE JUST NOT ALL THAT STRONG.
I KNOW!!! NOZAKI-SENPAI'S A MANGA-KA, ISN'T HE?
HOW ABOUT HE DRAWS SOMETHING TO EXPLAIN GROUND WORK?
SOME COOL PICTURES OF HOLDS OR SOMETHING.
...IF NII-SAN DRAWS THAT...
...THEY'LL PROBABLY TURN OUT LIKE THIS. YOU GOOD WITH THAT?
KAAA (BLUUSH)
OH NO ...!!! WHAT DO I DO...?
IF I'M PRESSED UP AGAINST HIM LIKE THIS, MY HEART'LL START RACING ...!!!
THAT WOULD BE REALLY HARD TO WORK WITH.
AND THEN IT'D END UP LIKE THIS.
HA HA HA! I GIVE UP...
ドキン
DOKIN (BADUM)
I'VE BEEN CAUGHT IN A LOVE HOLD... AND I CAN'T MOVE...
THE JUDO'S JUST A SECOND THOUGHT NOW!

WHERE HE CAN'T SEE

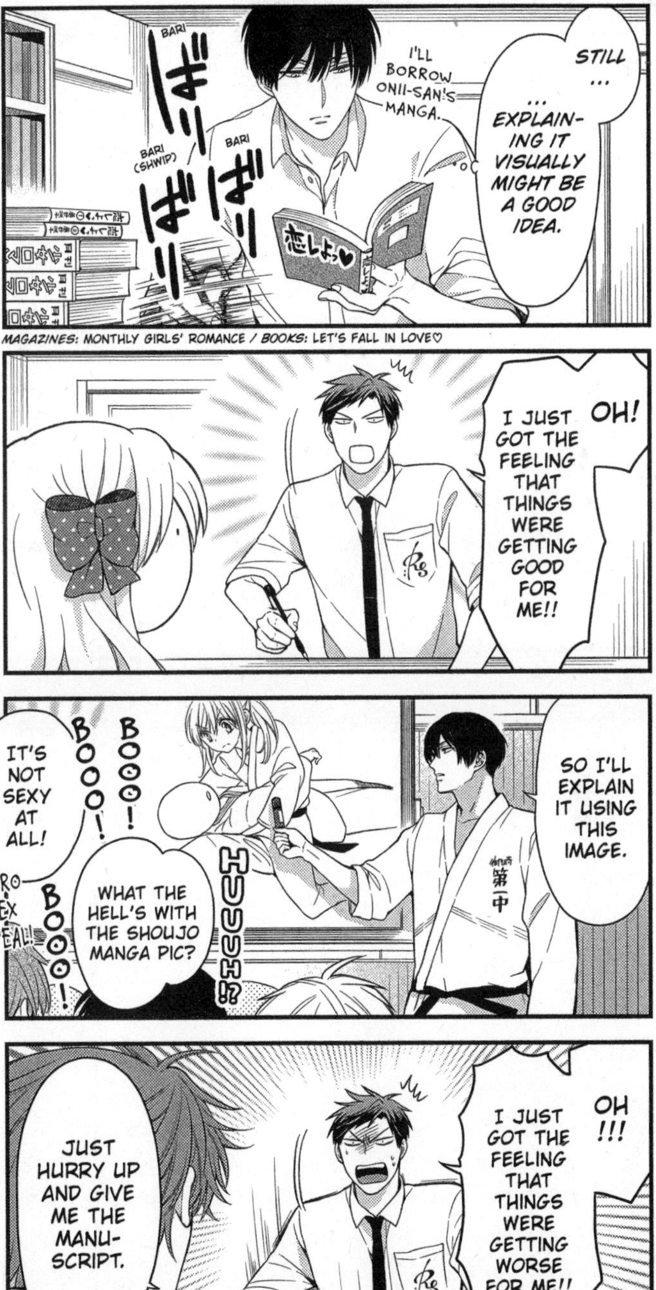
STILL ... ... EXPLAINING IT VISUALLY MIGHT BE A GOOD IDEA.
I'LL BORROW ONII-SAN'S MANGA.
BARI
BARI
BARI (SHWIP)
恋しよっ♥
OH!
I JUST GOT THE FEELING THAT THINGS WERE GETTING GOOD FOR ME!!
SO I'LL EXPLAIN IT USING THIS IMAGE.
HUUUH!?
BOOO!
BOOO!
IT'S NOT SEXY AT ALL!
WHAT THE HELL'S WITH THE SHOUJO MANGA PIC?
BOOO!
ZERO SEX APPEAL!
OH!!!
I JUST GOT THE FEELING THAT THINGS WERE GETTING WORSE FOR ME!!
JUST HURRY UP AND GIVE ME THE MANUSCRIPT.

MAGAZINES: MONTHLY GIRLS' ROMANCE / ***BOOKS:*** LET'S FALL IN LOVE♡

MIKOSHIBA-SENPAI'S EXISTENCE

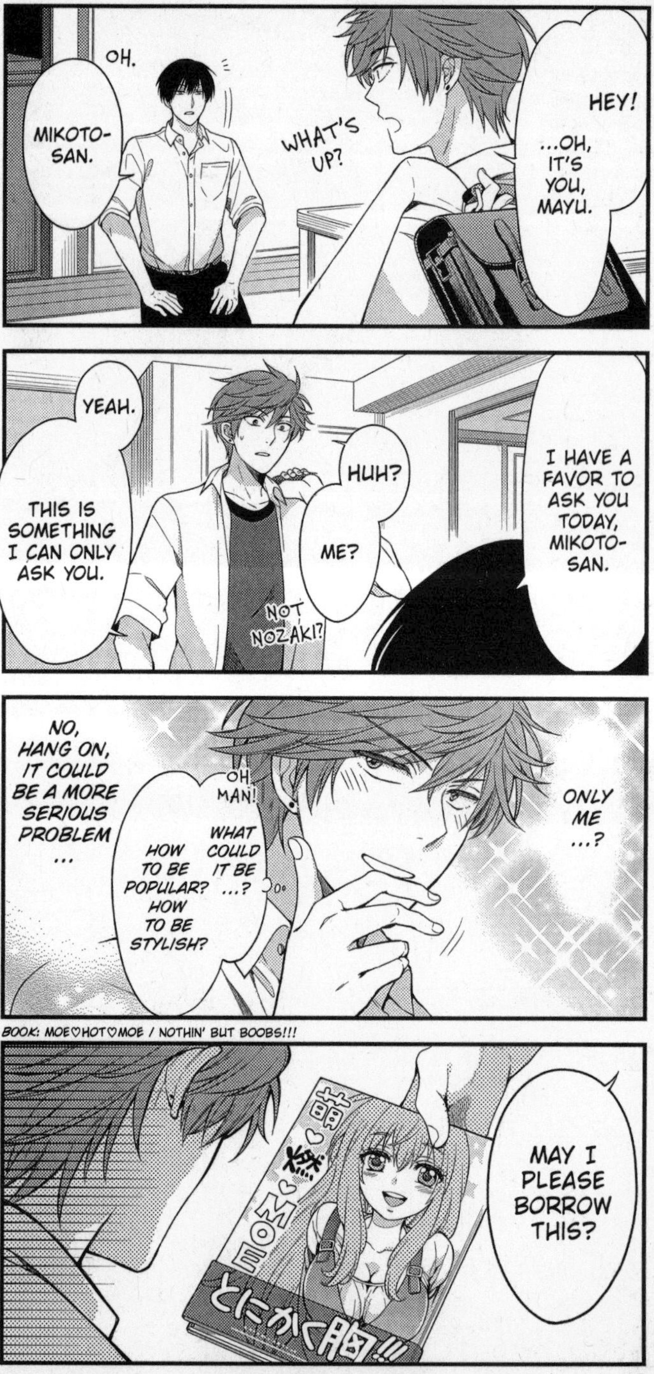
HEY!
...OH, IT'S YOU, MAYU.
WHAT'S UP?
OH.
MIKOTO-SAN.
I HAVE A FAVOR TO ASK YOU TODAY, MIKOTO-SAN.
HUH?
ME?
NOT NOZAKI?
YEAH.
THIS IS SOMETHING I CAN ONLY ASK YOU.
ONLY ME ...?
OH MAN!
WHAT COULD IT BE ...?
HOW TO BE POPULAR? HOW TO BE STYLISH?
NO, HANG ON, IT COULD BE A MORE SERIOUS PROBLEM ...
BOOK: MOE♡HOT♡MOE / NOTHIN' BUT BOOBS!!!
MAY I PLEASE BORROW THIS?
萌♡燃♡MOE
とにかく胸!!!

ACCELERATED LEVELING UP

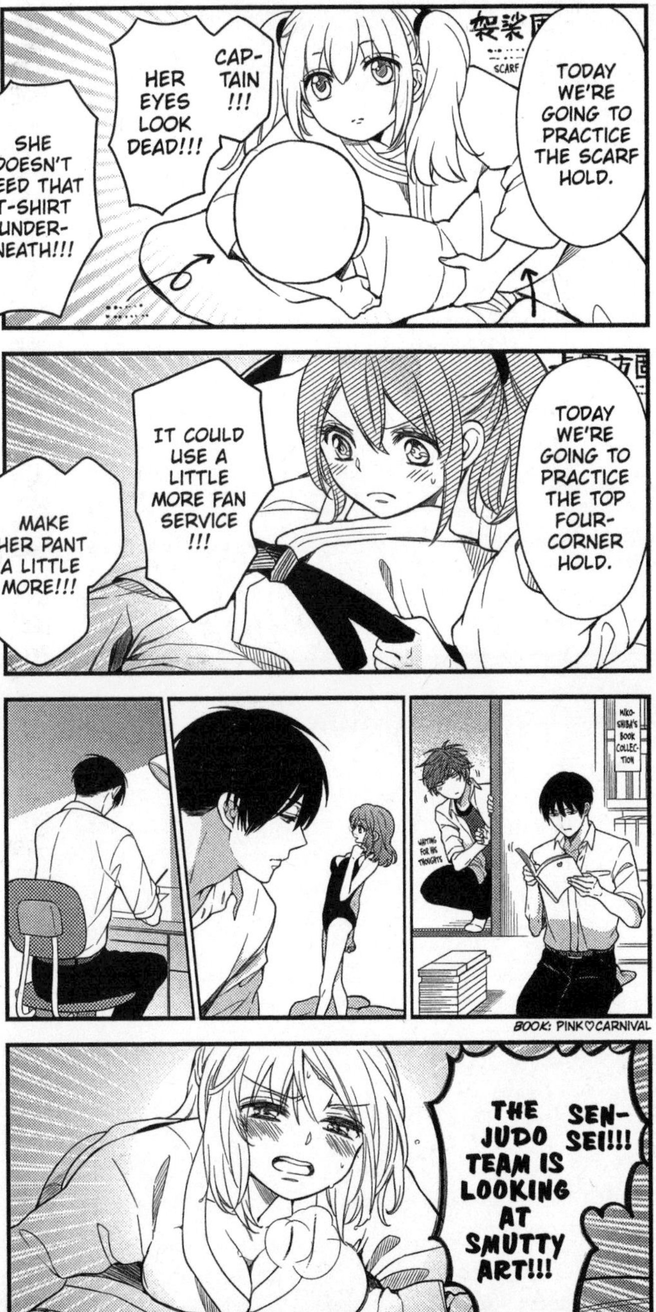
SCARF
TODAY WE'RE GOING TO PRACTICE THE SCARF HOLD.
CAP-TAIN!!!
HER EYES LOOK DEAD!!!
SHE DOESN'T NEED THAT T-SHIRT UNDER-NEATH!!!
TODAY WE'RE GOING TO PRACTICE THE TOP FOUR-CORNER HOLD.
IT COULD USE A LITTLE MORE FAN SERVICE!!!
MAKE HER PANT A LITTLE MORE!!!
MIKO-SHIBA'S BOOK COLLEC-TION
WAITING FOR HIS THOUGHTS
BOOK: PINK♡CARNIVAL
SEN-SEI!!! THE JUDO TEAM IS LOOKING AT SMUTTY ART!!!

THE RESULTS OF PRACTICE ①

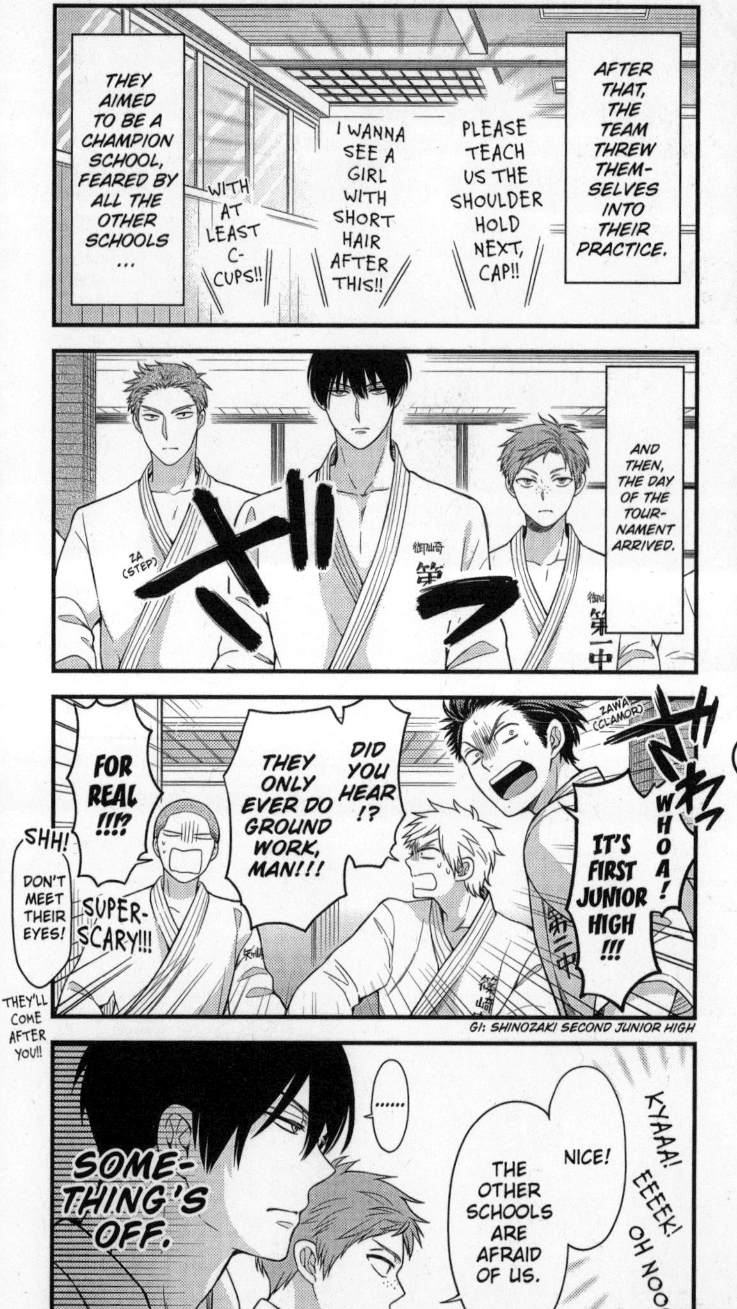

AFTER THAT, THE TEAM THREW THEMSELVES INTO THEIR PRACTICE.
PLEASE TEACH US THE SHOULDER HOLD NEXT, CAP!!
I WANNA SEE A GIRL WITH SHORT HAIR AFTER THIS!!
WITH AT LEAST C-CUPS!!
THEY AIMED TO BE A CHAMPION SCHOOL, FEARED BY ALL THE OTHER SCHOOLS ...
AND THEN, THE DAY OF THE TOURNAMENT ARRIVED.
ZA (STEP)
ZAWA (CLAMOR)
WHOA!
IT'S FIRST JUNIOR HIGH!!!
DID YOU HEAR!?
THEY ONLY EVER DO GROUND WORK, MAN!!!
FOR REAL!!!?
SUPER-SCARY!!!
SHH!
DON'T MEET THEIR EYES!
THEY'LL COME AFTER YOU!!
GI: SHINOZAKI SECOND JUNIOR HIGH
KYAAA! EEEEK! OH NOOO!
NICE!
THE OTHER SCHOOLS ARE AFRAID OF US.
......
SOMETHING'S OFF.

THE RESULTS OF PRACTICE ②

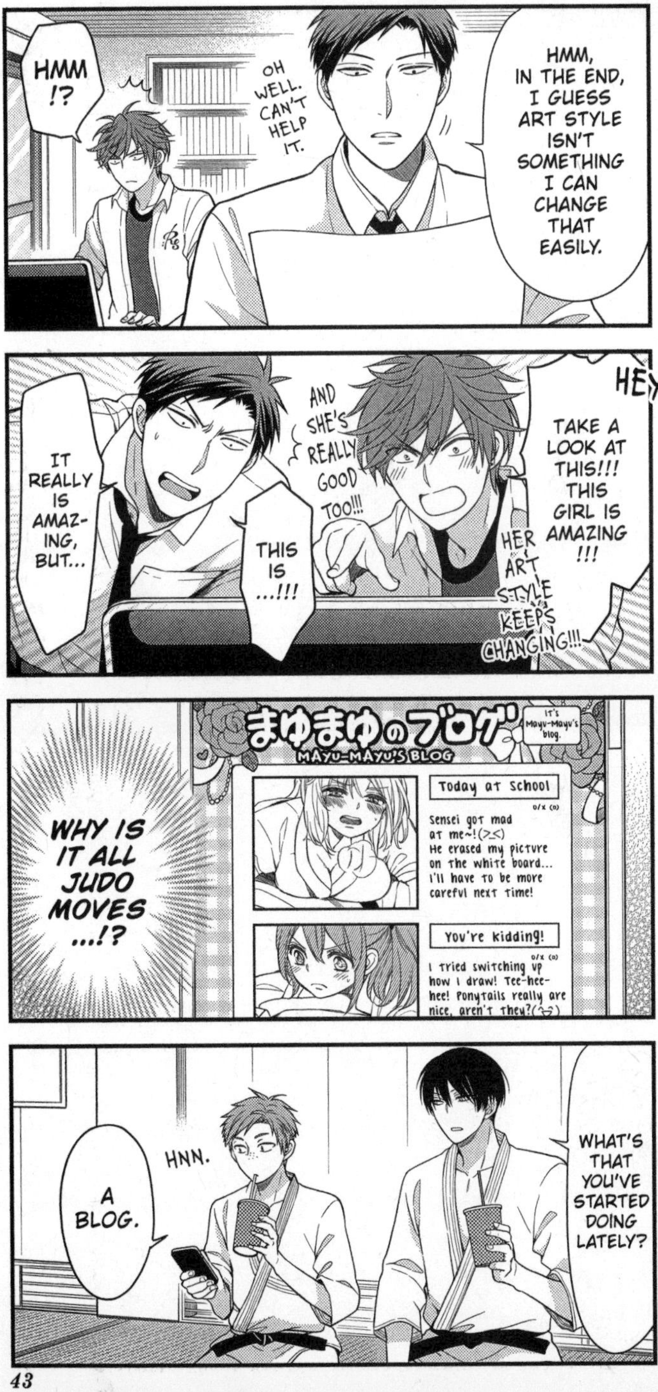
HMM, IN THE END, I GUESS ART STYLE ISN'T SOMETHING I CAN CHANGE THAT EASILY.
OH WELL. CAN'T HELP IT.
HMM!?
HEY!
TAKE A LOOK AT THIS!!! THIS GIRL IS AMAZING!!!
HER ART STYLE KEEPS CHANGING!!!
AND SHE'S REALLY GOOD TOO!!!
THIS IS ...!!!
IT REALLY IS AMAZING, BUT...
まゆまゆのブログ
MAYU-MAYU'S BLOG
It's Mayu-Mayu's blog.
Today at School
Sensei got mad at me~!(>_<) He erased my picture on the white board... I'll have to be more careful next time!
You're kidding!
I tried switching up how I draw! Tee-hee-hee! Ponytails really are nice, aren't they?
WHY IS IT ALL JUDO MOVES ...!?
WHAT'S THAT YOU'VE STARTED DOING LATELY?
HNN.
A BLOG.

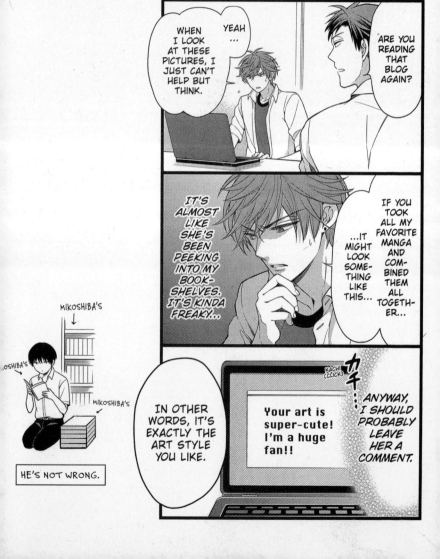

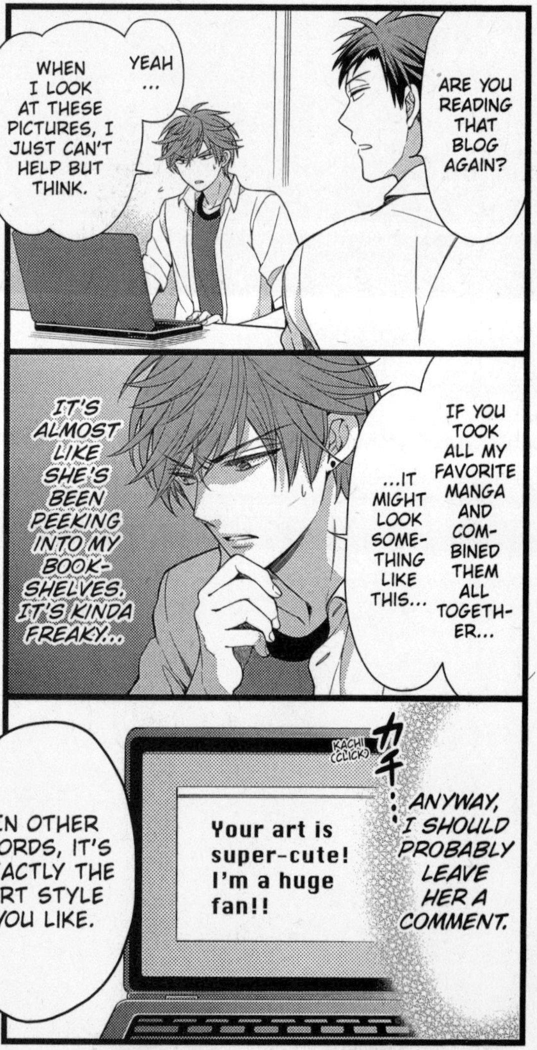
ARE YOU READING THAT BLOG AGAIN?
YEAH...
WHEN I LOOK AT THESE PICTURES, I JUST CAN'T HELP BUT THINK.
IF YOU TOOK ALL MY FAVORITE MANGA AND COM-BINED THEM ALL TOGETH-ER...
...IT MIGHT LOOK SOME-THING LIKE THIS...
IT'S ALMOST LIKE SHE'S BEEN PEEKING INTO MY BOOK-SHELVES. IT'S KINDA FREAKY...
KACHI (CLICK)
ANYWAY, I SHOULD PROBABLY LEAVE HER A COMMENT.
Your art is super-cute! I'm a huge fan!!
IN OTHER WORDS, IT'S EXACTLY THE ART STYLE YOU LIKE.

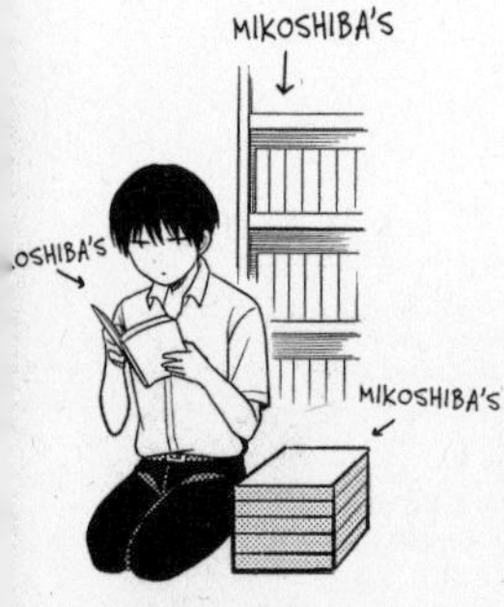
MIKOSHIBA'S
OSHIBA'S
MIKOSHIBA'S

HE'S NOT WRONG.

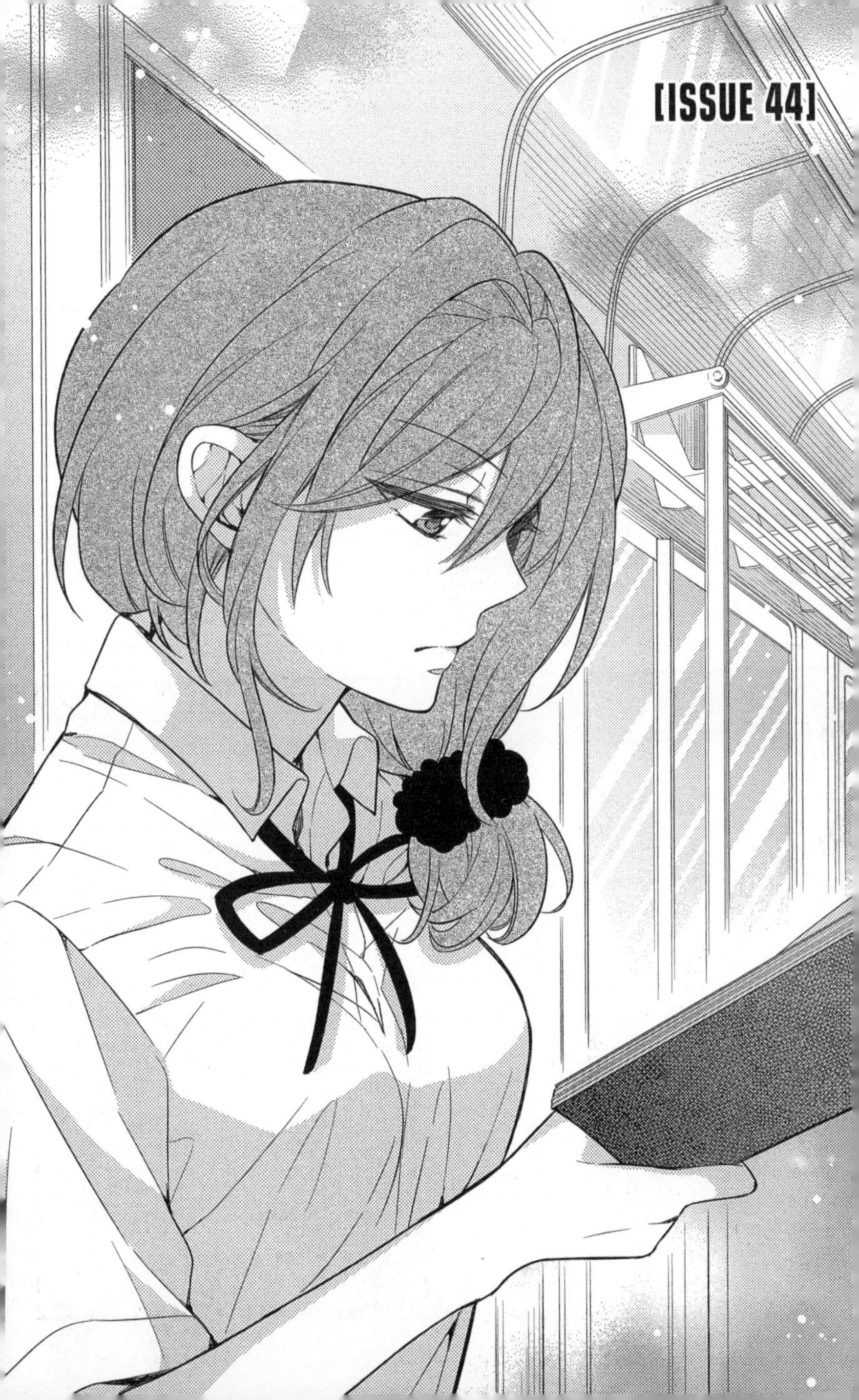
[ISSUE 44]

HE HAS SEVERAL PATTERNS READY

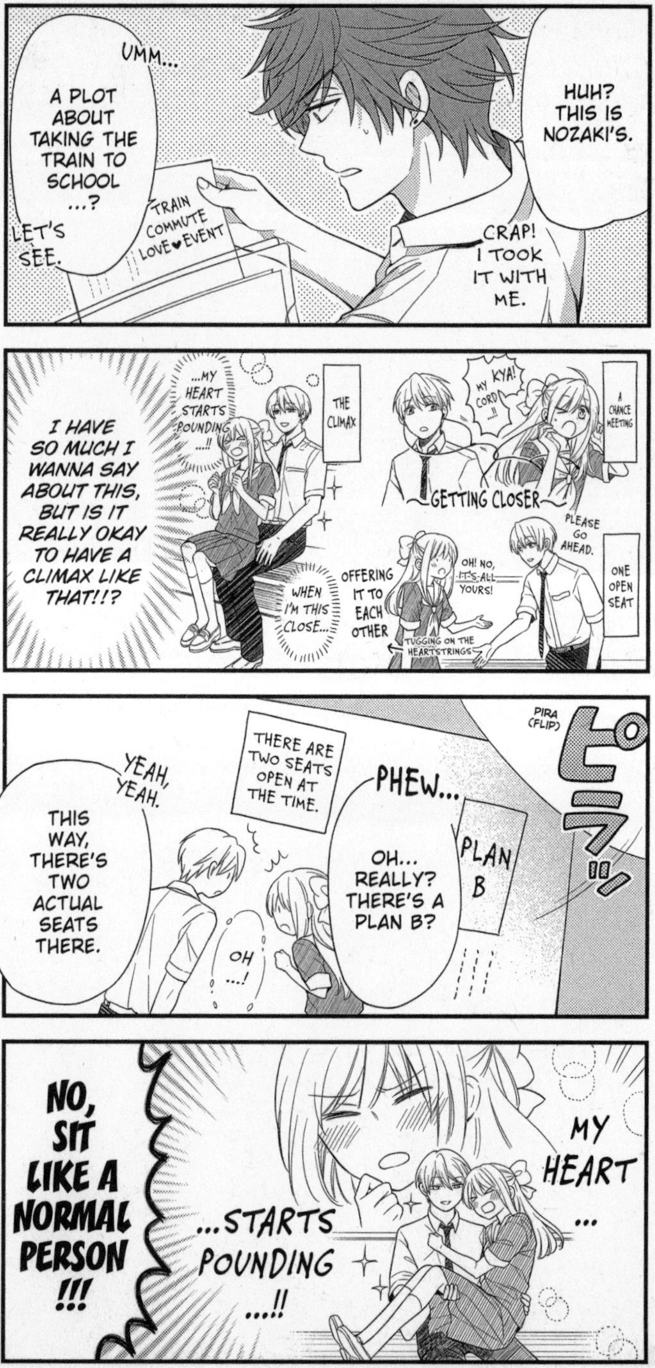

HUH? THIS IS NOZAKI'S.
CRAP! I TOOK IT WITH ME.
UMM... A PLOT ABOUT TAKING THE TRAIN TO SCHOOL ...?
TRAIN COMMUTE LOVE♥EVENT
LET'S SEE.
A CHANCE MEETING
KYA! MY CORD ...!!
GETTING CLOSER
THE CLIMAX
...MY HEART STARTS POUNDING ...!!
I HAVE SO MUCH I WANNA SAY ABOUT THIS, BUT IS IT REALLY OKAY TO HAVE A CLIMAX LIKE THAT!!?
ONE OPEN SEAT
PLEASE GO AHEAD.
OH! NO, IT'S ALL YOURS!
OFFERING IT TO EACH OTHER
TUGGING ON THE HEARTSTRINGS
WHEN I'M THIS CLOSE...
PIRA (FLIP)
ピラッ
PLAN B
PHEW...
OH... REALLY? THERE'S A PLAN B?
THERE ARE TWO SEATS OPEN AT THE TIME.
YEAH, YEAH.
THIS WAY, THERE'S TWO ACTUAL SEATS THERE.
OH ...!
MY HEART ...
...STARTS POUNDING ...!!
NO, SIT LIKE A NORMAL PERSON!!!

THIS LEADS TO...

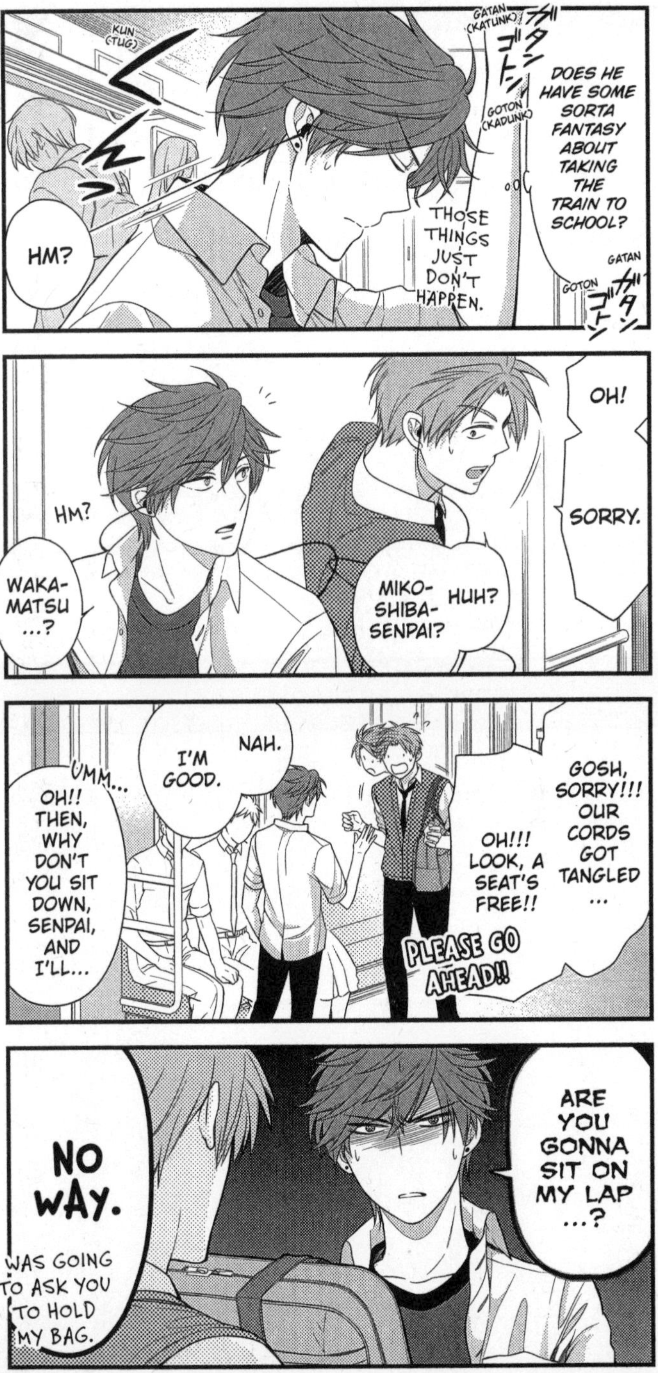

GATAN (KATUNK)
ガタ
ゴトン
GOTON (KADUNK)
DOES HE HAVE SOME SORTA FANTASY ABOUT TAKING THE TRAIN TO SCHOOL?
THOSE THINGS JUST DON'T HAPPEN.
GATAN
ガタン
GOTON
ゴトン
KUN (TUG)
HM?
OH!
SORRY.
HUH?
MIKO-SHIBA-SENPAI?
HM?
WAKA-MATSU ...?
GOSH, SORRY!!! OUR CORDS GOT TANGLED ...
OH!!! LOOK, A SEAT'S FREE!!
PLEASE GO AHEAD!!
NAH.
I'M GOOD.
UMM...
OH!! THEN, WHY DON'T YOU SIT DOWN, SENPAI, AND I'LL...
ARE YOU GONNA SIT ON MY LAP ...?
NO WAY.
I WAS GOING TO ASK YOU TO HOLD MY BAG.

POWER

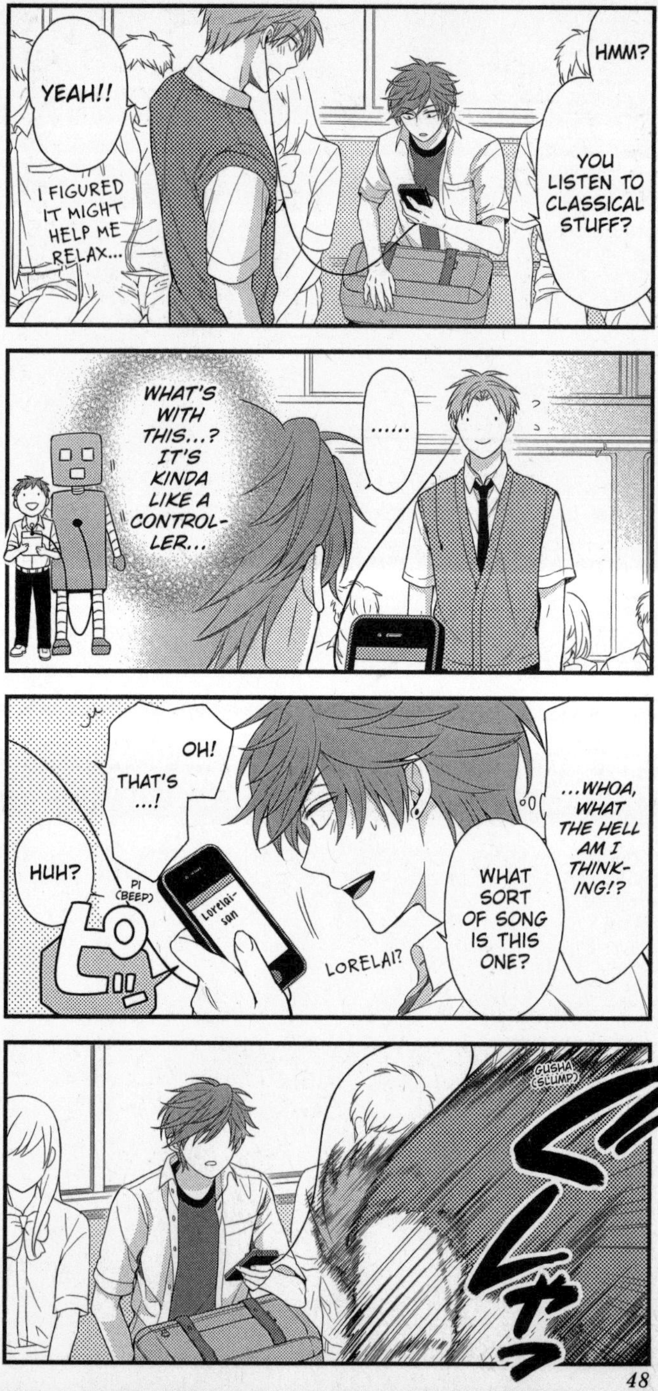
HMM?
YOU LISTEN TO CLASSICAL STUFF?
YEAH!!
I FIGURED IT MIGHT HELP ME RELAX...
......
WHAT'S WITH THIS...? IT'S KINDA LIKE A CONTROLLER...
...WHOA, WHAT THE HELL AM I THINKING!?
WHAT SORT OF SONG IS THIS ONE?
LORELAI?
Lorelai-san
OH! THAT'S ...!
HUH?
ピッ
PI (BEEP)
GUSHA (SLUMP)
ぐしゃっ

"LORELAI OF THE GLEE CLUB"

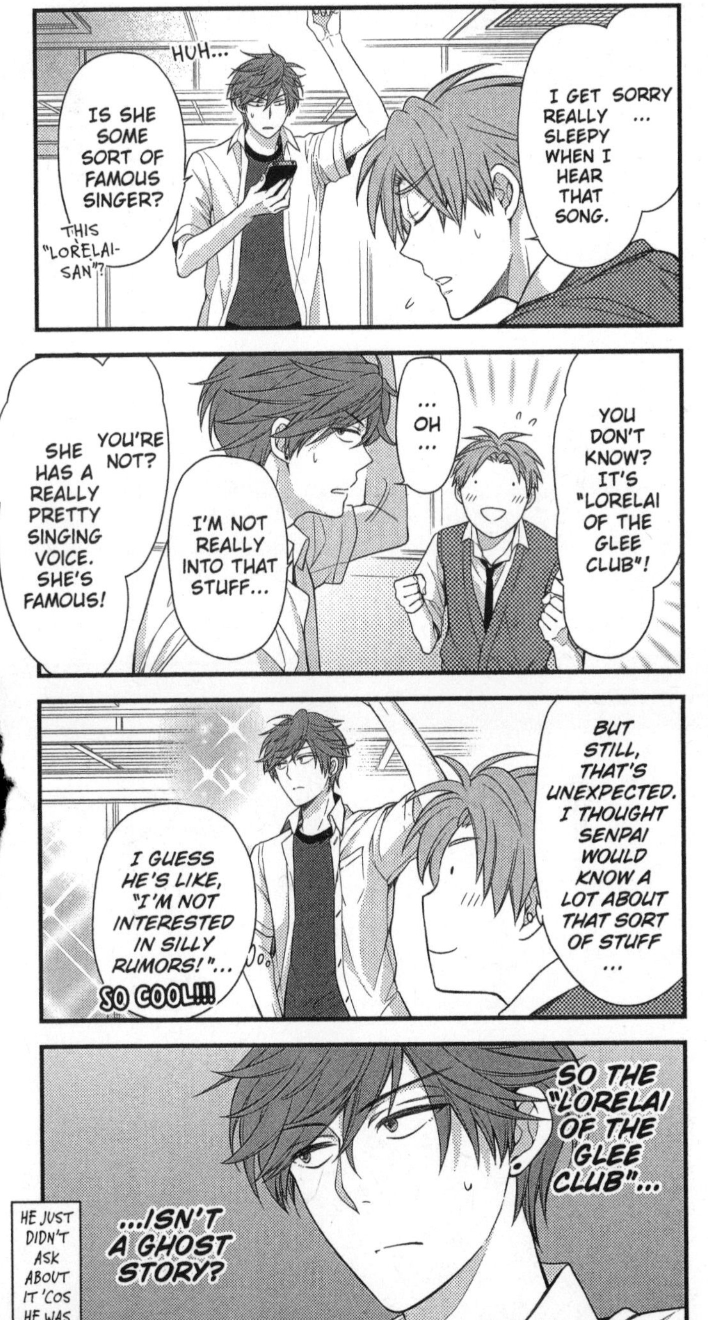
SORRY ... I GET REALLY SLEEPY WHEN I HEAR THAT SONG.
HUH...
IS SHE SOME SORT OF FAMOUS SINGER?
THIS "LORELAI-SAN"?
YOU DON'T KNOW? IT'S "LORELAI OF THE GLEE CLUB"!
... OH ...
I'M NOT REALLY INTO THAT STUFF...
YOU'RE NOT? SHE HAS A REALLY PRETTY SINGING VOICE. SHE'S FAMOUS!
BUT STILL, THAT'S UNEXPECTED. I THOUGHT SENPAI WOULD KNOW A LOT ABOUT THAT SORT OF STUFF ...
I GUESS HE'S LIKE, "I'M NOT INTERESTED IN SILLY RUMORS!"...
SO COOL!!!
SO THE "LORELAI OF THE GLEE CLUB"...
...ISN'T A GHOST STORY?
HE JUST DIDN'T ASK ABOUT IT 'COS HE WAS SCARED.

SENPAI'S HIGH LEVEL CONVERSATION

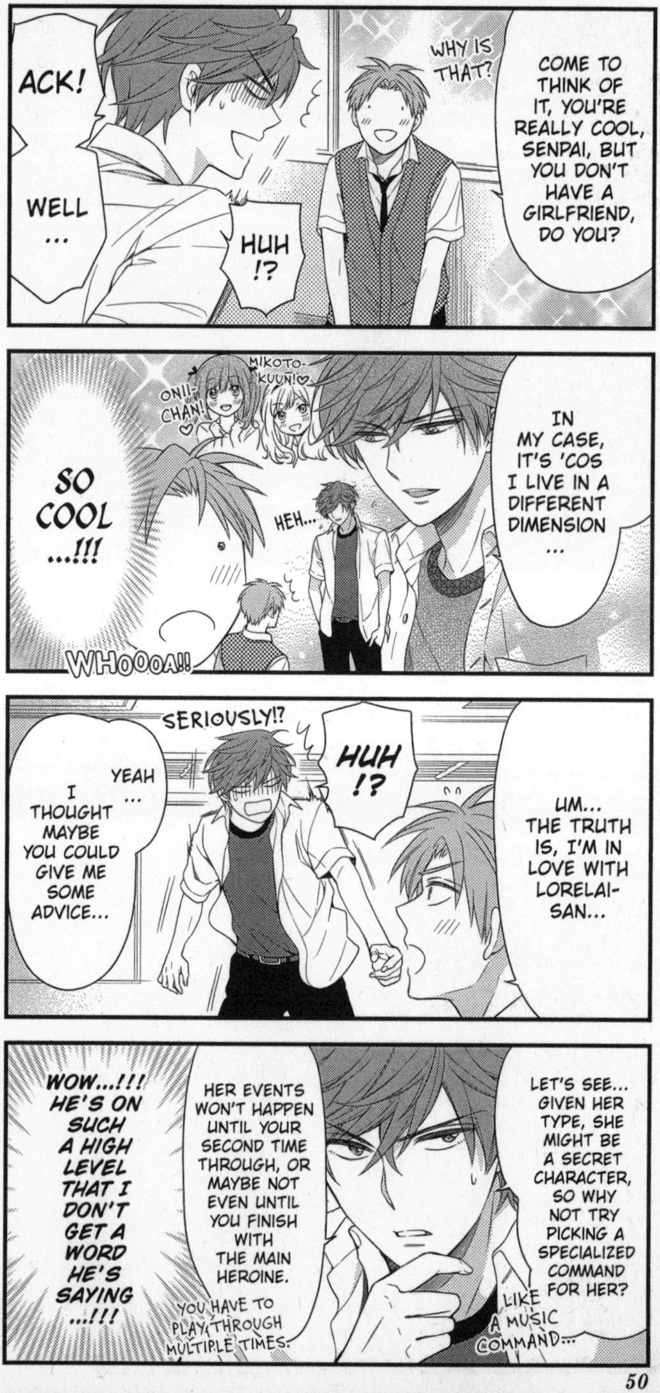
COME TO THINK OF IT, YOU'RE REALLY COOL, SENPAI, BUT YOU DON'T HAVE A GIRLFRIEND, DO YOU?
WHY IS THAT?
HUH!?
ACK!
WELL...
IN MY CASE, IT'S 'COS I LIVE IN A DIFFERENT DIMENSION...
MIKOTO-KUUN!♡
ONII-CHAN!♡
HEH...
SO COOL...!!!
WHOOOA!!
UM... THE TRUTH IS, I'M IN LOVE WITH LORELAI-SAN...
HUH!?
SERIOUSLY!?
YEAH... I THOUGHT MAYBE YOU COULD GIVE ME SOME ADVICE...
LET'S SEE... GIVEN HER TYPE, SHE MIGHT BE A SECRET CHARACTER, SO WHY NOT TRY PICKING A SPECIALIZED COMMAND FOR HER?
LIKE A MUSIC COMMAND...
HER EVENTS WON'T HAPPEN UNTIL YOUR SECOND TIME THROUGH, OR MAYBE NOT EVEN UNTIL YOU FINISH WITH THE MAIN HEROINE.
YOU HAVE TO PLAY THROUGH MULTIPLE TIMES.
WOW...!!! HE'S ON SUCH A HIGH LEVEL THAT I DON'T GET A WORD HE'S SAYING...!!!

ADVANCE NOTICE

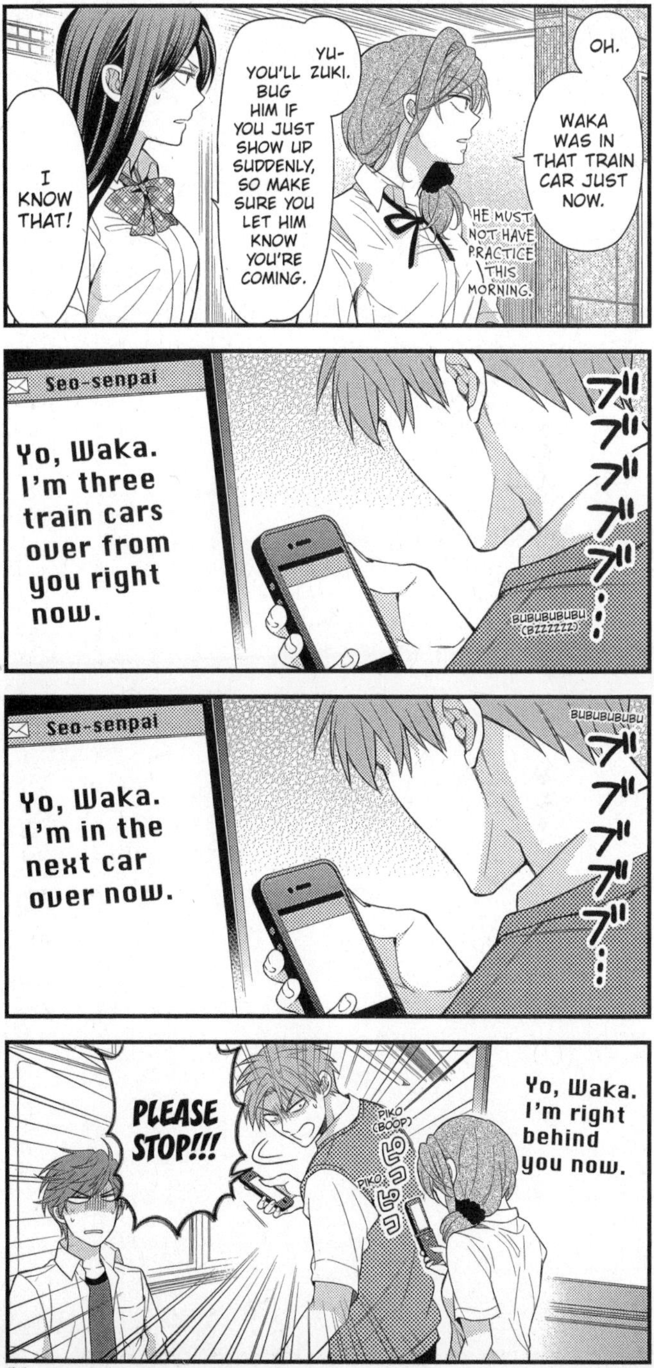

OH.
WAKA WAS IN THAT TRAIN CAR JUST NOW.
HE MUST NOT HAVE PRACTICE THIS MORNING.
YUZUKI. YOU'LL BUG HIM IF YOU JUST SHOW UP SUDDENLY, SO MAKE SURE YOU LET HIM KNOW YOU'RE COMING.
I KNOW THAT!
ブブブブブ…
BUBUBUBUBU (BZZZZZZ)
Seo-senpai
Yo, Waka. I'm three train cars over from you right now.
BUBUBUBUBU
ブブブブブ…
Seo-senpai
Yo, Waka. I'm in the next car over now.
Yo, Waka. I'm right behind you now.
PIKO (BOOP)
PIKO
PLEASE STOP!!!

THE TRUTH HE DIDN'T REALLY WANT TO KNOW

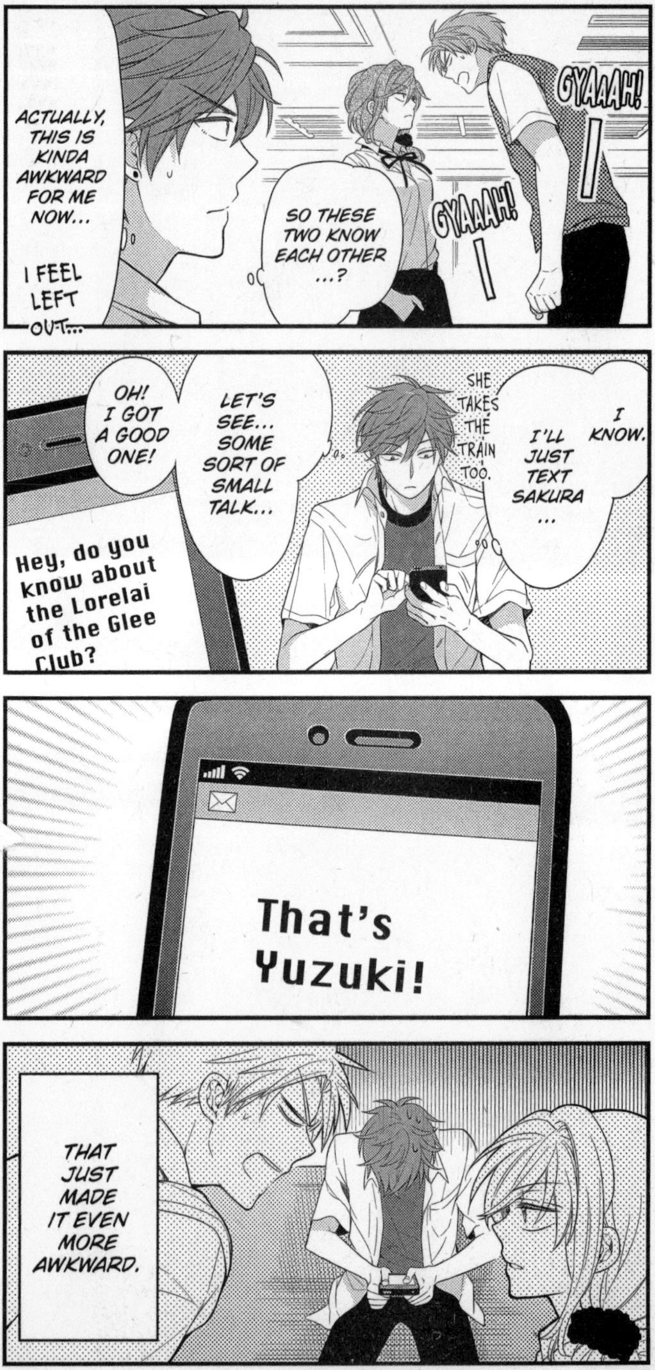
GYAAAH!
GYAAAH!
SO THESE TWO KNOW EACH OTHER ...?
ACTUALLY, THIS IS KINDA AWKWARD FOR ME NOW...
I FEEL LEFT OUT...
I KNOW.
I'LL JUST TEXT SAKURA...
SHE TAKES THE TRAIN TOO.
LET'S SEE... SOME SORT OF SMALL TALK...
OH! I GOT A GOOD ONE!
Hey, do you know about the Lorelai of the Glee Club?
That's Yuzuki!
THAT JUST MADE IT EVEN MORE AWKWARD.

TAKING A STEP BACK

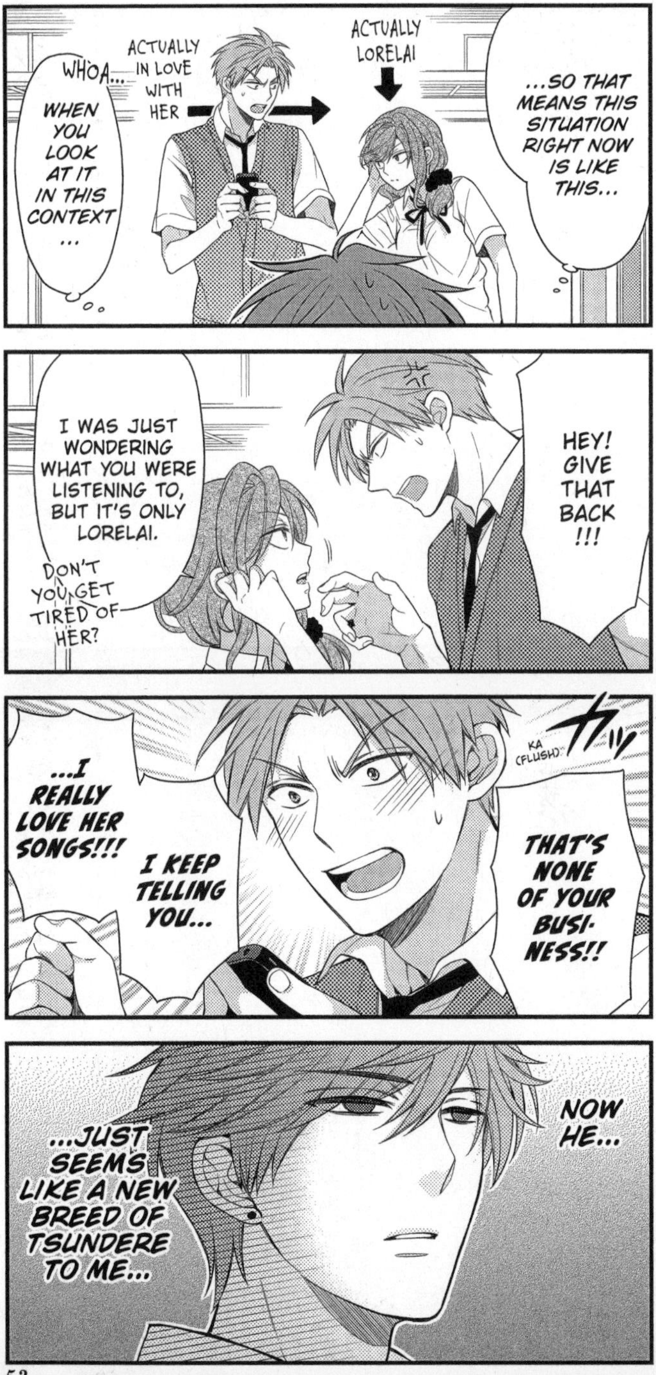

...SO THAT MEANS THIS SITUATION RIGHT NOW IS LIKE THIS...
ACTUALLY LORELAI
ACTUALLY IN LOVE WITH HER
WHOA... WHEN YOU LOOK AT IT IN THIS CONTEXT...
HEY! GIVE THAT BACK!!!
I WAS JUST WONDERING WHAT YOU WERE LISTENING TO, BUT IT'S ONLY LORELAI.
DON'T YOU GET TIRED OF HER?
KA (FLUSH)
THAT'S NONE OF YOUR BUSI-NESS!!
I KEEP TELLING YOU...
...I REALLY LOVE HER SONGS!!!
NOW HE...
...JUST SEEMS LIKE A NEW BREED OF TSUNDERE TO ME...

INNOCENCE AND STABILITY

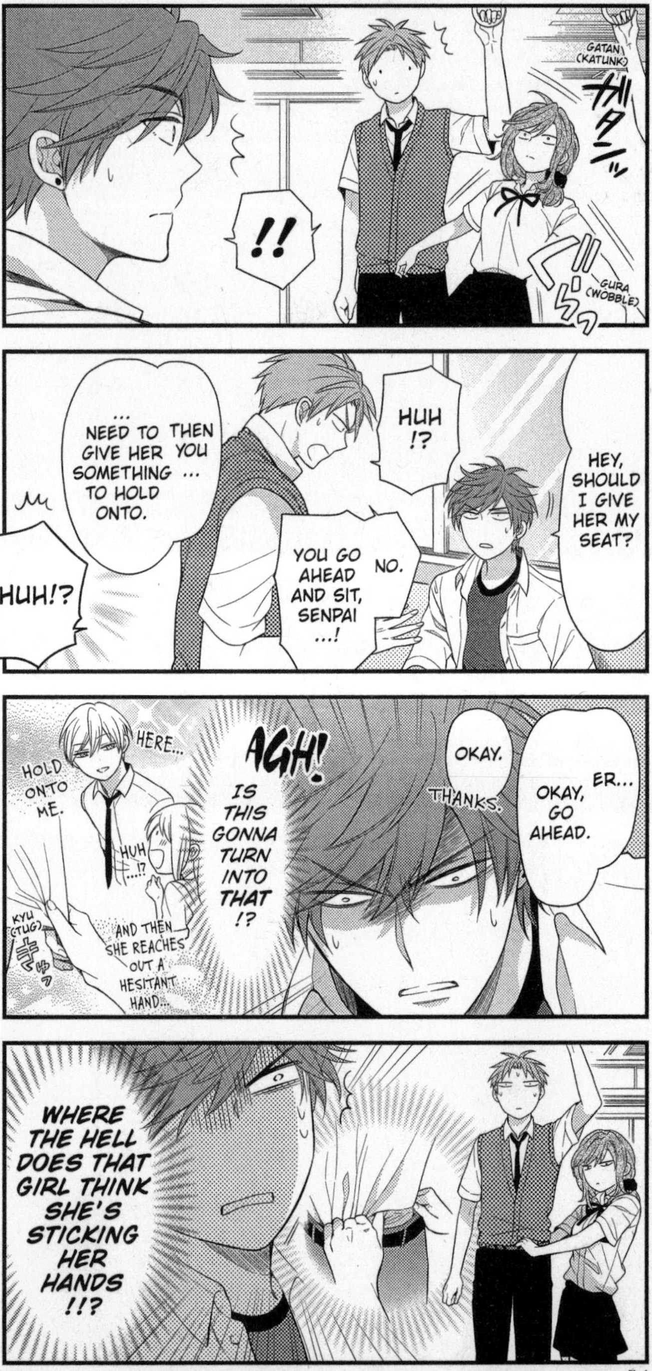
GATAN (KATUNK)
!!
GURA (WOBBLE)
HEY, SHOULD I GIVE HER MY SEAT?
HUH !?
NO.
YOU GO AHEAD AND SIT, SENPAI ...!
... NEED TO THEN GIVE HER YOU SOMETHING ... TO HOLD ONTO.
HUH!?
ER... OKAY, GO AHEAD.
OKAY.
THANKS.
AGH!
IS THIS GONNA TURN INTO THAT !?
HERE...
HOLD ONTO ME.
HUH ...!?
AND THEN SHE REACHES OUT A HESITANT HAND...
KYU (TUG)
WHERE THE HELL DOES THAT GIRL THINK SHE'S STICKING HER HANDS !!?

DEAL WITH IT

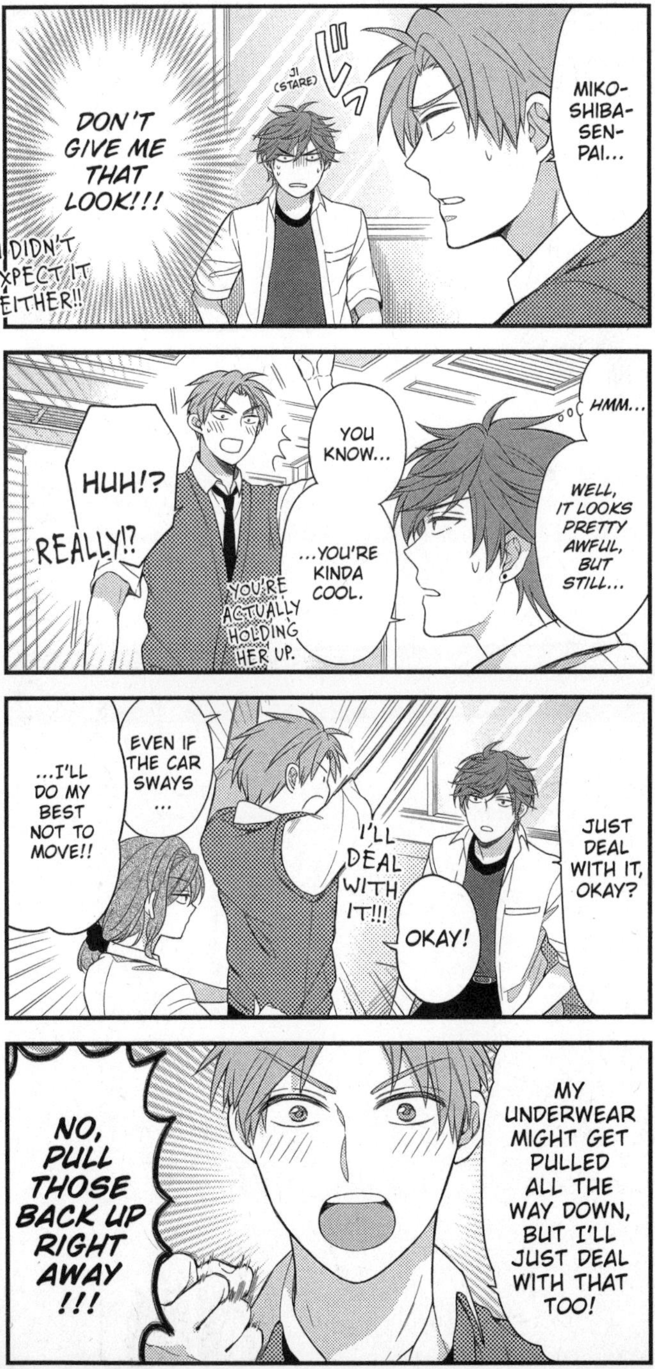
MIKO-SHIBA-SEN-PAI...
JI (STARE)
DON'T GIVE ME THAT LOOK!!!
I DIDN'T EXPECT IT EITHER!!
HMM...
WELL, IT LOOKS PRETTY AWFUL, BUT STILL...
YOU KNOW...
...YOU'RE KINDA COOL.
YOU'RE ACTUALLY HOLDING HER UP.
HUH!?
REALLY!?
JUST DEAL WITH IT, OKAY?
OKAY!
I'LL DEAL WITH IT!!!
EVEN IF THE CAR SWAYS...
...I'LL DO MY BEST NOT TO MOVE!!
MY UNDERWEAR MIGHT GET PULLED ALL THE WAY DOWN, BUT I'LL JUST DEAL WITH THAT TOO!
NO, PULL THOSE BACK UP RIGHT AWAY!!!

THIS LEADS TO... ②

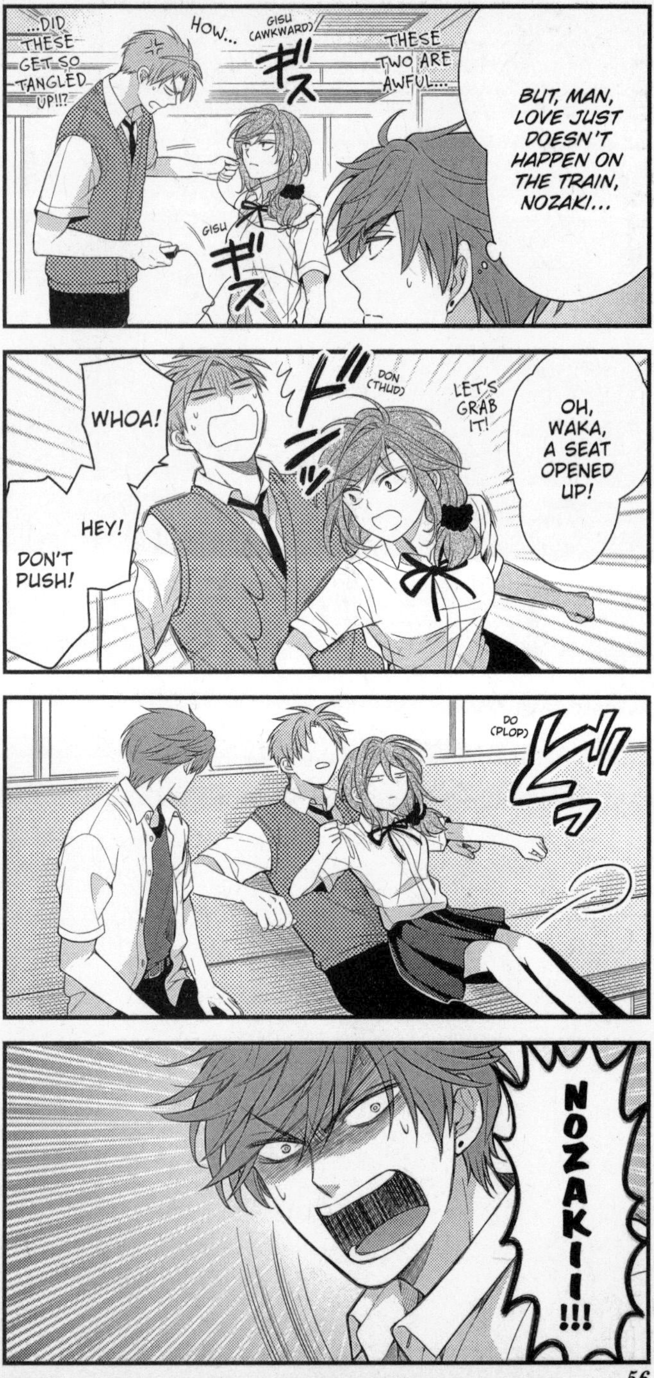
BUT, MAN, LOVE JUST DOESN'T HAPPEN ON THE TRAIN, NOZAKI...
THESE TWO ARE AWFUL...
GISU (AWKWARD)
HOW...
...DID THESE GET SO TANGLED UP!!?
GISU
OH, WAKA, A SEAT OPENED UP!
LET'S GRAB IT!
DON (THUD)
WHOA!
HEY!
DON'T PUSH!
DO (PLOP)
NOZAKI!!!

WHY IT WAS REJECTED

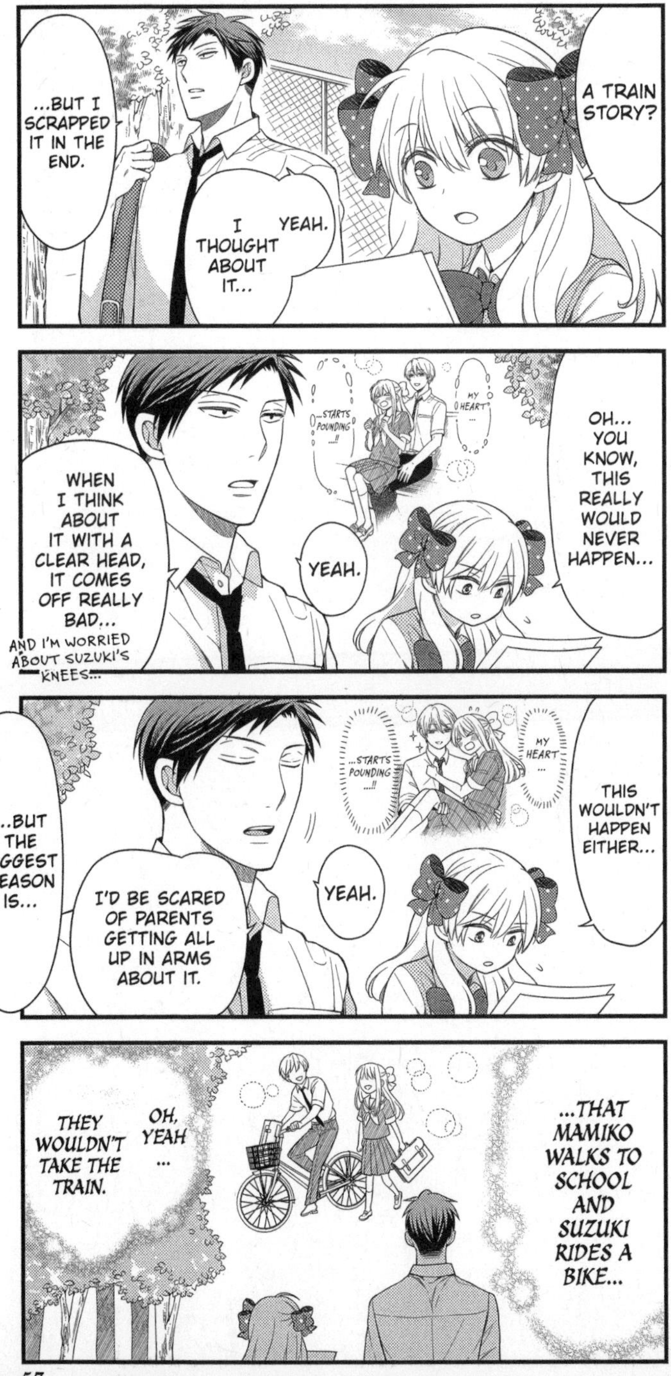
A TRAIN STORY?
YEAH.
I THOUGHT ABOUT IT...
...BUT I SCRAPPED IT IN THE END.
OH... YOU KNOW, THIS REALLY WOULD NEVER HAPPEN...
MY HEART...
...STARTS POUNDING...!!
YEAH.
WHEN I THINK ABOUT IT WITH A CLEAR HEAD, IT COMES OFF REALLY BAD...
AND I'M WORRIED ABOUT SUZUKI'S KNEES...
THIS WOULDN'T HAPPEN EITHER...
MY HEART...
...STARTS POUNDING...!!
YEAH.
...BUT THE BIGGEST REASON IS...
I'D BE SCARED OF PARENTS GETTING ALL UP IN ARMS ABOUT IT.
...THAT MAMIKO WALKS TO SCHOOL AND SUZUKI RIDES A BIKE...
OH, YEAH...
THEY WOULDN'T TAKE THE TRAIN.

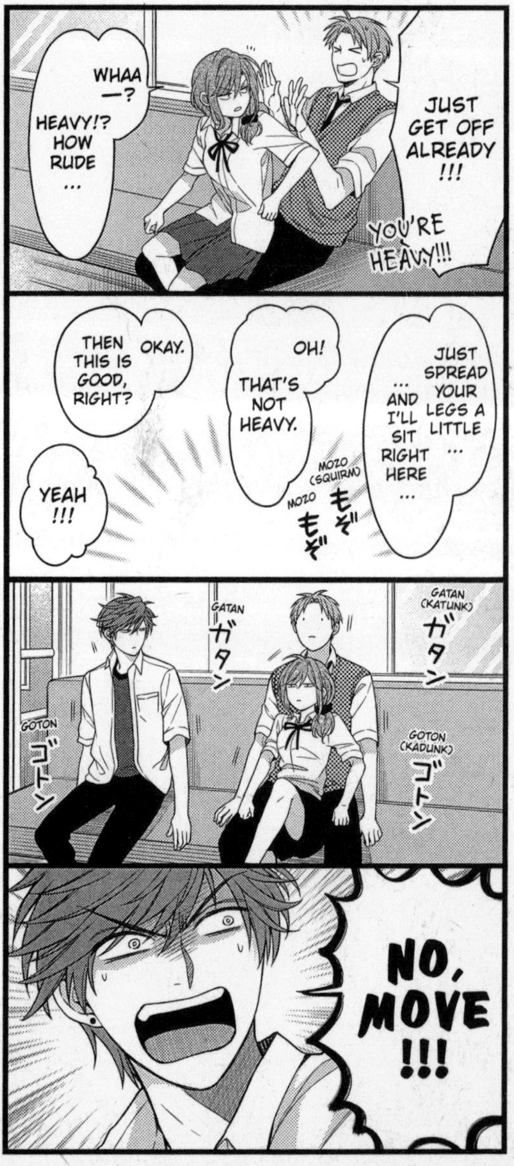
JUST GET OFF ALREADY!!!
YOU'RE HEAVY!!!
WHAA—?
HEAVY!? HOW RUDE...
JUST SPREAD YOUR LEGS A LITTLE...
...AND I'LL SIT RIGHT HERE...
MOZO (SQUIRM) もぞ
MOZO もぞ
OH!
THAT'S NOT HEAVY.
OKAY.
THEN THIS IS GOOD, RIGHT?
YEAH!!!
GATAN (KATUNK) ガタン
GOTON (KADUNK) ゴトン
GATAN ガタン
GOTON ゴトン
NO, MOVE!!!

[ISSUE 45]

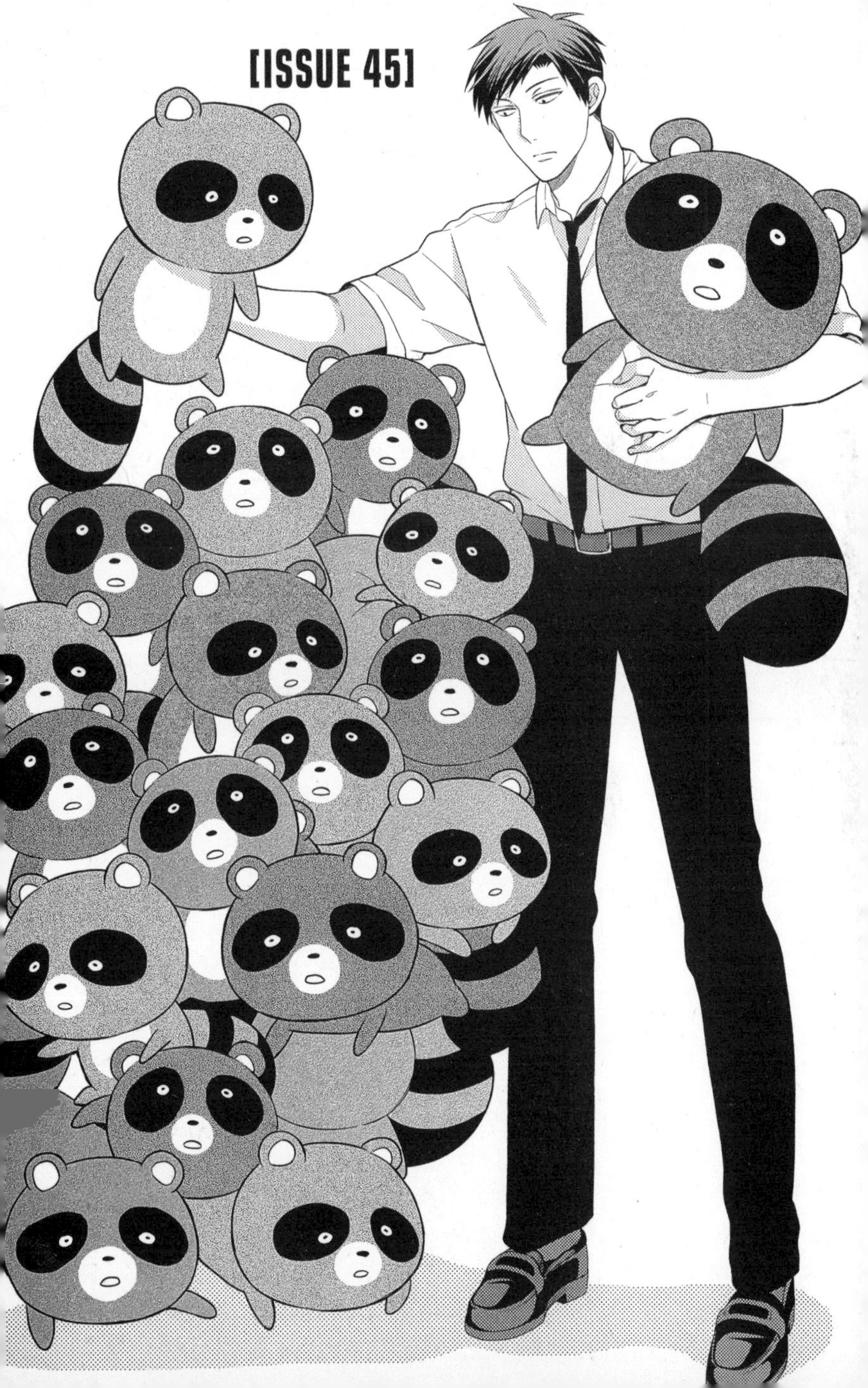

CHIBI CHARACTERS

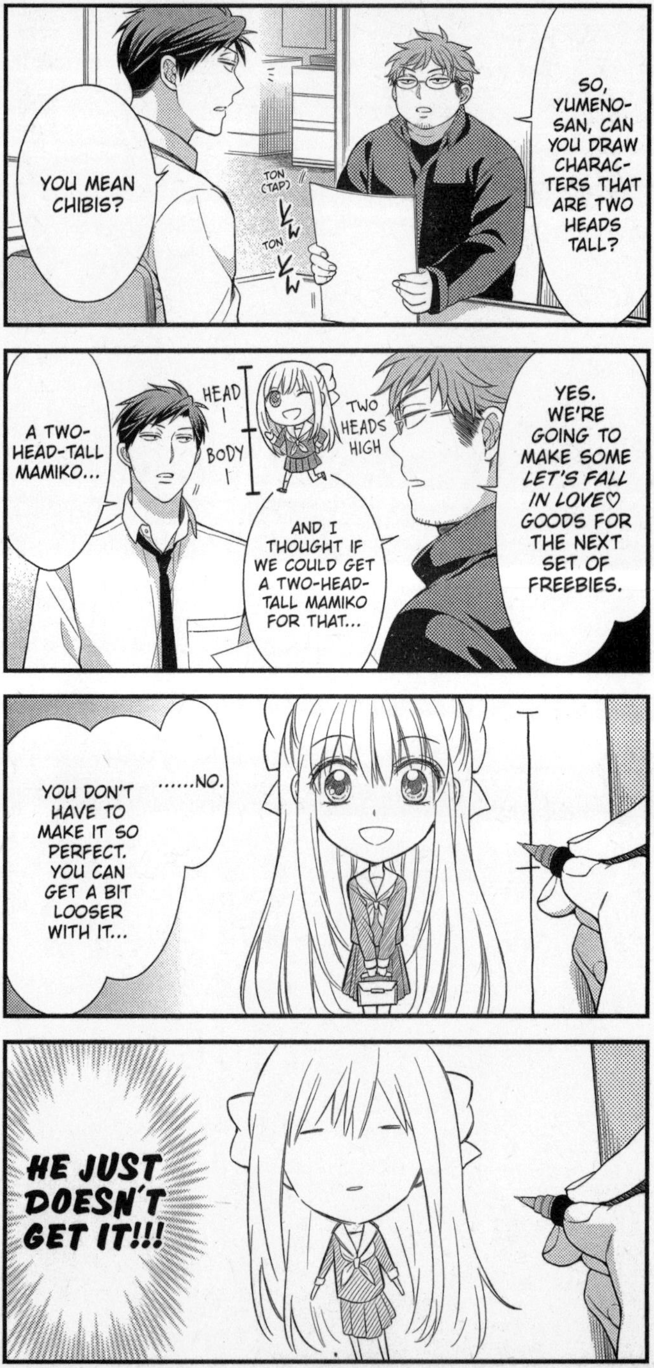

SO, YUMENO-SAN, CAN YOU DRAW CHARACTERS THAT ARE TWO HEADS TALL?
TON (TAP)
TON
YOU MEAN CHIBIS?
YES. WE'RE GOING TO MAKE SOME LET'S FALL IN LOVE♡ GOODS FOR THE NEXT SET OF FREEBIES.
TWO HEADS HIGH
HEAD
BODY
AND I THOUGHT IF WE COULD GET A TWO-HEAD-TALL MAMIKO FOR THAT...
A TWO-HEAD-TALL MAMIKO...
......NO.
YOU DON'T HAVE TO MAKE IT SO PERFECT. YOU CAN GET A BIT LOOSER WITH IT...
HE JUST DOESN'T GET IT!!!

HE WORKS AT EVERYTHING

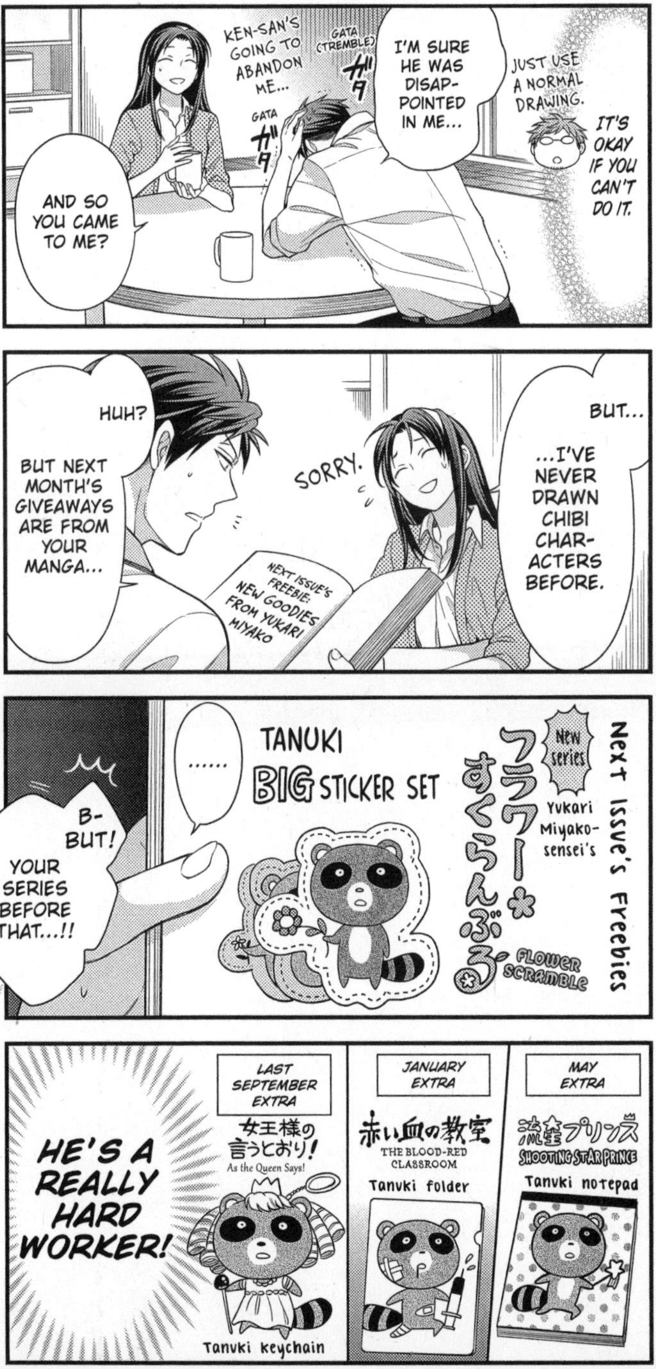

JUST USE A NORMAL DRAWING.
IT'S OKAY IF YOU CAN'T DO IT.
I'M SURE HE WAS DISAP-POINTED IN ME...
GATA (TREMBLE)
KEN-SAN'S GOING TO ABANDON ME...
GATA
AND SO YOU CAME TO ME?
BUT...
...I'VE NEVER DRAWN CHIBI CHAR-ACTERS BEFORE.
SORRY.
HUH?
BUT NEXT MONTH'S GIVEAWAYS ARE FROM YOUR MANGA...
NEXT ISSUE'S FREEBIE: NEW GOODIES FROM YUKARI MIYAKO
Next Issue's Freebies
New series
Yukari Miyako-sensei's
フラワー✿すくらんぶる
FLOWER SCRAMBLE
TANUKI BIG STICKER SET
......
B-BUT!
YOUR SERIES BEFORE THAT...!!
MAY EXTRA
流星プリンス
SHOOTING STAR PRINCE
Tanuki notepad
JANUARY EXTRA
赤い血の教室
THE BLOOD-RED CLASSROOM
Tanuki folder
LAST SEPTEMBER EXTRA
女王様の言うとおり!
As the Queen Says!
Tanuki keychain
HE'S A REALLY HARD WORKER!

ADVICE

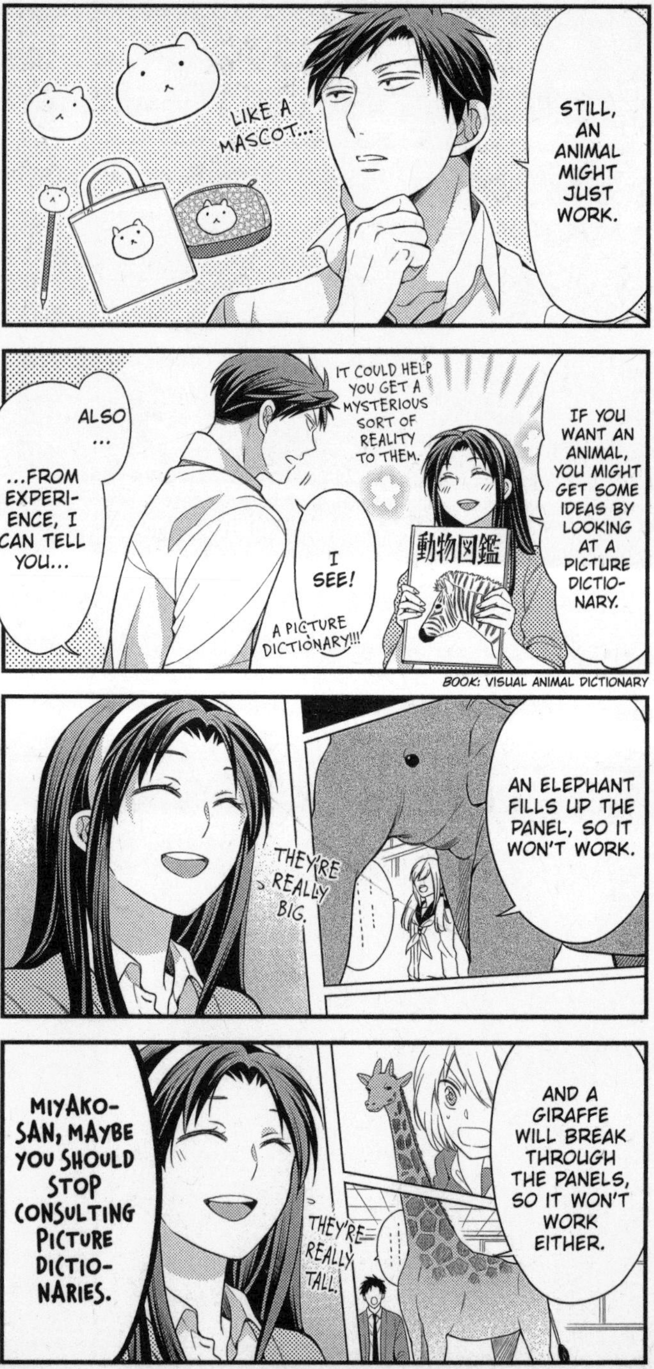
STILL, AN ANIMAL MIGHT JUST WORK.
LIKE A MASCOT...
IF YOU WANT AN ANIMAL, YOU MIGHT GET SOME IDEAS BY LOOKING AT A PICTURE DICTIONARY.
IT COULD HELP YOU GET A MYSTERIOUS SORT OF REALITY TO THEM.
動物図鑑
I SEE!
A PICTURE DICTIONARY!!!
ALSO ...
...FROM EXPERIENCE, I CAN TELL YOU...
BOOK: VISUAL ANIMAL DICTIONARY
AN ELEPHANT FILLS UP THE PANEL, SO IT WON'T WORK.
THEY'RE REALLY BIG.
AND A GIRAFFE WILL BREAK THROUGH THE PANELS, SO IT WON'T WORK EITHER.
THEY'RE REALLY TALL.
MIYAKO-SAN, MAYBE YOU SHOULD STOP CONSULTING PICTURE DICTIONARIES.

THINKING WHILE OVERTIRED

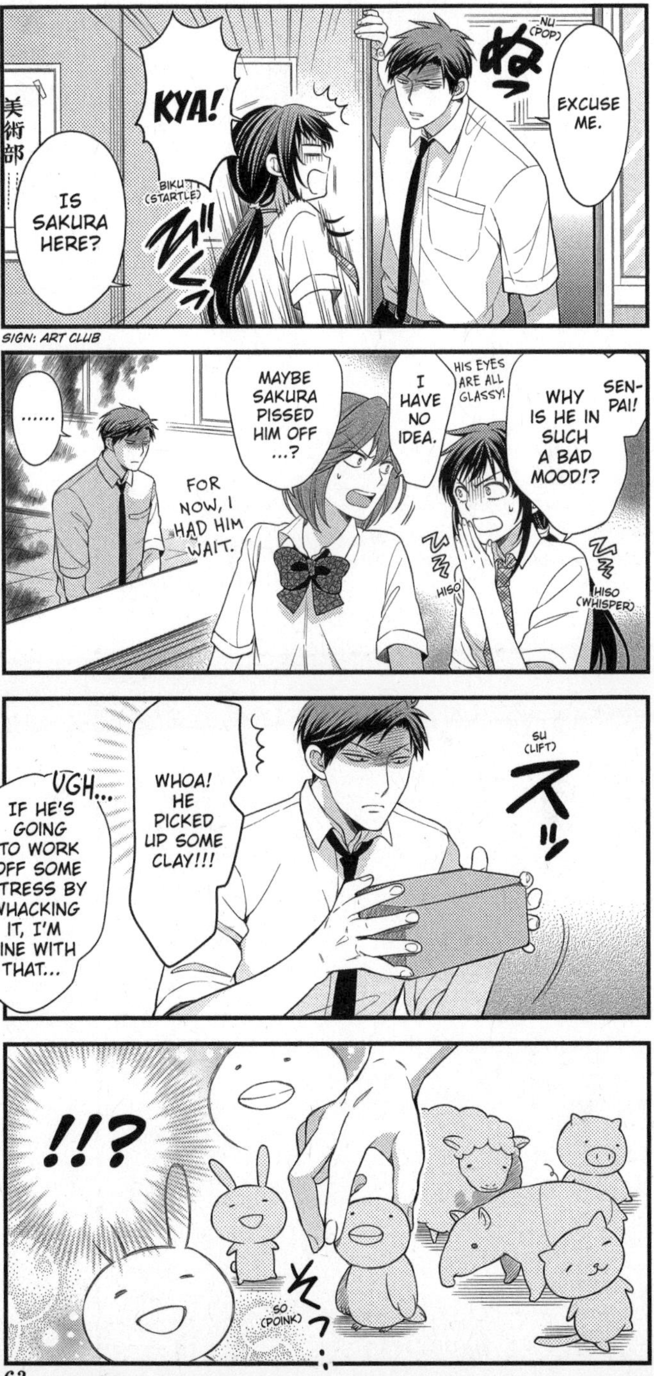
NU (POP)
ぬっ
EXCUSE ME.
KYA!
BIKU (STARTLE)
IS SAKURA HERE?
美術部……
SIGN: ART CLUB
SEN-PAI!
WHY IS HE IN SUCH A BAD MOOD!?
HIS EYES ARE ALL GLASSY!
I HAVE NO IDEA.
MAYBE SAKURA PISSED HIM OFF ...?
FOR NOW, I HAD HIM WAIT.
HISO (WHISPER)
HISO
......
SU (LIFT)
スッ
WHOA! HE PICKED UP SOME CLAY!!!
UGH... IF HE'S GOING TO WORK OFF SOME STRESS BY WHACKING IT, I'M FINE WITH THAT...
!!?
SO (POINK)
...

AS A FREEBIE

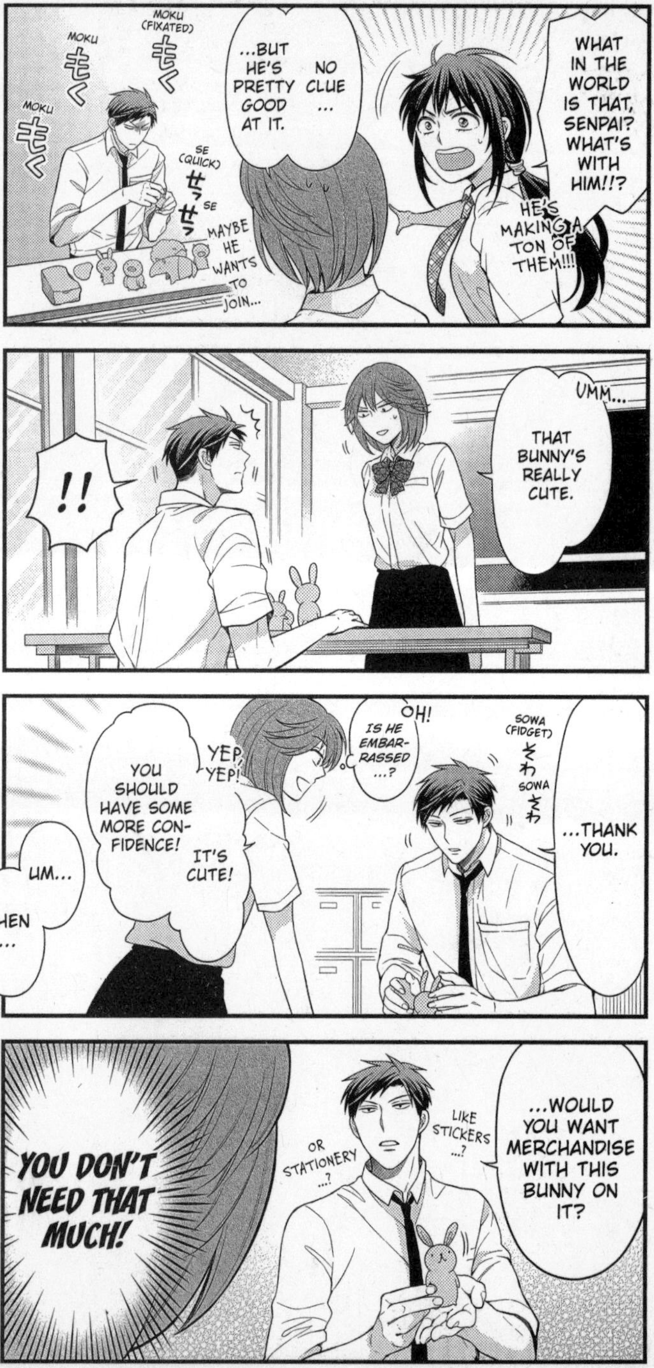
WHAT IN THE WORLD IS THAT, SENPAI? WHAT'S WITH HIM!!?
HE'S MAKING A TON OF THEM!!!
NO CLUE ...
...BUT HE'S PRETTY GOOD AT IT.
MOKU (FIXATED) もく
MOKU もく
MOKU もく
SE (QUICK) せっ
SE せっ
MAYBE HE WANTS TO JOIN...
UMM...
THAT BUNNY'S REALLY CUTE.
!!
...THANK YOU.
SOWA (FIDGET) そわ
SOWA そわ
OH!
IS HE EMBAR-RASSED ...?
YEP, YEP!
YOU SHOULD HAVE SOME MORE CON-FIDENCE!
IT'S CUTE!
UM...
THEN ...
...WOULD YOU WANT MERCHANDISE WITH THIS BUNNY ON IT?
LIKE STICKERS ...?
OR STATIONERY ...?
YOU DON'T NEED THAT MUCH!

FOR THE MAGAZINE

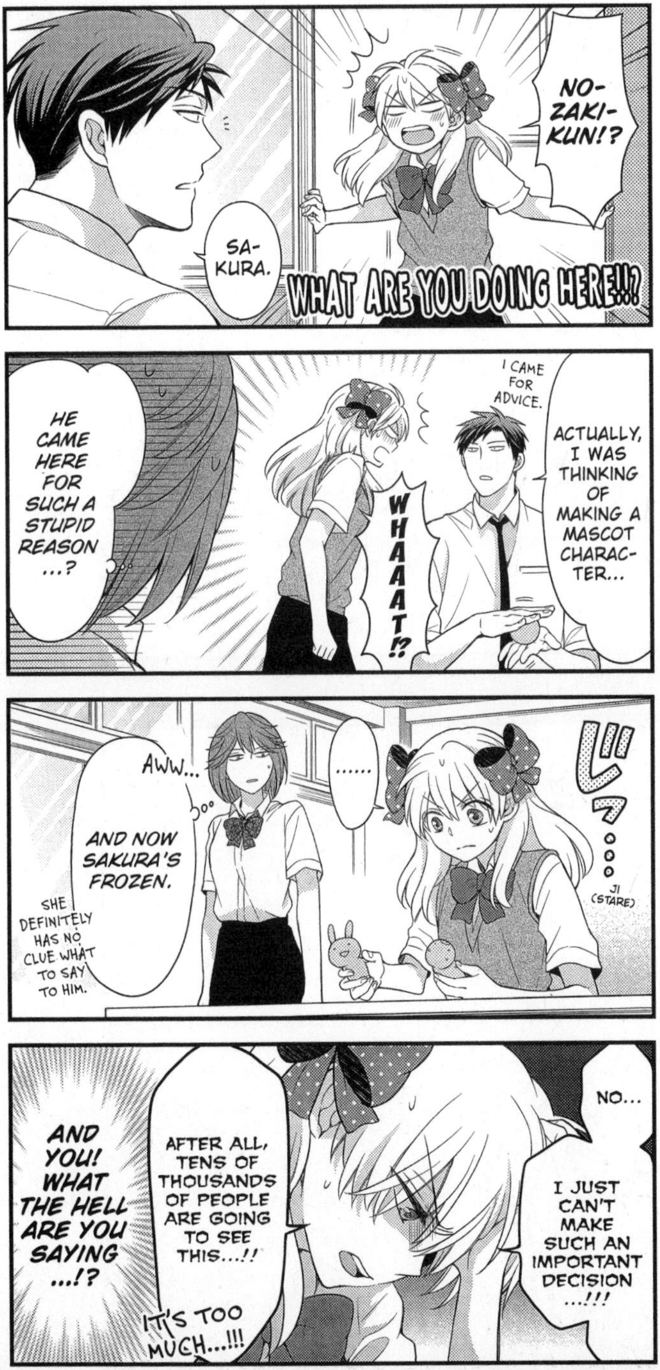
NO-ZAKI-KUN!?
WHAT ARE YOU DOING HERE!!?
SA-KURA.
I CAME FOR ADVICE.
ACTUALLY, I WAS THINKING OF MAKING A MASCOT CHARACTER...
WHAAAAT!?
HE CAME HERE FOR SUCH A STUPID REASON...?
ジー
JI (STARE)
......
AWW...
AND NOW SAKURA'S FROZEN.
SHE DEFINITELY HAS NO CLUE WHAT TO SAY TO HIM.
NO...
I JUST CAN'T MAKE SUCH AN IMPORTANT DECISION...!!!
AFTER ALL, TENS OF THOUSANDS OF PEOPLE ARE GOING TO SEE THIS...!!
IT'S TOO MUCH...!!!
AND YOU! WHAT THE HELL ARE YOU SAYING...!?

MEAL CONVERSATION

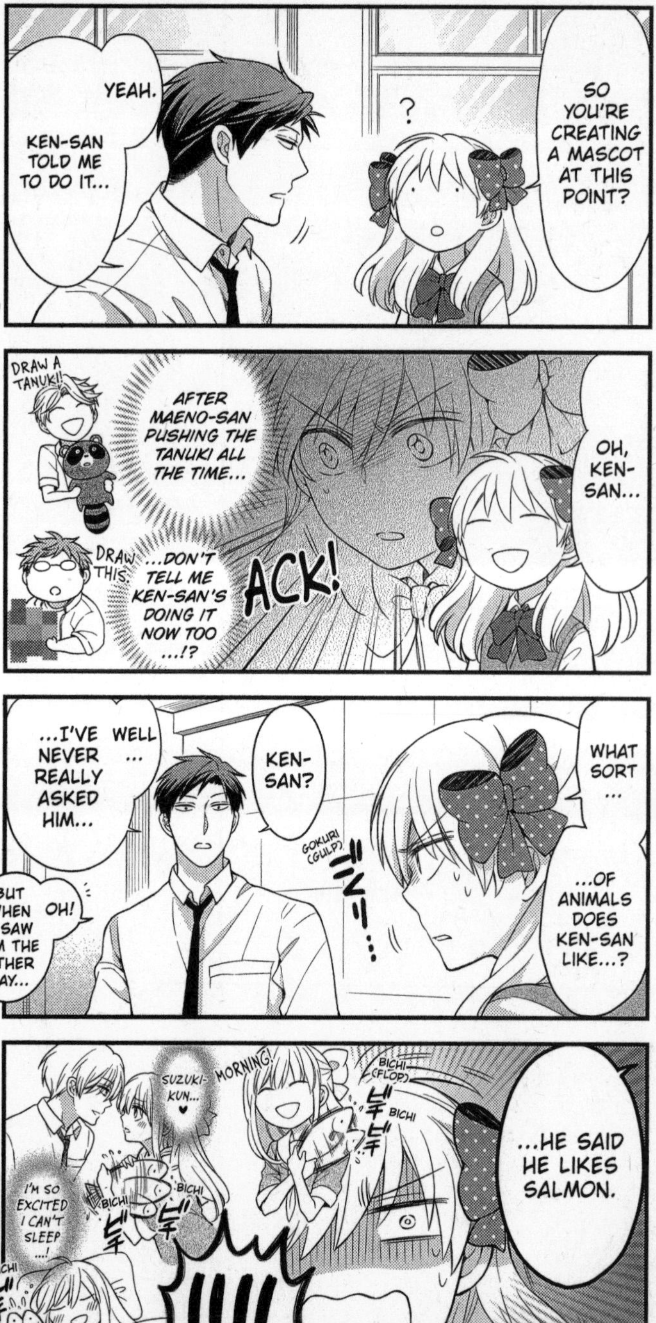
SO YOU'RE CREATING A MASCOT AT THIS POINT?
?
YEAH.
KEN-SAN TOLD ME TO DO IT...
OH, KEN-SAN...
ACK!
AFTER MAENO-SAN PUSHING THE TANUKI ALL THE TIME...
...DON'T TELL ME KEN-SAN'S DOING IT NOW TOO...!?
DRAW A TANUKI!
DRAW THIS.
WHAT SORT ...
...OF ANIMALS DOES KEN-SAN LIKE...?
GOKURI (GULP)
KEN-SAN?
WELL ...
...I'VE NEVER REALLY ASKED HIM...
OH!
BUT WHEN I SAW HIM THE OTHER DAY...
...HE SAID HE LIKES SALMON.
BICHI (FLOP)
BICHI
MORNING!
SUZUKI-KUN... ♥
BICHI
BICHI
I'M SO EXCITED I CAN'T SLEEP ...!
!!!!!
BICHI
BICHI
BICHI

THEIR WORRYING DISCUSSION

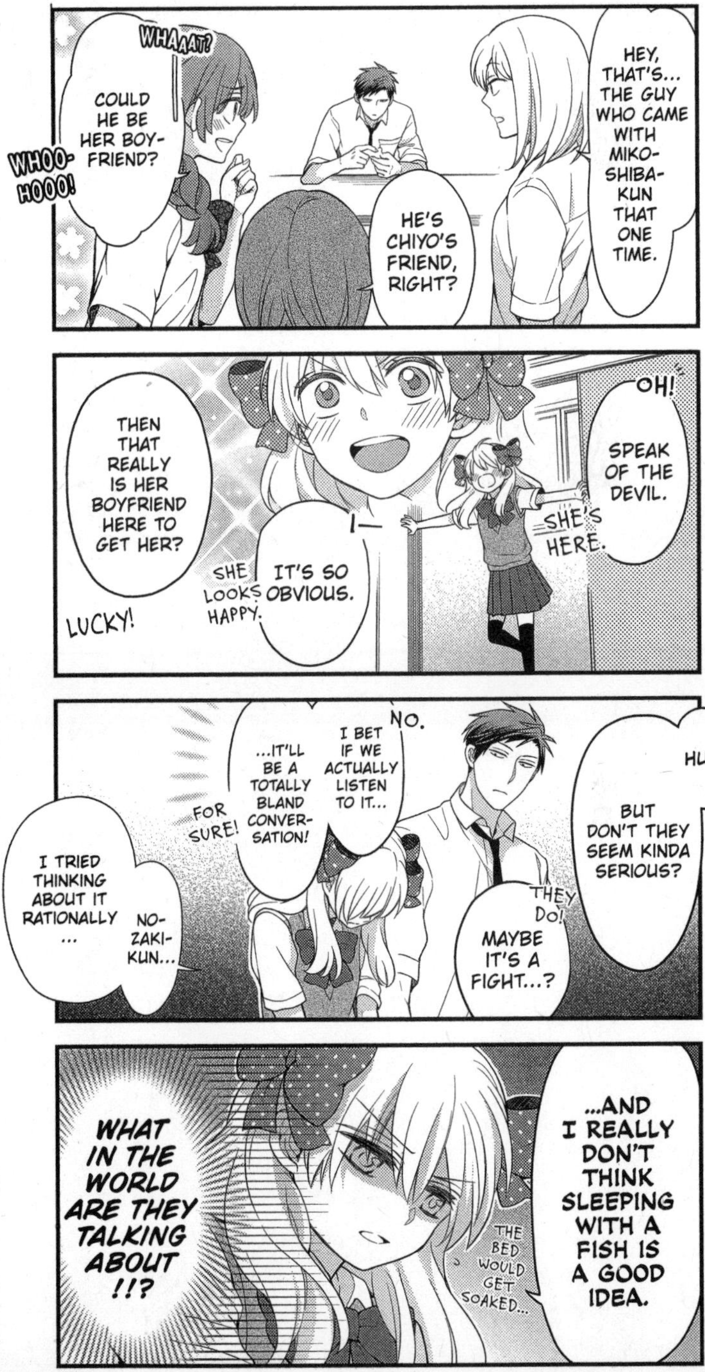

HEY, THAT'S... THE GUY WHO CAME WITH MIKO-SHIBA-KUN THAT ONE TIME.
HE'S CHIYO'S FRIEND, RIGHT?
WHAAAT?
COULD HE BE HER BOY-FRIEND?
WHOO-HOOO!
OH!
SPEAK OF THE DEVIL.
SHE'S HERE.
I—
IT'S SO OBVIOUS.
SHE LOOKS HAPPY.
THEN THAT REALLY IS HER BOYFRIEND HERE TO GET HER?
LUCKY!
HUH?
BUT DON'T THEY SEEM KINDA SERIOUS?
THEY DO!
MAYBE IT'S A FIGHT...?
NO.
I BET IF WE ACTUALLY LISTEN TO IT...
...IT'LL BE A TOTALLY BLAND CONVERSATION!
FOR SURE!
NO-ZAKI-KUN...
I TRIED THINKING ABOUT IT RATIONALLY...
...AND I REALLY DON'T THINK SLEEPING WITH A FISH IS A GOOD IDEA.
THE BED WOULD GET SOAKED...
WHAT IN THE WORLD ARE THEY TALKING ABOUT!!?

SOMEONE ELSE'S PROBLEM IN THE END

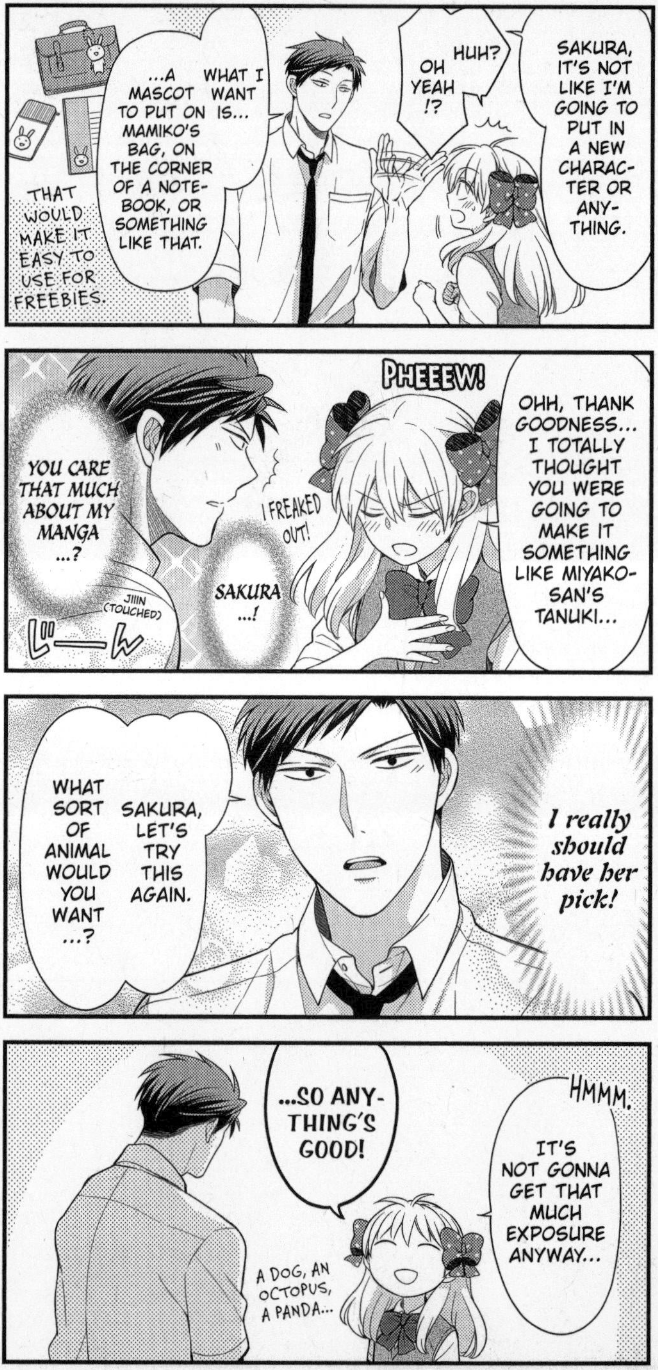
SAKURA, IT'S NOT LIKE I'M GOING TO PUT IN A NEW CHARACTER OR ANYTHING.
HUH?
OH YEAH !?
WHAT I WANT IS...
...A MASCOT TO PUT ON MAMIKO'S BAG, ON THE CORNER OF A NOTEBOOK, OR SOMETHING LIKE THAT.
THAT WOULD MAKE IT EASY TO USE FOR FREEBIES.
PHEEEW!
OHH, THANK GOODNESS... I TOTALLY THOUGHT YOU WERE GOING TO MAKE IT SOMETHING LIKE MIYAKO-SAN'S TANUKI...
I FREAKED OUT!
SAKURA ...!
YOU CARE THAT MUCH ABOUT MY MANGA ...?
JIIN (TOUCHED)
ジーん
I really should have her pick!
SAKURA, LET'S TRY THIS AGAIN.
WHAT SORT OF ANIMAL WOULD YOU WANT ...?
HMMM.
IT'S NOT GONNA GET THAT MUCH EXPOSURE ANYWAY...
...SO ANYTHING'S GOOD!
A DOG, AN OCTOPUS, A PANDA...

BALANCING ITS VALUE

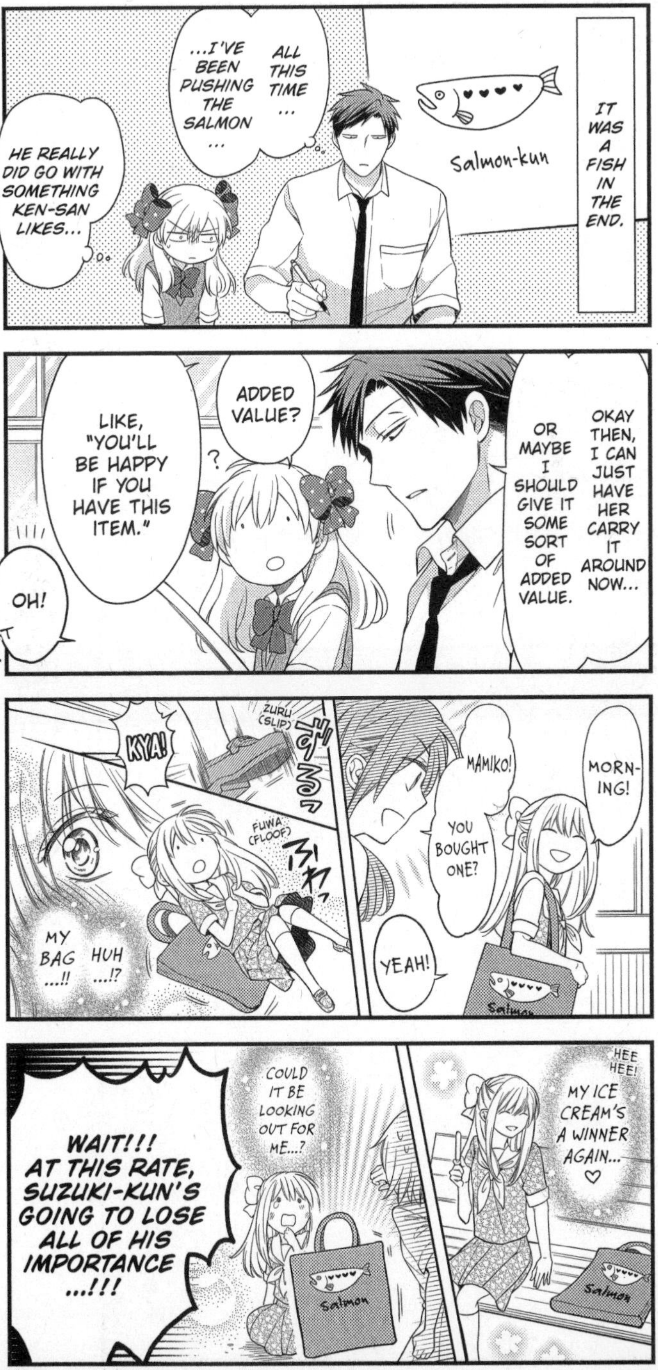
IT WAS A FISH IN THE END.
Salmon-kun
ALL THIS TIME...
...I'VE BEEN PUSHING THE SALMON...
HE REALLY DID GO WITH SOMETHING KEN-SAN LIKES...
OKAY THEN, I CAN JUST HAVE HER CARRY IT AROUND NOW...
OR MAYBE I SHOULD GIVE IT SOME SORT OF ADDED VALUE.
ADDED VALUE?
?
LIKE, "YOU'LL BE HAPPY IF YOU HAVE THIS ITEM."
OH!
I GET IT.
MORN-ING!
MAMIKO!
YOU BOUGHT ONE?
YEAH!
ZURU (SLIP)
する
KYA!
FUWA (FLOOF)
ふわ
HUH ...!?
MY BAG ...!!
HEE HEE!
MY ICE CREAM'S A WINNER AGAIN... ♡
Salmon
COULD IT BE LOOKING OUT FOR ME...?
WAIT!!! AT THIS RATE, SUZUKI-KUN'S GOING TO LOSE ALL OF HIS IMPORTANCE ...!!!
Salmon

AS A WAY TO INTRODUCE IT

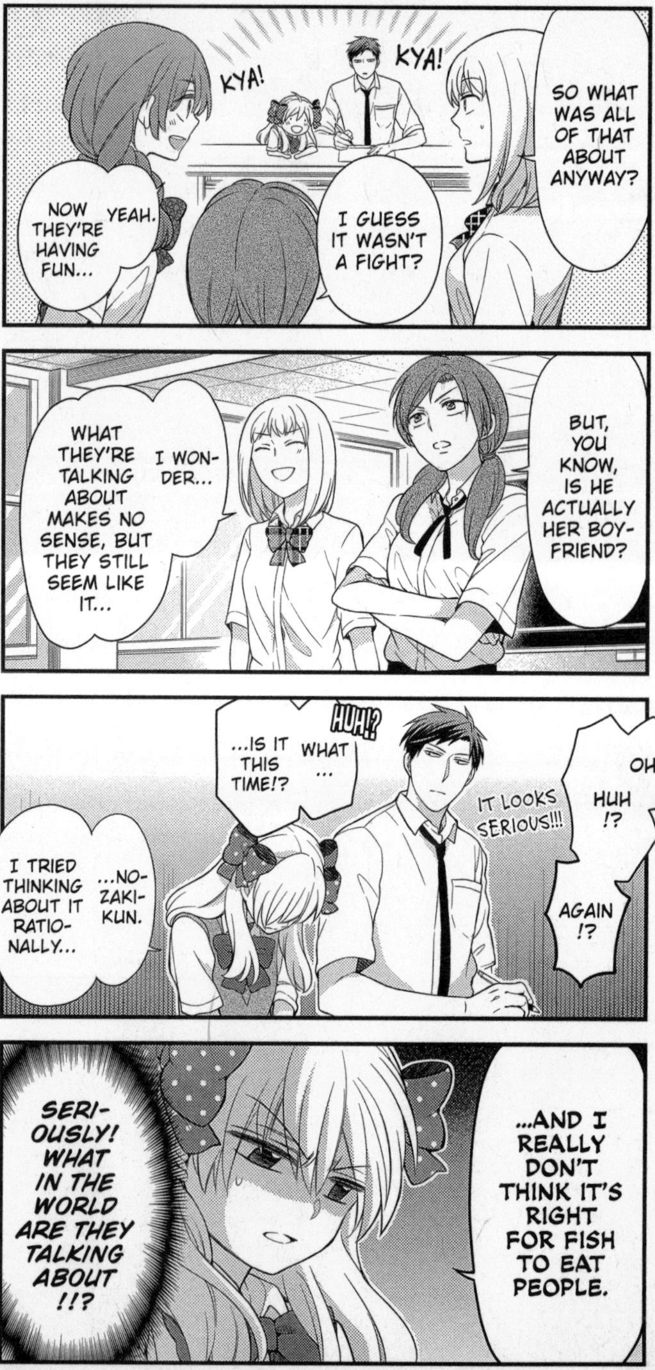
SO WHAT WAS ALL OF THAT ABOUT ANYWAY?
KYA!
I GUESS IT WASN'T A FIGHT?
KYA!
YEAH.
NOW THEY'RE HAVING FUN...
BUT, YOU KNOW, IS HE ACTUALLY HER BOY-FRIEND?
I WONDER...
WHAT THEY'RE TALKING ABOUT MAKES NO SENSE, BUT THEY STILL SEEM LIKE IT...
OH!
HUH!?
AGAIN!?
IT LOOKS SERIOUS!!!
HUH!?
WHAT...
...IS IT THIS TIME!?
...NOZAKI-KUN.
I TRIED THINKING ABOUT IT RATIONALLY...
...AND I REALLY DON'T THINK IT'S RIGHT FOR FISH TO EAT PEOPLE.
SERIOUSLY! WHAT IN THE WORLD ARE THEY TALKING ABOUT!!?

HE GOT IT OUT JUST FINE

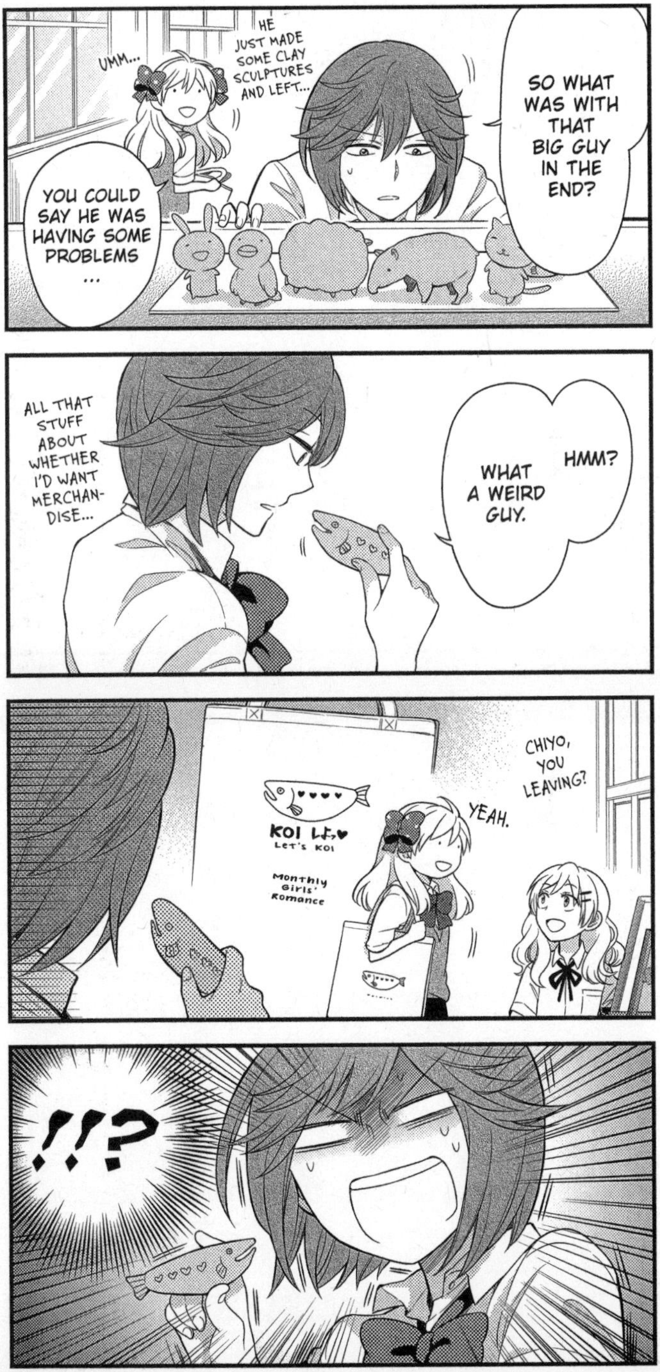
SO WHAT WAS WITH THAT BIG GUY IN THE END?
HE JUST MADE SOME CLAY SCULPTURES AND LEFT...
UMM...
YOU COULD SAY HE WAS HAVING SOME PROBLEMS ...
HMM?
WHAT A WEIRD GUY.
ALL THAT STUFF ABOUT WHETHER I'D WANT MERCHANDISE...
CHIYO, YOU LEAVING?
YEAH.
KOI しよっ♥
Let's KOI
Monthly Girls' Romance
!!?

A CREATOR'S INSISTENCE

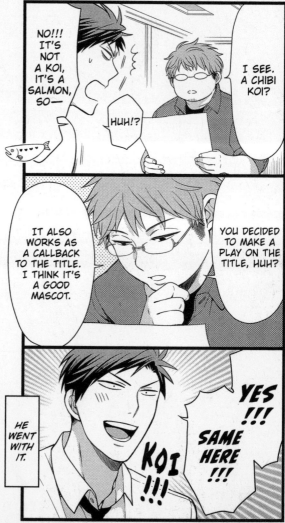

I SEE. A CHIBI KOI?
HUH!?
NO!!! IT'S NOT A KOI, IT'S A SALMON, SO—
YOU DECIDED TO MAKE A PLAY ON THE TITLE, HUH?
IT ALSO WORKS AS A CALLBACK TO THE TITLE. I THINK IT'S A GOOD MASCOT.
YES!!! SAME HERE!!!
KOI!!!
HE WENT WITH IT.

※KOI CAN MEAN BOTH "LOVE" AND THE FISH, SO THE KOI MASCOT IS A PLAY ON THE TITLE OF NOZAKI'S MANGA, LET'S FALL IN LOVE♡, THE JAPANESE TITLE OF WHICH IS KOI SHIYO♡.

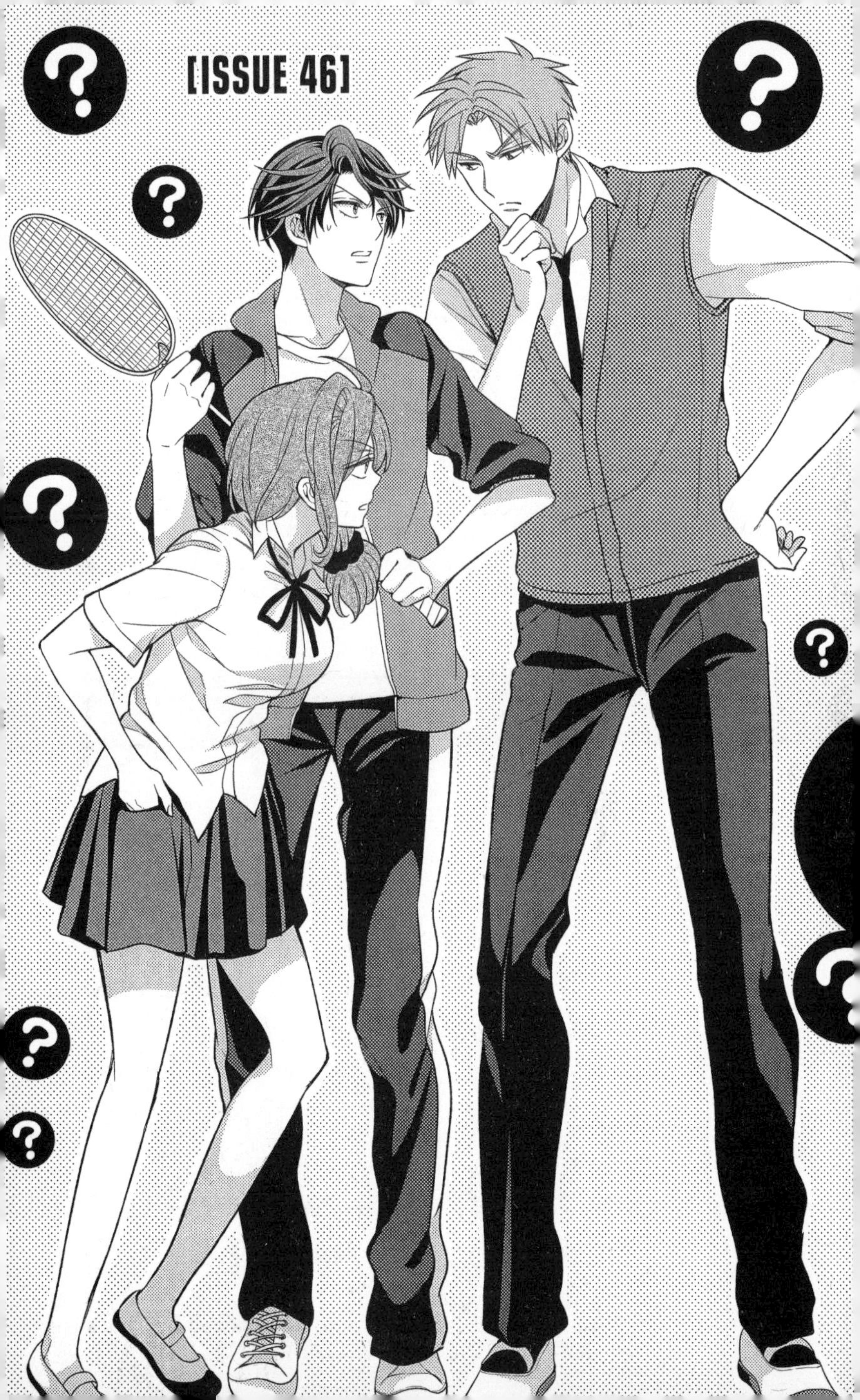
[ISSUE 46]

HIS ADVISOR'S INTERESTS ①

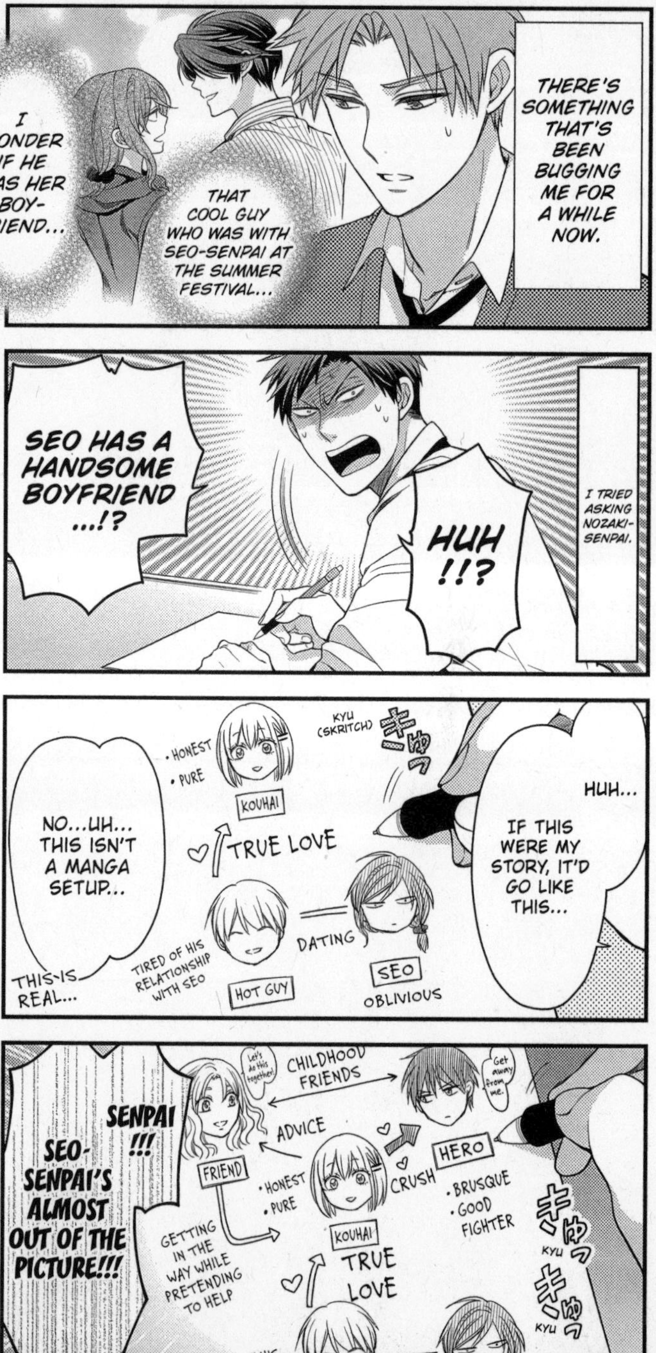

THERE'S SOMETHING THAT'S BEEN BUGGING ME FOR A WHILE NOW.
THAT COOL GUY WHO WAS WITH SEO-SENPAI AT THE SUMMER FESTIVAL...
I WONDER IF HE WAS HER BOY-FRIEND...
I TRIED ASKING NOZAKI-SENPAI.
HUH!!?
SEO HAS A HANDSOME BOYFRIEND ...!?
HUH...
IF THIS WERE MY STORY, IT'D GO LIKE THIS...
KYU (SKRITCH)
• HONEST
• PURE
KOUHAI
TRUE LOVE
DATING
SEO
OBLIVIOUS
HOT GUY
TIRED OF HIS RELATIONSHIP WITH SEO
NO...UH... THIS ISN'T A MANGA SETUP...
THIS IS REAL...
KYU
KYU
Get away from me.
HERO
• BRUSQUE
• GOOD FIGHTER
CHILDHOOD FRIENDS
Let's do this together!
CRUSH
ADVICE
FRIEND
• HONEST
• PURE
KOUHAI
TRUE LOVE
GETTING IN THE WAY WHILE PRETENDING TO HELP
SENPAI!!!
SEO-SENPAI'S ALMOST OUT OF THE PICTURE!!!

HIS ADVISOR'S INTERESTS ②

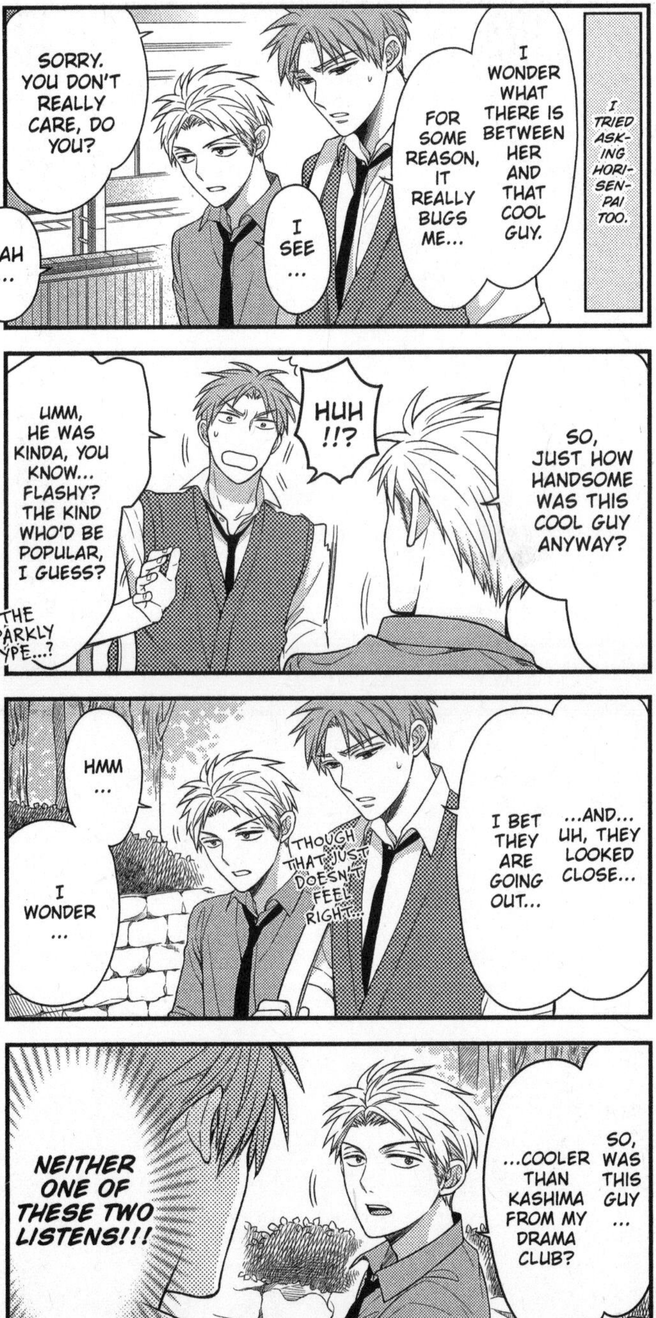
I TRIED ASKING HORI-SENPAI TOO.
I WONDER WHAT THERE IS BETWEEN HER AND THAT COOL GUY.
FOR SOME REASON, IT REALLY BUGS ME...
I SEE...
SORRY. YOU DON'T REALLY CARE, DO YOU?
NAH...
SO, JUST HOW HANDSOME WAS THIS COOL GUY ANYWAY?
HUH!!?
UMM, HE WAS KINDA, YOU KNOW... FLASHY? THE KIND WHO'D BE POPULAR, I GUESS?
THE SPARKLY TYPE...?
...AND... UH, THEY LOOKED CLOSE...
I BET THEY ARE GOING OUT...
THOUGH THAT JUST DOESN'T FEEL RIGHT...
HMM...
I WONDER...
SO, WAS THIS GUY...
...COOLER THAN KASHIMA FROM MY DRAMA CLUB?
NEITHER ONE OF THESE TWO LISTENS!!!

FUN TRAVEL PLANS

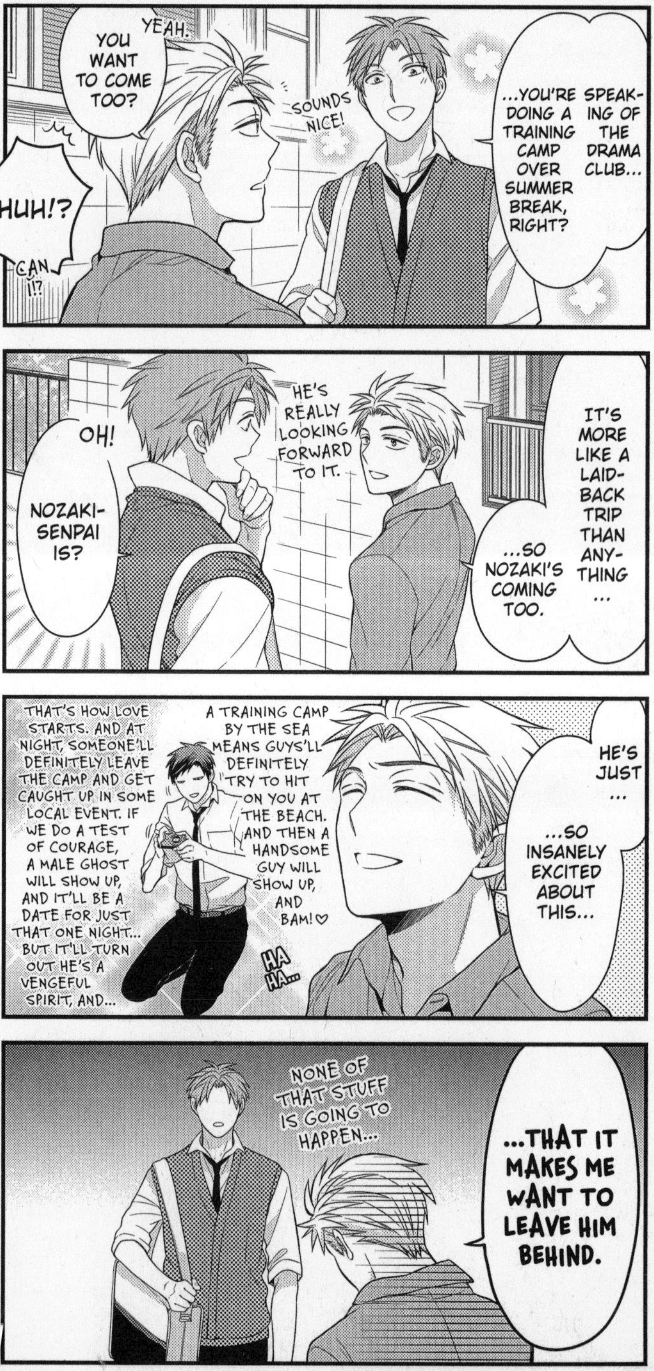
SPEAKING OF THE DRAMA CLUB...
...YOU'RE DOING A TRAINING CAMP OVER SUMMER BREAK, RIGHT?
SOUNDS NICE!
YEAH.
YOU WANT TO COME TOO?
HUH!?
CAN I!?
IT'S MORE LIKE A LAID-BACK TRIP THAN ANYTHING...
...SO NOZAKI'S COMING TOO.
HE'S REALLY LOOKING FORWARD TO IT.
OH!
NOZAKI-SENPAI IS?
HE'S JUST...
...SO INSANELY EXCITED ABOUT THIS...
HA HA...
A TRAINING CAMP BY THE SEA MEANS GUYS'LL DEFINITELY TRY TO HIT ON YOU AT THE BEACH. AND THEN A HANDSOME GUY WILL SHOW UP, AND BAM! ♡
THAT'S HOW LOVE STARTS. AND AT NIGHT, SOMEONE'LL DEFINITELY LEAVE THE CAMP AND GET CAUGHT UP IN SOME LOCAL EVENT. IF WE DO A TEST OF COURAGE, A MALE GHOST WILL SHOW UP, AND IT'LL BE A DATE FOR JUST THAT ONE NIGHT... BUT IT'LL TURN OUT HE'S A VENGEFUL SPIRIT, AND...
...THAT IT MAKES ME WANT TO LEAVE HIM BEHIND.
NONE OF THAT STUFF IS GOING TO HAPPEN...

BEST FRIENDS

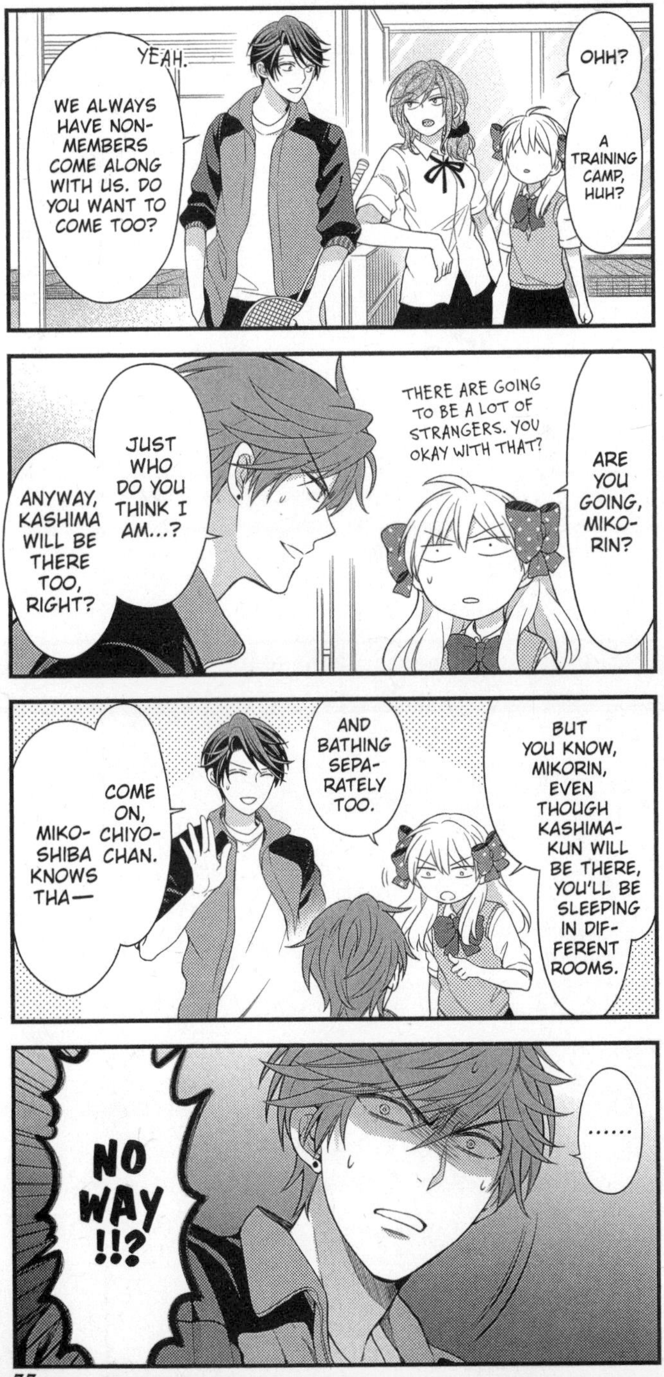
OHH?
A TRAINING CAMP, HUH?
YEAH.
WE ALWAYS HAVE NON-MEMBERS COME ALONG WITH US. DO YOU WANT TO COME TOO?
ARE YOU GOING, MIKO-RIN?
THERE ARE GOING TO BE A LOT OF STRANGERS. YOU OKAY WITH THAT?
JUST WHO DO YOU THINK I AM...?
ANYWAY, KASHIMA WILL BE THERE TOO, RIGHT?
BUT YOU KNOW, MIKORIN, EVEN THOUGH KASHIMA-KUN WILL BE THERE, YOU'LL BE SLEEPING IN DIF-FERENT ROOMS.
AND BATHING SEPA-RATELY TOO.
COME ON, CHIYO-CHAN.
MIKO-SHIBA KNOWS THA—
......
NO WAY !!?

SEO-SENPAI, THE ADULT

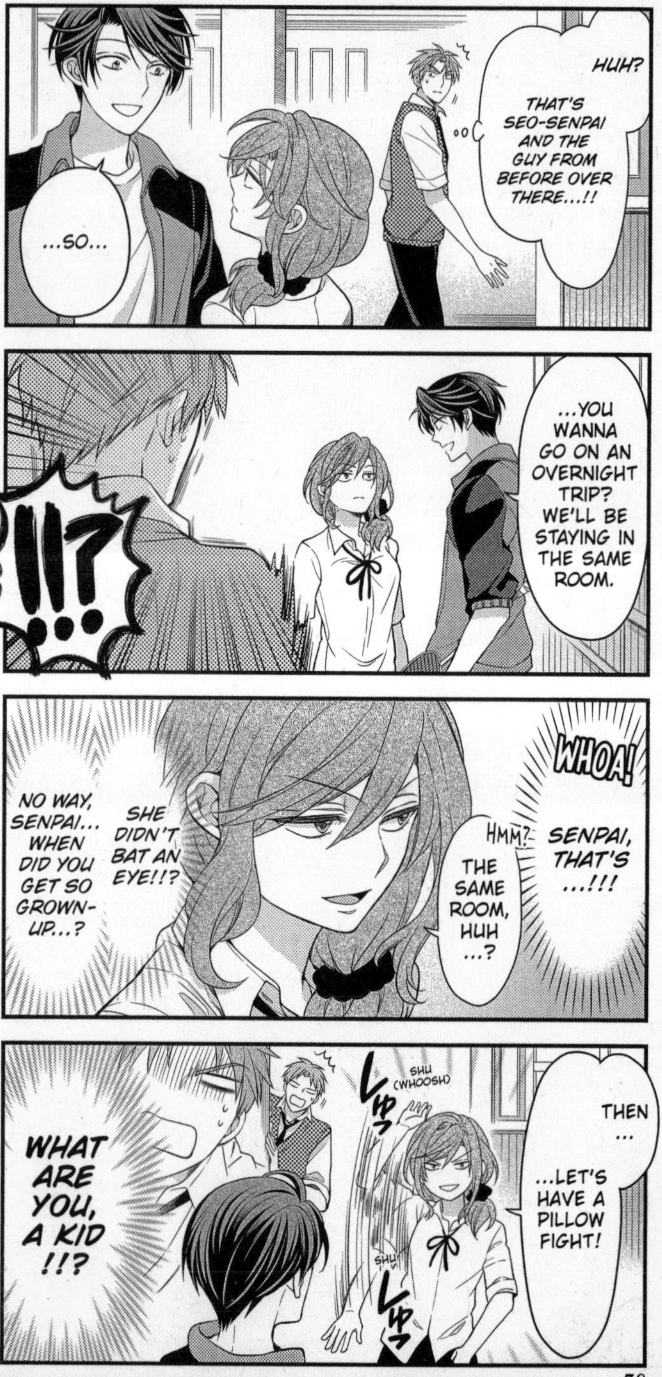
HUH?
THAT'S SEO-SENPAI AND THE GUY FROM BEFORE OVER THERE...!!
...SO...
...YOU WANNA GO ON AN OVERNIGHT TRIP? WE'LL BE STAYING IN THE SAME ROOM.
!!?
WHOA!
SENPAI, THAT'S ...!!!
HMM?
THE SAME ROOM, HUH ...?
SHE DIDN'T BAT AN EYE!!?
NO WAY, SENPAI... WHEN DID YOU GET SO GROWN-UP...?
THEN ...
...LET'S HAVE A PILLOW FIGHT!
SHU (WHOOSH)
SHU
WHAT ARE YOU, A KID!!?

THE PROPER REACTION IS...

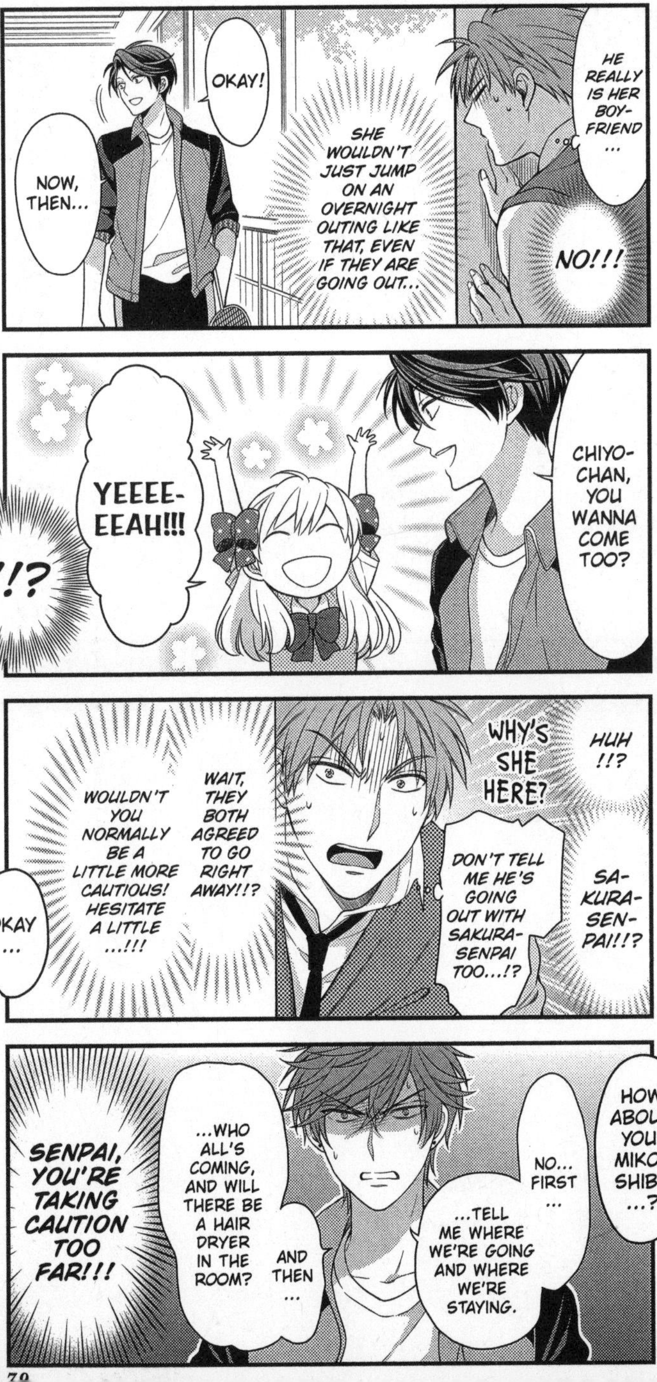
HE REALLY IS HER BOYFRIEND...
NO!!!
SHE WOULDN'T JUST JUMP ON AN OVERNIGHT OUTING LIKE THAT, EVEN IF THEY ARE GOING OUT...
OKAY!
NOW, THEN...
CHIYO-CHAN, YOU WANNA COME TOO?
YEEEE-EEAH!!!
!!?
HUH!!?
SA-KURA-SEN-PAI!!?
WHY'S SHE HERE?
DON'T TELL ME HE'S GOING OUT WITH SAKURA-SENPAI TOO...!?
WAIT, THEY BOTH AGREED TO GO RIGHT AWAY!!?
WOULDN'T YOU NORMALLY BE A LITTLE MORE CAUTIOUS! HESITATE A LITTLE...!!!
OKAY...
HOW ABOUT YOU, MIKOSHIBA...?
NO... FIRST...
...TELL ME WHERE WE'RE GOING AND WHERE WE'RE STAYING.
AND THEN...
...WHO ALL'S COMING, AND WILL THERE BE A HAIR DRYER IN THE ROOM?
SENPAI, YOU'RE TAKING CAUTION TOO FAR!!!

THE ONLY PERVERT

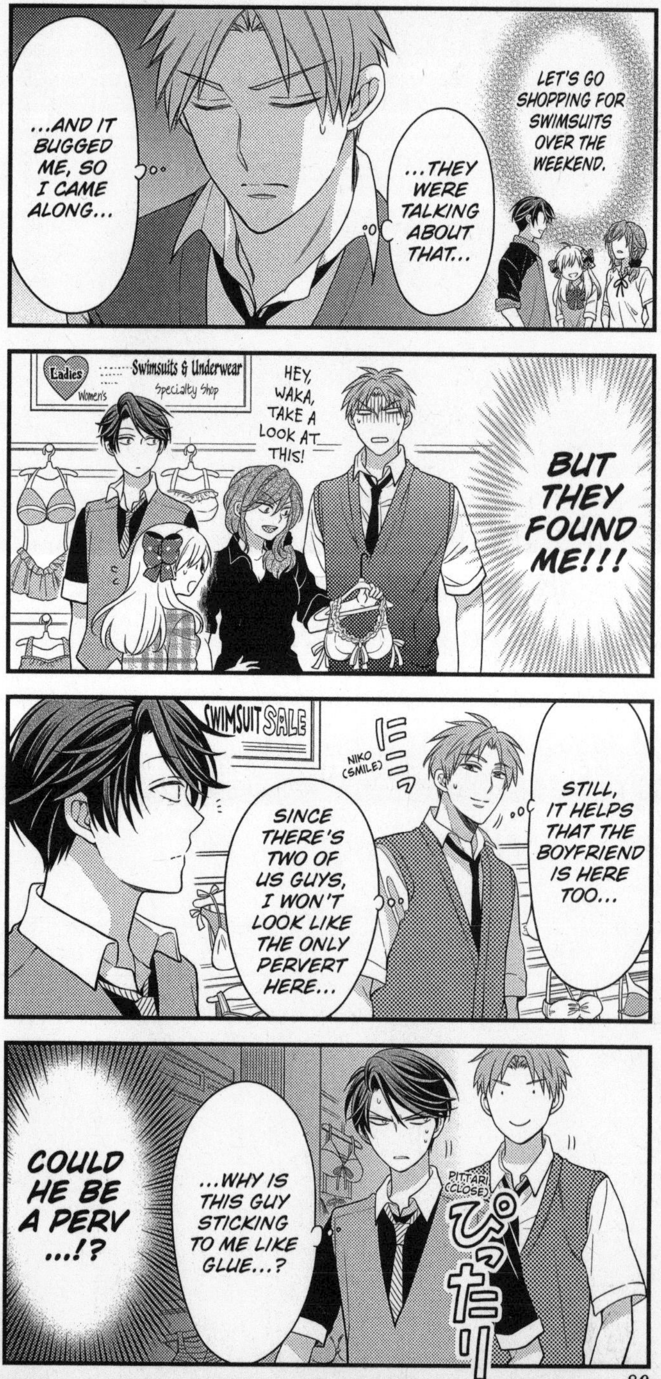

LET'S GO SHOPPING FOR SWIMSUITS OVER THE WEEKEND.
...THEY WERE TALKING ABOUT THAT...
...AND IT BUGGED ME, SO I CAME ALONG...
BUT THEY FOUND ME!!!
HEY, WAKA, TAKE A LOOK AT THIS!
Ladies Women's Swimsuits & Underwear Specialty Shop
STILL, IT HELPS THAT THE BOYFRIEND IS HERE TOO...
NIKO (SMILE)
SINCE THERE'S TWO OF US GUYS, I WON'T LOOK LIKE THE ONLY PERVERT HERE...
SWIMSUIT SALE
PITTARI (CLOSE)
ぴったり
...WHY IS THIS GUY STICKING TO ME LIKE GLUE...?
COULD HE BE A PERV ...!?

A GOOD SPORT

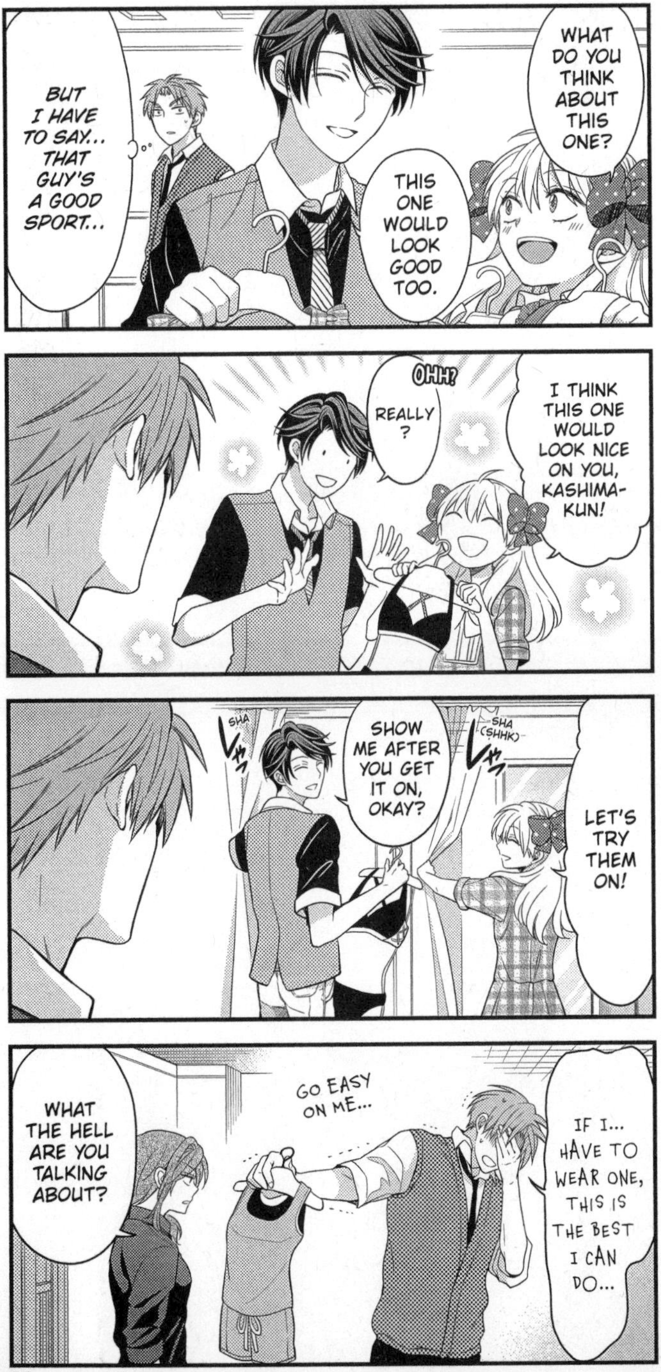
WHAT DO YOU THINK ABOUT THIS ONE?
THIS ONE WOULD LOOK GOOD TOO.
BUT I HAVE TO SAY... THAT GUY'S A GOOD SPORT...
I THINK THIS ONE WOULD LOOK NICE ON YOU, KASHIMA-KUN!
OHH?
REALLY?
LET'S TRY THEM ON!
SHA (SHHK)
SHOW ME AFTER YOU GET IT ON, OKAY?
SHA
IF I... HAVE TO WEAR ONE, THIS IS THE BEST I CAN DO...
GO EASY ON ME...
WHAT THE HELL ARE YOU TALKING ABOUT?

COULDN'T TELL THE DIFFERENCE

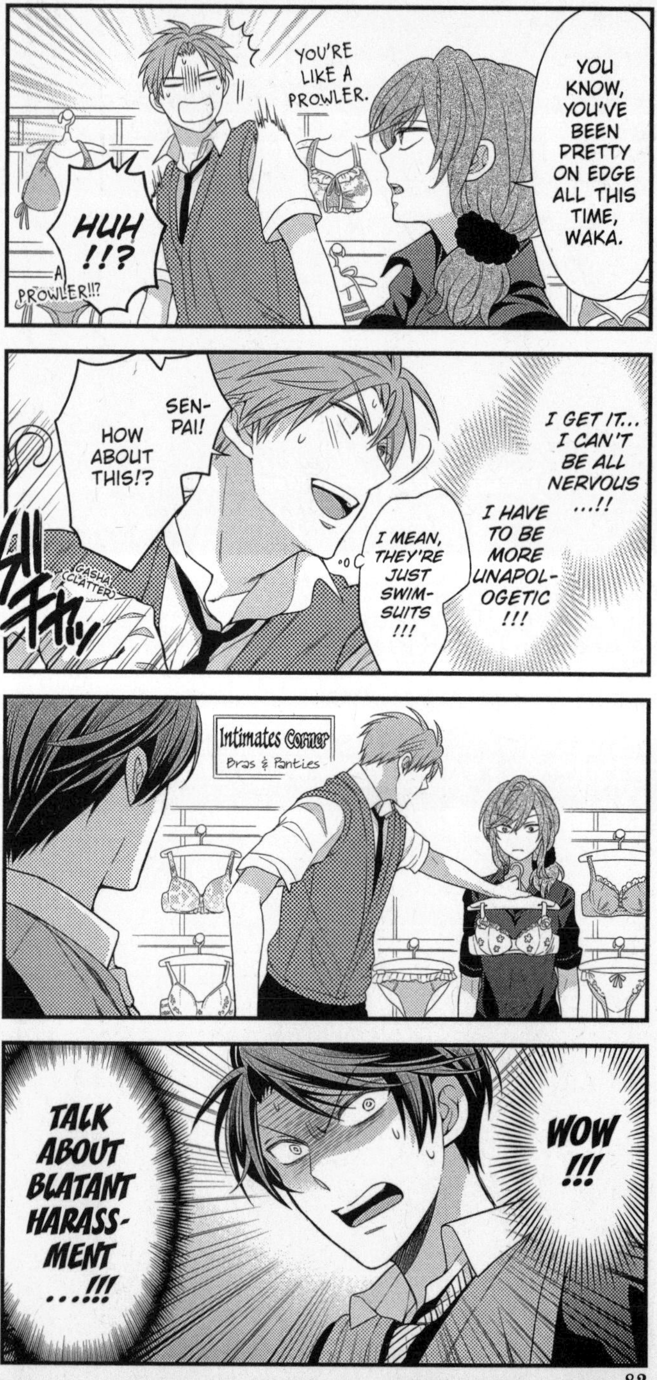
YOU KNOW, YOU'VE BEEN PRETTY ON EDGE ALL THIS TIME, WAKA.
YOU'RE LIKE A PROWLER.
HUH!!?
A PROWLER!!?
I GET IT... I CAN'T BE ALL NERVOUS...!!
I HAVE TO BE MORE UNAPOLOGETIC!!!
I MEAN, THEY'RE JUST SWIMSUITS!!!
SENPAI!
HOW ABOUT THIS!?
(GASHA) (CLATTER)
Intimates Corner
Bras & Panties
WOW!!!
TALK ABOUT BLATANT HARASSMENT...!!!

NOWHERE TO RUN

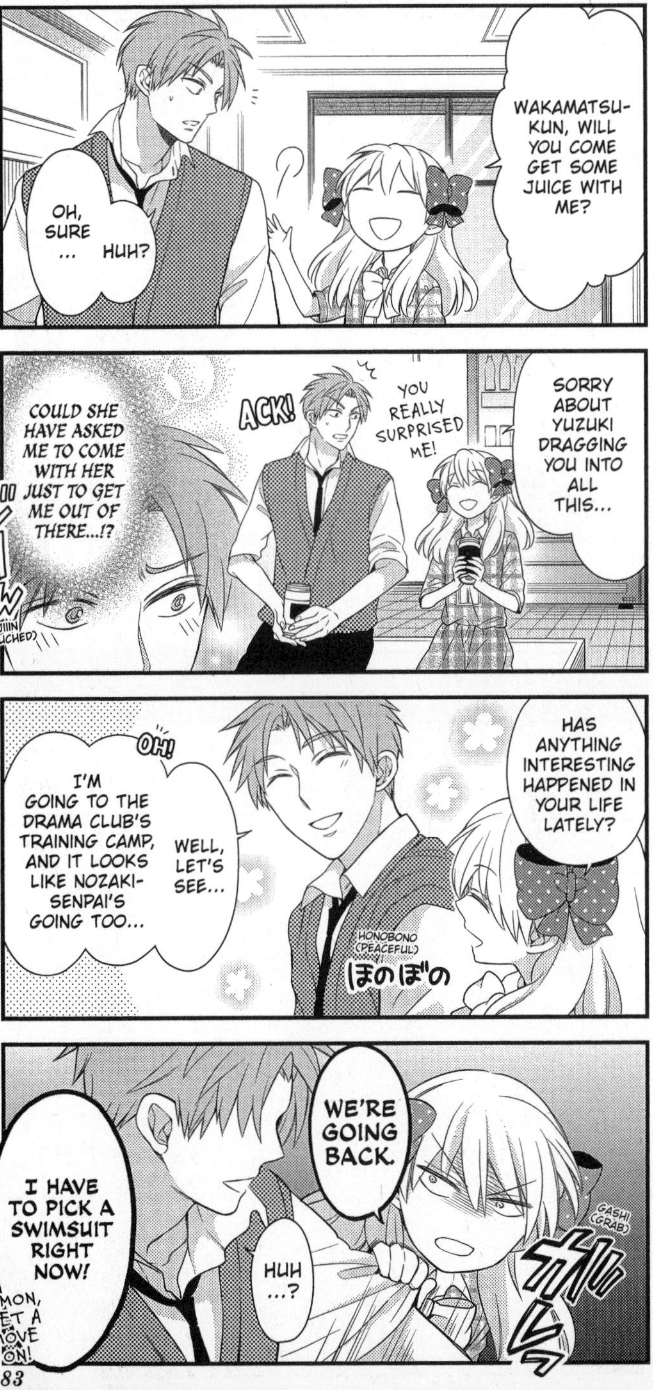
WAKAMATSU-KUN, WILL YOU COME GET SOME JUICE WITH ME?
OH, SURE ... HUH?
SORRY ABOUT YUZUKI DRAGGING YOU INTO ALL THIS...
YOU REALLY SURPRISED ME!
ACK!
COULD SHE HAVE ASKED ME TO COME WITH HER JUST TO GET ME OUT OF THERE...!?
JIIIN (TOUCHED)
HAS ANYTHING INTERESTING HAPPENED IN YOUR LIFE LATELY?
WELL, LET'S SEE...
OH!
I'M GOING TO THE DRAMA CLUB'S TRAINING CAMP, AND IT LOOKS LIKE NOZAKI-SENPAI'S GOING TOO...
HONOBONO (PEACEFUL)
ほのぼの
GASHI (GRAB)
WE'RE GOING BACK.
HUH ...?
I HAVE TO PICK A SWIMSUIT RIGHT NOW!
C'MON, GET A MOVE ON!

WHAT I WANT TO TELL YOU

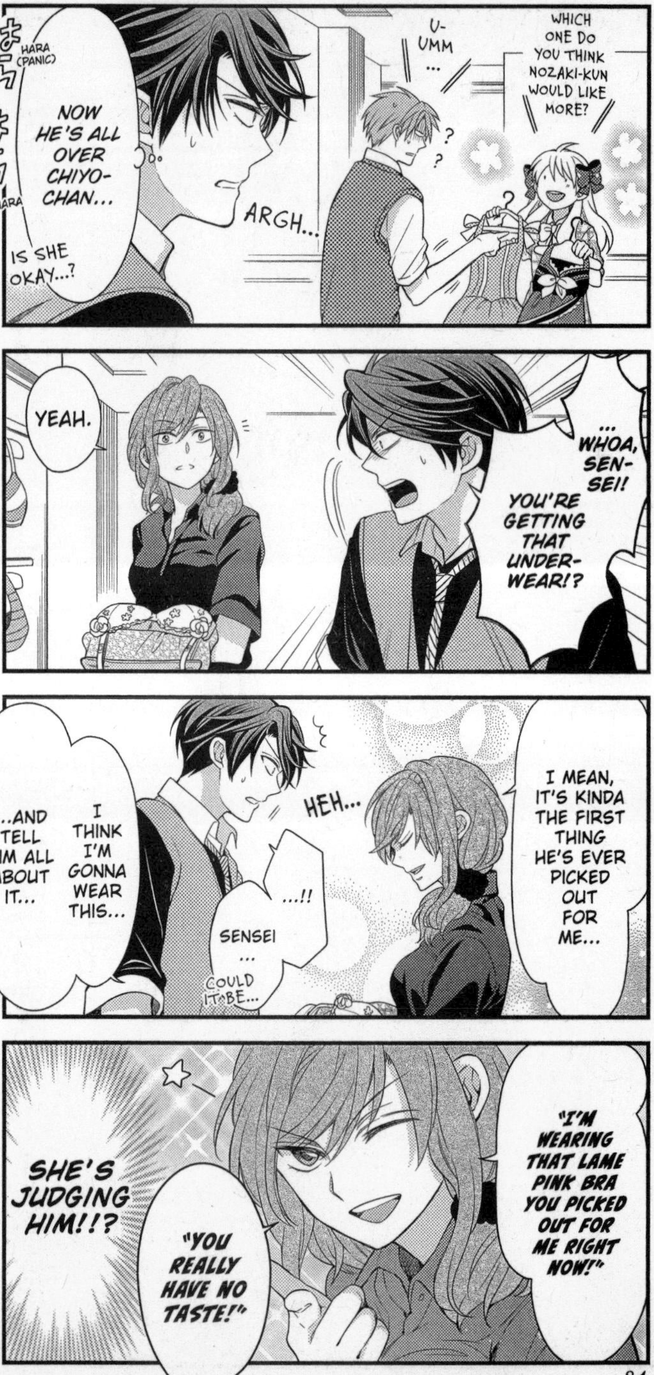
WHICH ONE DO YOU THINK NOZAKI-KUN WOULD LIKE MORE?
U-UMM...
ARGH...
NOW HE'S ALL OVER CHIYO-CHAN...
はら HARA (PANIC)
はら HARA
IS SHE OKAY...?
...WHOA, SENSEI! YOU'RE GETTING THAT UNDERWEAR!?
YEAH.
I MEAN, IT'S KINDA THE FIRST THING HE'S EVER PICKED OUT FOR ME...
HEH...
...!!
SENSEI... COULD IT BE...
I THINK I'M GONNA WEAR THIS...
...AND TELL HIM ALL ABOUT IT...
"I'M WEARING THAT LAME PINK BRA YOU PICKED OUT FOR ME RIGHT NOW!"
"YOU REALLY HAVE NO TASTE!"
SHE'S JUDGING HIM!!?

THE RELATIONSHIP DIAGRAM THAT TIES THEM ALL TOGETHER

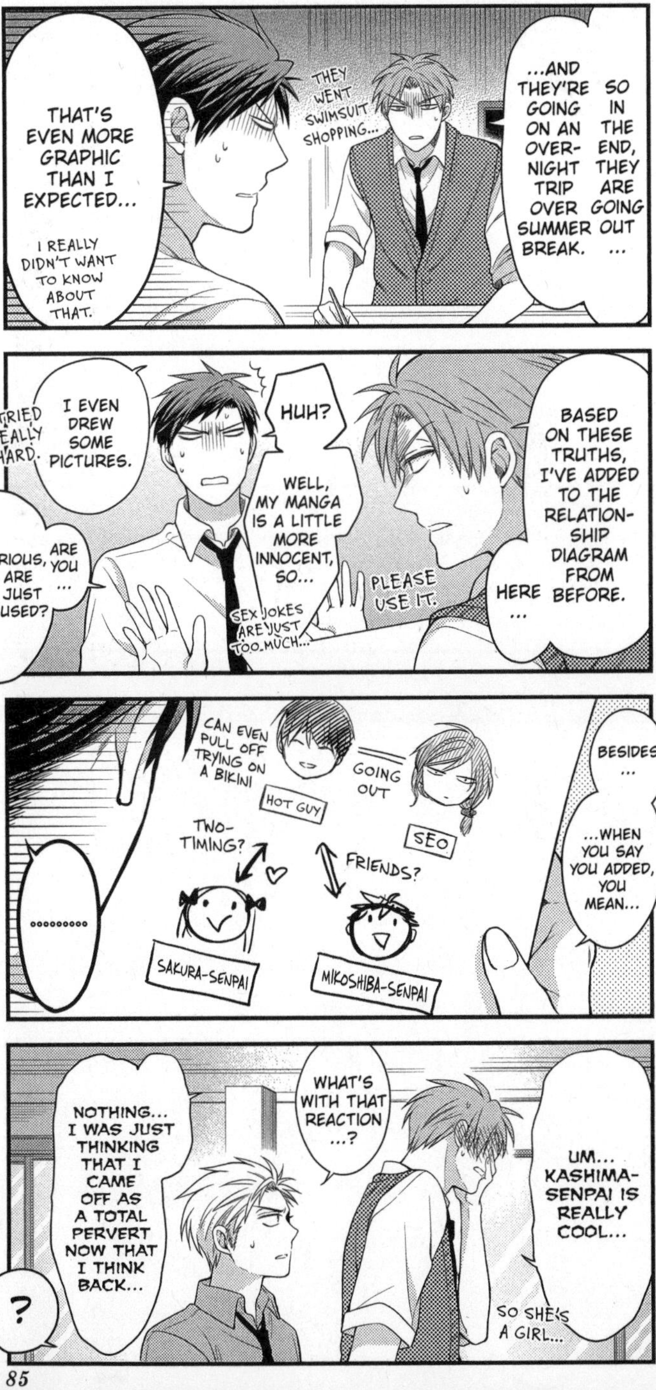
SO IN THE END, THEY ARE GOING OUT ...
...AND THEY'RE GOING ON AN OVERNIGHT TRIP OVER SUMMER BREAK.
THEY WENT SWIMSUIT SHOPPING...
THAT'S EVEN MORE GRAPHIC THAN I EXPECTED...
I REALLY DIDN'T WANT TO KNOW ABOUT THAT.
BASED ON THESE TRUTHS, I'VE ADDED TO THE RELATIONSHIP DIAGRAM FROM BEFORE.
HERE ...
PLEASE USE IT.
HUH?
WELL, MY MANGA IS A LITTLE MORE INNOCENT, SO...
SEX JOKES ARE JUST TOO MUCH...
I EVEN DREW SOME PICTURES.
I TRIED REALLY HARD.
ARE YOU ...
...SERIOUS, OR ARE YOU JUST CONFUSED?
BESIDES ...
...WHEN YOU SAY YOU ADDED, YOU MEAN...
SEO
GOING OUT
HOT GUY
CAN EVEN PULL OFF TRYING ON A BIKINI
FRIENDS?
MIKOSHIBA-SENPAI
TWO-TIMING?
SAKURA-SENPAI
....
UM... KASHIMA-SENPAI IS REALLY COOL...
SO SHE'S A GIRL...
WHAT'S WITH THAT REACTION ...?
NOTHING... I WAS JUST THINKING THAT I CAME OFF AS A TOTAL PERVERT NOW THAT I THINK BACK...
?

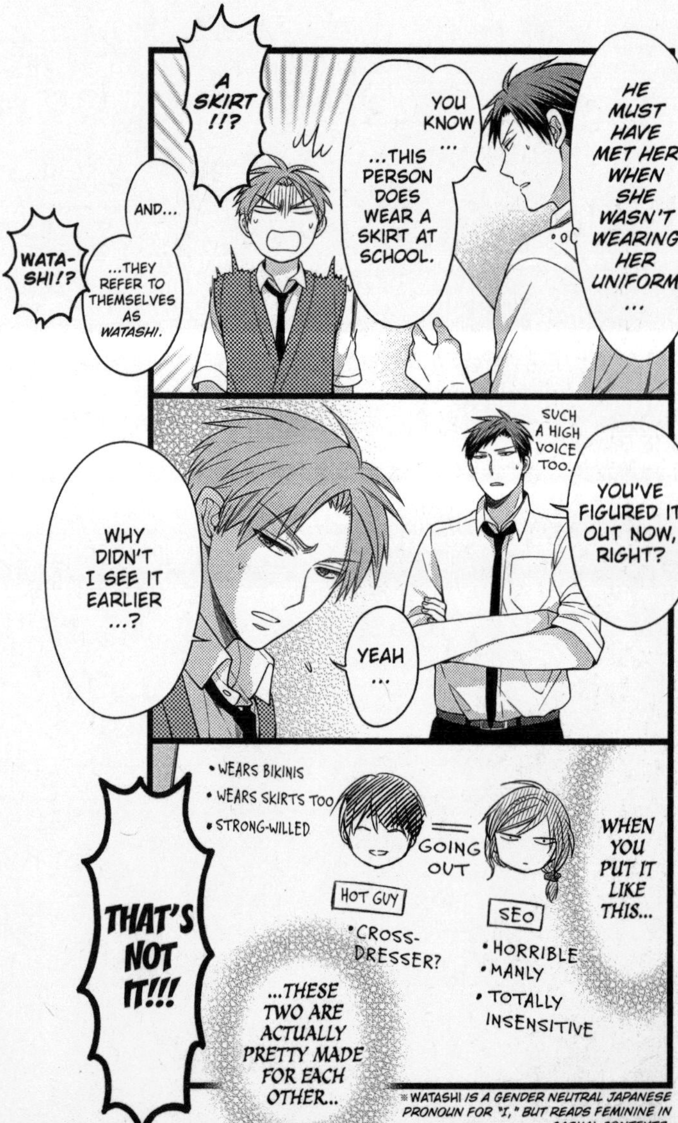
HE MUST HAVE MET HER WHEN SHE WASN'T WEARING HER UNIFORM...
YOU KNOW...
...THIS PERSON DOES WEAR A SKIRT AT SCHOOL.
A SKIRT!!?
AND...
...THEY REFER TO THEMSELVES AS WATASHI.
WATA-SHI!?
SUCH A HIGH VOICE TOO.
YOU'VE FIGURED IT OUT NOW, RIGHT?
YEAH...
WHY DIDN'T I SEE IT EARLIER...?
WHEN YOU PUT IT LIKE THIS...
• WEARS BIKINIS
• WEARS SKIRTS TOO
• STRONG-WILLED
GOING OUT
SEO
• HORRIBLE
• MANLY
• TOTALLY INSENSITIVE
HOT GUY
• CROSS-DRESSER?
...THESE TWO ARE ACTUALLY PRETTY MADE FOR EACH OTHER...
THAT'S NOT IT!!!

※ *WATASHI IS A GENDER NEUTRAL JAPANESE PRONOUN FOR "I," BUT READS FEMININE IN CASUAL CONTEXTS.*

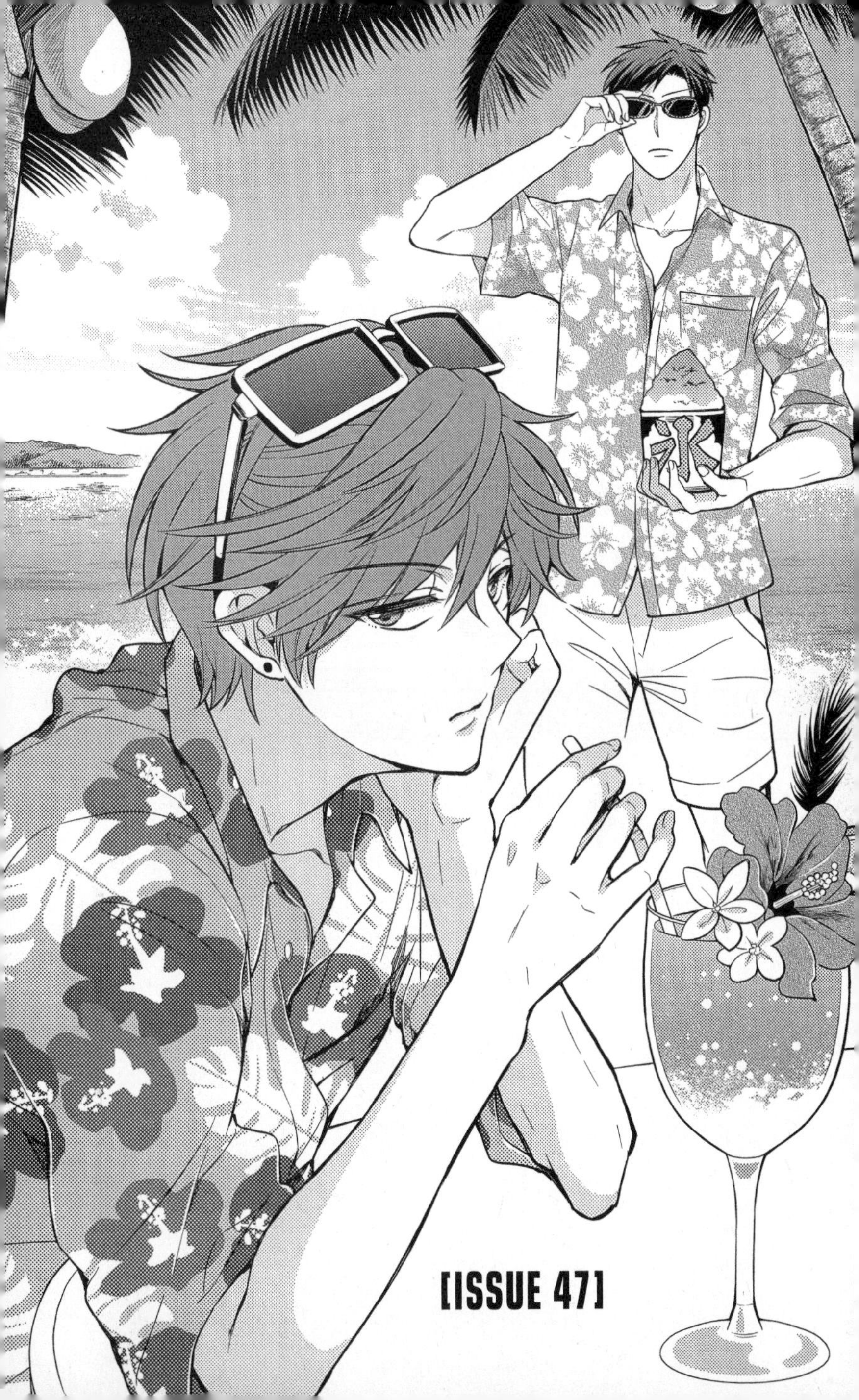
氷

[ISSUE 47]

FANTASY BEACH

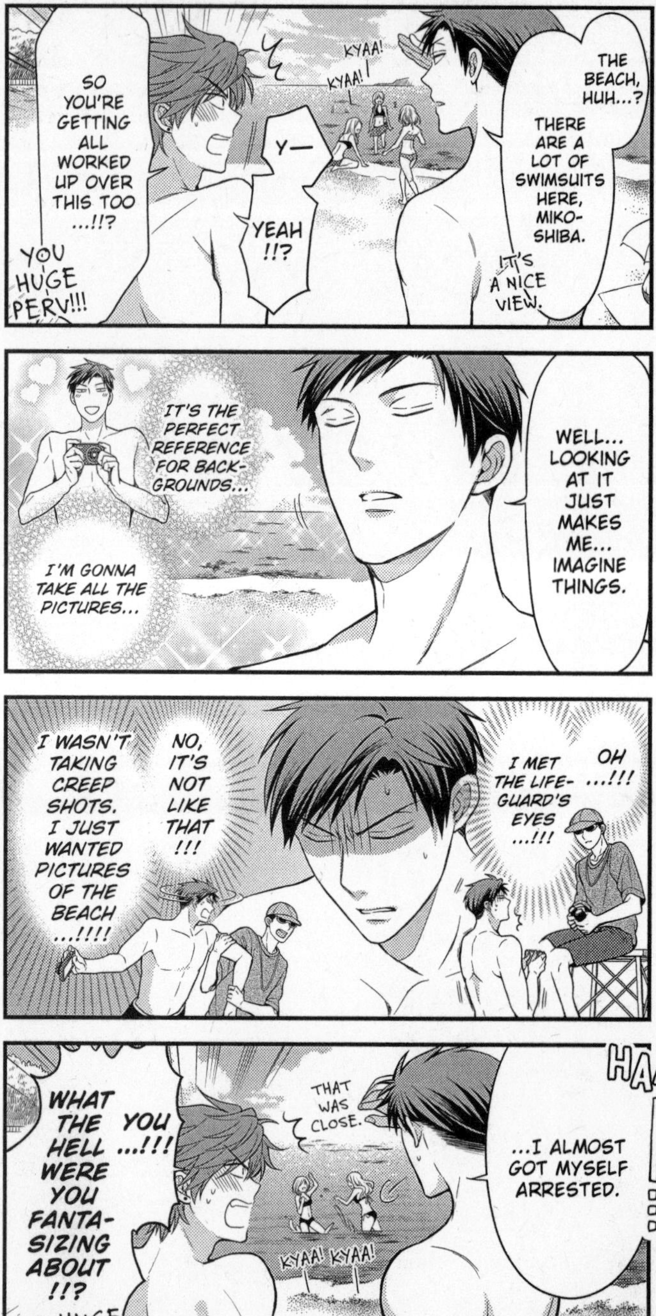

THE BEACH, HUH...? THERE ARE A LOT OF SWIMSUITS HERE, MIKO-SHIBA.
IT'S A NICE VIEW.
KYAA!
KYAA!
Y—
YEAH!!?
SO YOU'RE GETTING ALL WORKED UP OVER THIS TOO...!!?
YOU HUGE PERV!!!
WELL... LOOKING AT IT JUST MAKES ME... IMAGINE THINGS.
IT'S THE PERFECT REFERENCE FOR BACK-GROUNDS...
I'M GONNA TAKE ALL THE PICTURES...
OH ...!!!
I MET THE LIFE-GUARD'S EYES ...!!!
NO, IT'S NOT LIKE THAT!!!
I WASN'T TAKING CREEP SHOTS. I JUST WANTED PICTURES OF THE BEACH ...!!!!
HAAAH
...I ALMOST GOT MYSELF ARRESTED.
THAT WAS CLOSE.
YOU ...!!!
WHAT THE HELL WERE YOU FANTA-SIZING ABOUT!!?
KYAA! KYAA!
YOU HUGE PERV!!!

THEY'RE ALL GOOD!

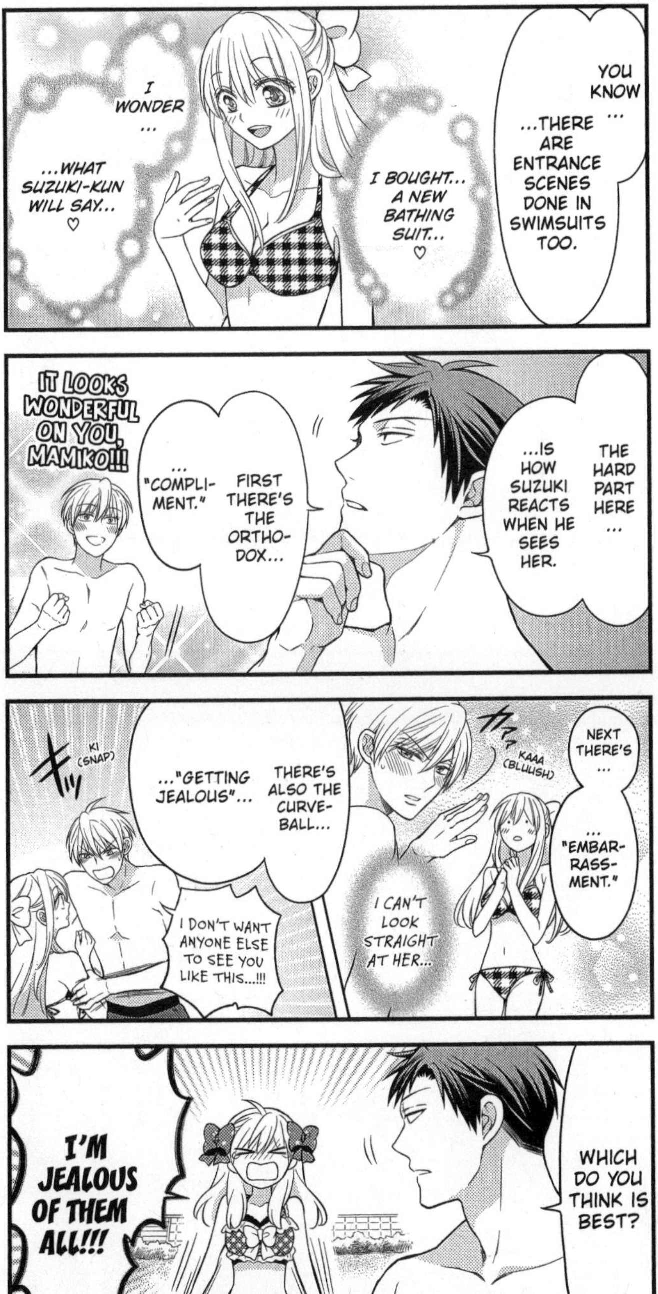
YOU KNOW ...
...THERE ARE ENTRANCE SCENES DONE IN SWIMSUITS TOO.
I BOUGHT... A NEW BATHING SUIT... ♡
I WONDER ...
...WHAT SUZUKI-KUN WILL SAY... ♡
THE HARD PART HERE ...
...IS HOW SUZUKI REACTS WHEN HE SEES HER.
FIRST THERE'S THE ORTHO-DOX...
... "COMPLI-MENT."
IT LOOKS WONDERFUL ON YOU, MAMIKO!!!
NEXT THERE'S ...
... "EMBAR-RASS-MENT."
KAAA (BLUUSH)
I CAN'T LOOK STRAIGHT AT HER...
THERE'S ALSO THE CURVE-BALL...
..."GETTING JEALOUS"...
KI (SNAP)
I DON'T WANT ANYONE ELSE TO SEE YOU LIKE THIS...!!!
WHICH DO YOU THINK IS BEST?
I'M JEALOUS OF THEM ALL!!!

DISAPPOINTMENT

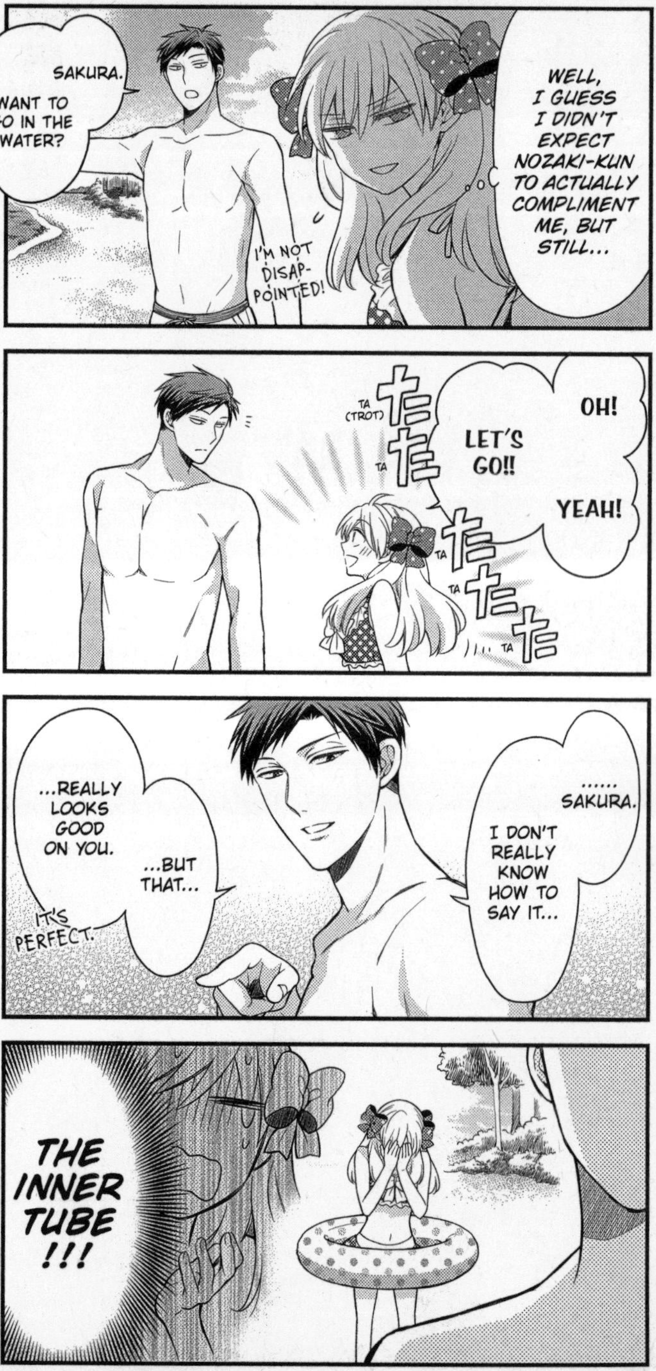
WELL, I GUESS I DIDN'T EXPECT NOZAKI-KUN TO ACTUALLY COMPLIMENT ME, BUT STILL...
I'M NOT DISAPPOINTED!
SAKURA. WANT TO GO IN THE WATER?
OH! LET'S GO!! YEAH!
TA (TROT) TA TA TA TA
...... SAKURA. I DON'T REALLY KNOW HOW TO SAY IT...
...BUT THAT...
...REALLY LOOKS GOOD ON YOU.
IT'S PERFECT.
THE INNER TUBE!!!

THE SPOT WITH THE PERFECT VIEW

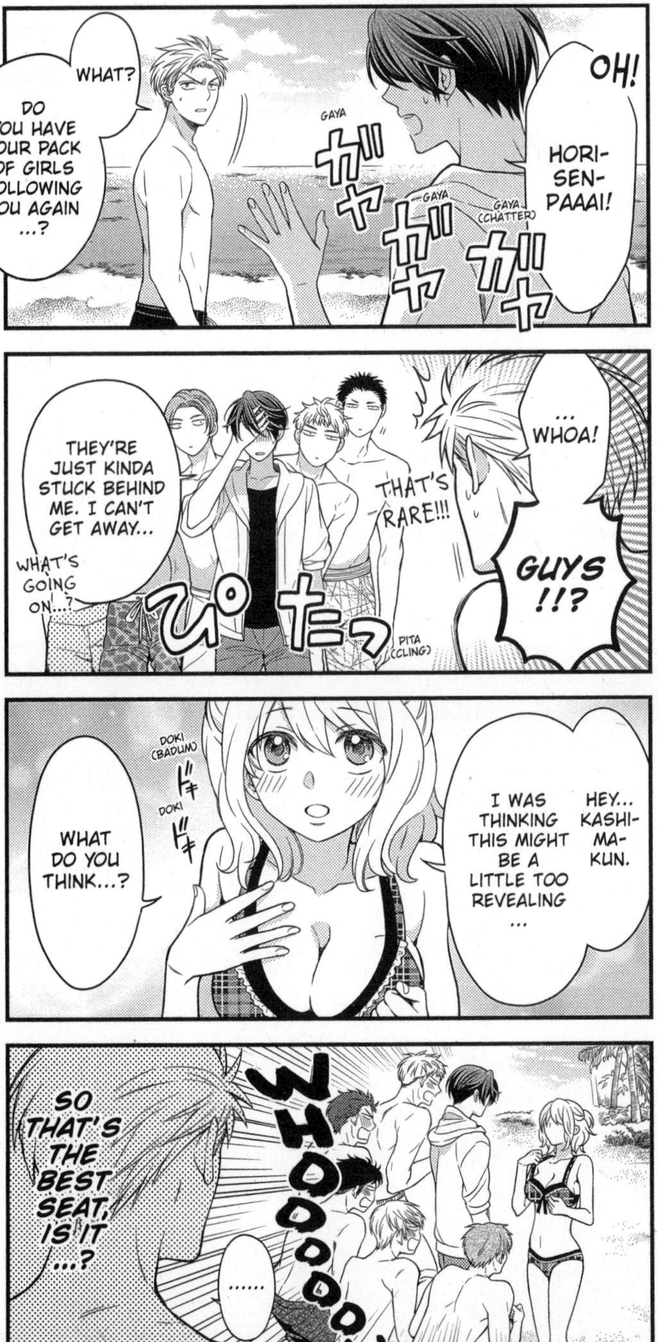
OH!
HORI-SEN-PAAAI!
GAYA (CHATTER)
ガヤ
GAYA
ガヤ
GAYA
ガヤ
WHAT?
DO YOU HAVE YOUR PACK OF GIRLS FOLLOWING YOU AGAIN ...?
... WHOA!
GUYS !!?
THAT'S RARE!!!
THEY'RE JUST KINDA STUCK BEHIND ME. I CAN'T GET AWAY...
PITA (CLING)
ぴたっ
WHAT'S GOING ON...?
HEY... KASHIMA-KUN.
I WAS THINKING THIS MIGHT BE A LITTLE TOO REVEALING ...
DOKI (BADUM)
ドキ
DOKI
ドキ
WHAT DO YOU THINK...?
WHOOOOOA!
SO THAT'S THE BEST SEAT, IS IT ...?
......

A CONSIDERATE KOUHAI

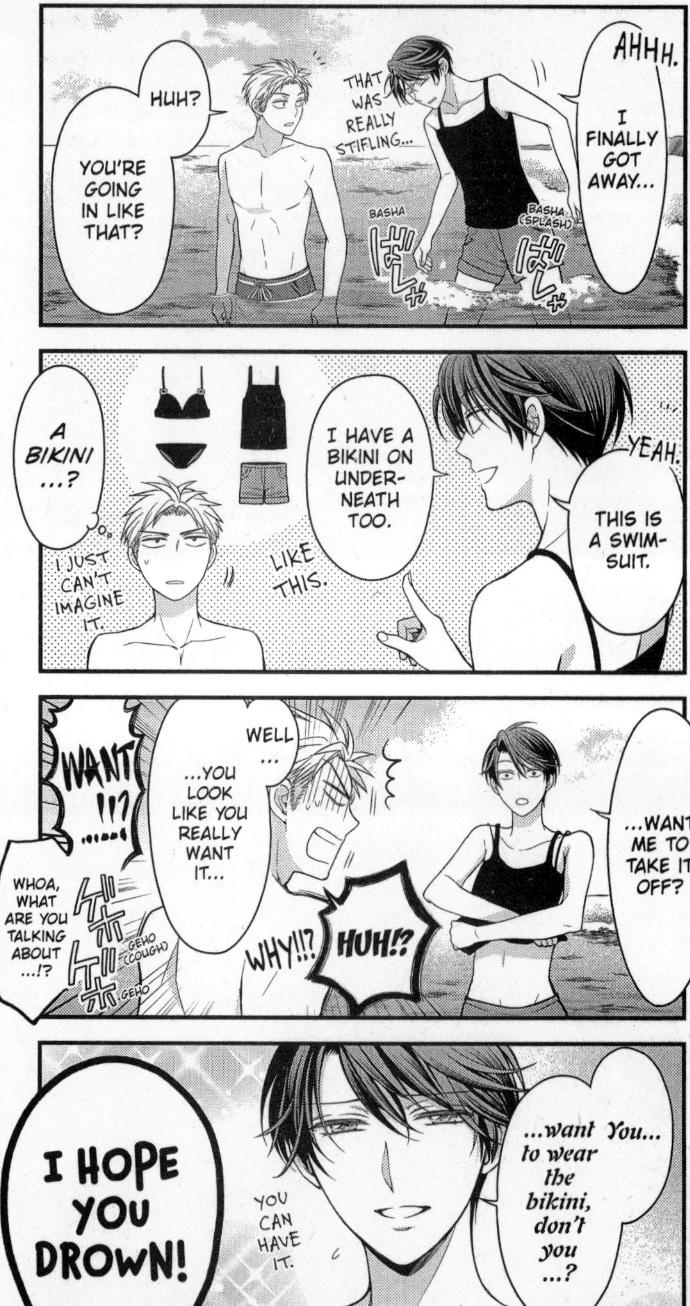
AHHH.
I FINALLY GOT AWAY...
BASHA (SPLASH)
THAT WAS REALLY STIFLING...
BASHA
HUH?
YOU'RE GOING IN LIKE THAT?
YEAH.
THIS IS A SWIMSUIT.
I HAVE A BIKINI ON UNDERNEATH TOO.
LIKE THIS.
A BIKINI ...?
I JUST CAN'T IMAGINE IT.
...WANT ME TO TAKE IT OFF?
HUH!?
WHY!!?
WELL ...
...YOU LOOK LIKE YOU REALLY WANT IT...
WANT !!?
GEHO (COUGH)
GEHO
WHOA, WHAT ARE YOU TALKING ABOUT ...!?
You... ...want to wear the bikini, don't you ...?
YOU CAN HAVE IT.
I HOPE YOU DROWN!

GAME-BRAINED MIKORIN

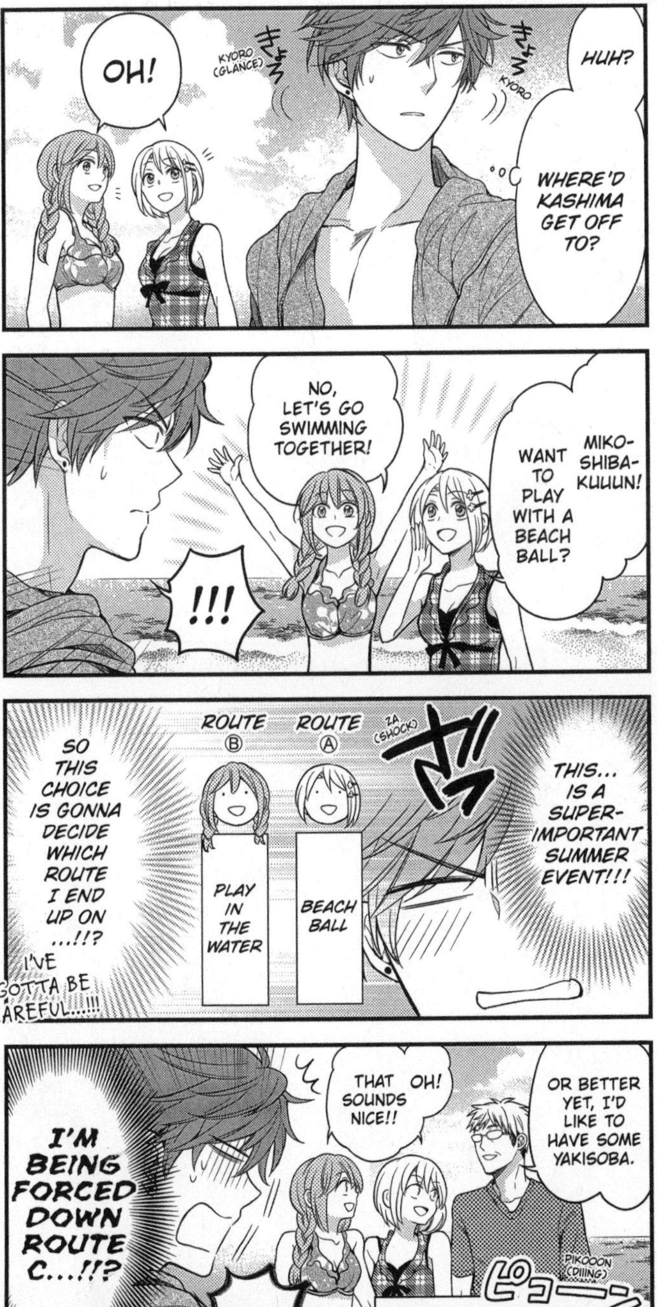
HUH?
WHERE'D KASHIMA GET OFF TO?
KYORO
KYORO (GLANCE)
OH!
MIKO-SHIBA-KUUUN!
WANT TO PLAY WITH A BEACH BALL?
NO, LET'S GO SWIMMING TOGETHER!
!!!
THIS... IS A SUPER-IMPORTANT SUMMER EVENT!!!
ZA (SHOCK)
ROUTE Ⓐ
BEACH BALL
ROUTE Ⓑ
PLAY IN THE WATER
SO THIS CHOICE IS GONNA DECIDE WHICH ROUTE I END UP ON ...!!?
I'VE GOTTA BE CAREFUL...!!!!
OR BETTER YET, I'D LIKE TO HAVE SOME YAKISOBA.
OH! THAT SOUNDS NICE!!
PIKOOON (DIIING)
© GO GET YAKISOBA
I'M BEING FORCED DOWN ROUTE C...!!?
!!?

THAT HAPPENS AT THE BEACH

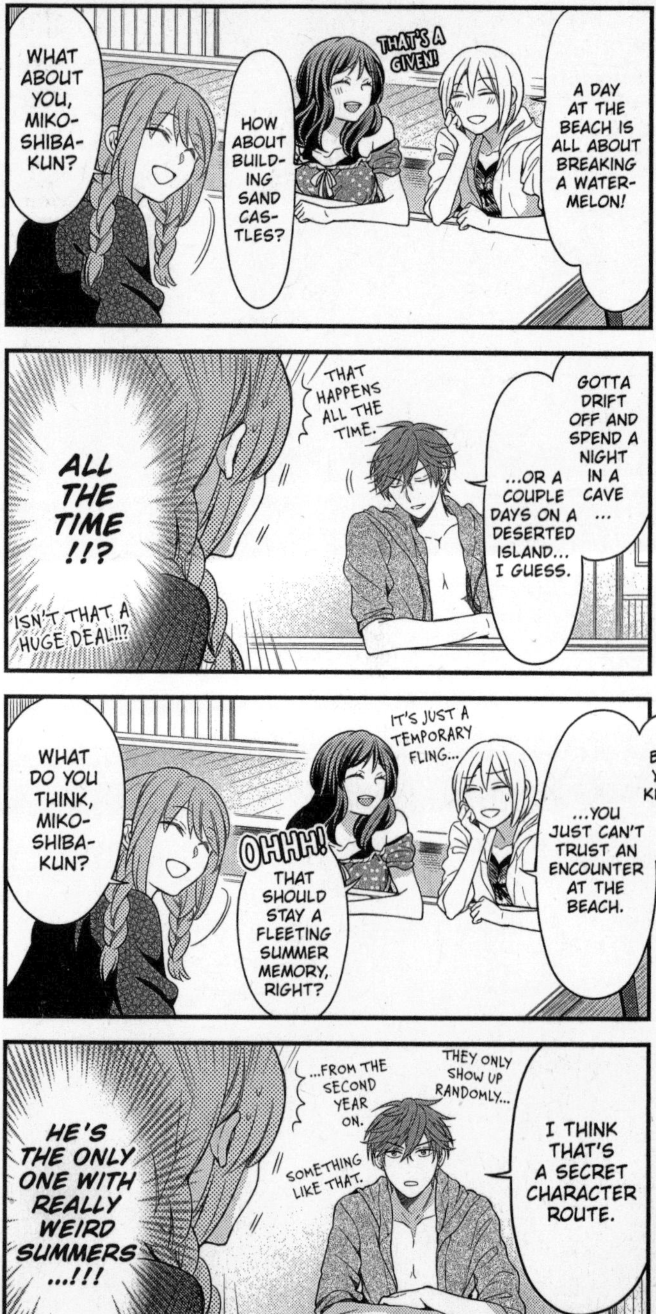
A DAY AT THE BEACH IS ALL ABOUT BREAKING A WATERMELON!
THAT'S A GIVEN!
HOW ABOUT BUILDING SAND CASTLES?
WHAT ABOUT YOU, MIKOSHIBA-KUN?
GOTTA DRIFT OFF AND SPEND A NIGHT IN A CAVE ...
...OR A COUPLE DAYS ON A DESERTED ISLAND... I GUESS.
THAT HAPPENS ALL THE TIME.
ALL THE TIME!!?
ISN'T THAT A HUGE DEAL!!?
BUT, YOU KNOW ...
...YOU JUST CAN'T TRUST AN ENCOUNTER AT THE BEACH.
IT'S JUST A TEMPORARY FLING...
OHHH!
THAT SHOULD STAY A FLEETING SUMMER MEMORY, RIGHT?
WHAT DO YOU THINK, MIKOSHIBA-KUN?
I THINK THAT'S A SECRET CHARACTER ROUTE.
THEY ONLY SHOW UP RANDOMLY...
...FROM THE SECOND YEAR ON.
SOMETHING LIKE THAT.
HE'S THE ONLY ONE WITH REALLY WEIRD SUMMERS ...!!!

A SPECIAL BOY

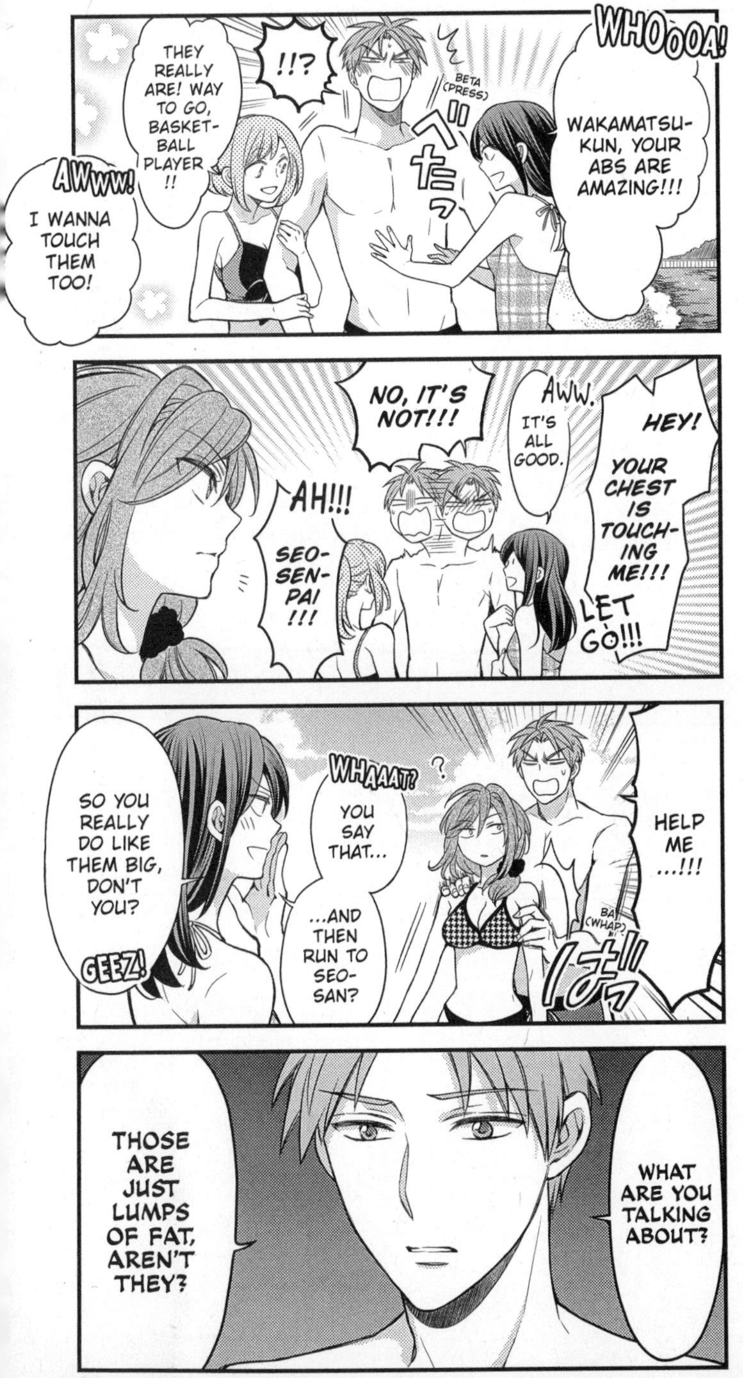
WHOOOOA!
WAKAMATSU-KUN, YOUR ABS ARE AMAZING!!!
BETA (PRESS)
!!?
THEY REALLY ARE! WAY TO GO, BASKET-BALL PLAYER!!
AWWW!
I WANNA TOUCH THEM TOO!
HEY!
YOUR CHEST IS TOUCH-ING ME!!!
LET GO!!!
AWW.
IT'S ALL GOOD.
NO, IT'S NOT!!!
AH!!!
SEO-SEN-PAI!!!
HELP ME...!!!
BA (WHAP)
WHAAAT?
YOU SAY THAT...
...AND THEN RUN TO SEO-SAN?
SO YOU REALLY DO LIKE THEM BIG, DON'T YOU?
GEEZ!
WHAT ARE YOU TALKING ABOUT?
THOSE ARE JUST LUMPS OF FAT, AREN'T THEY?

THE LIKELY CONVERSATION

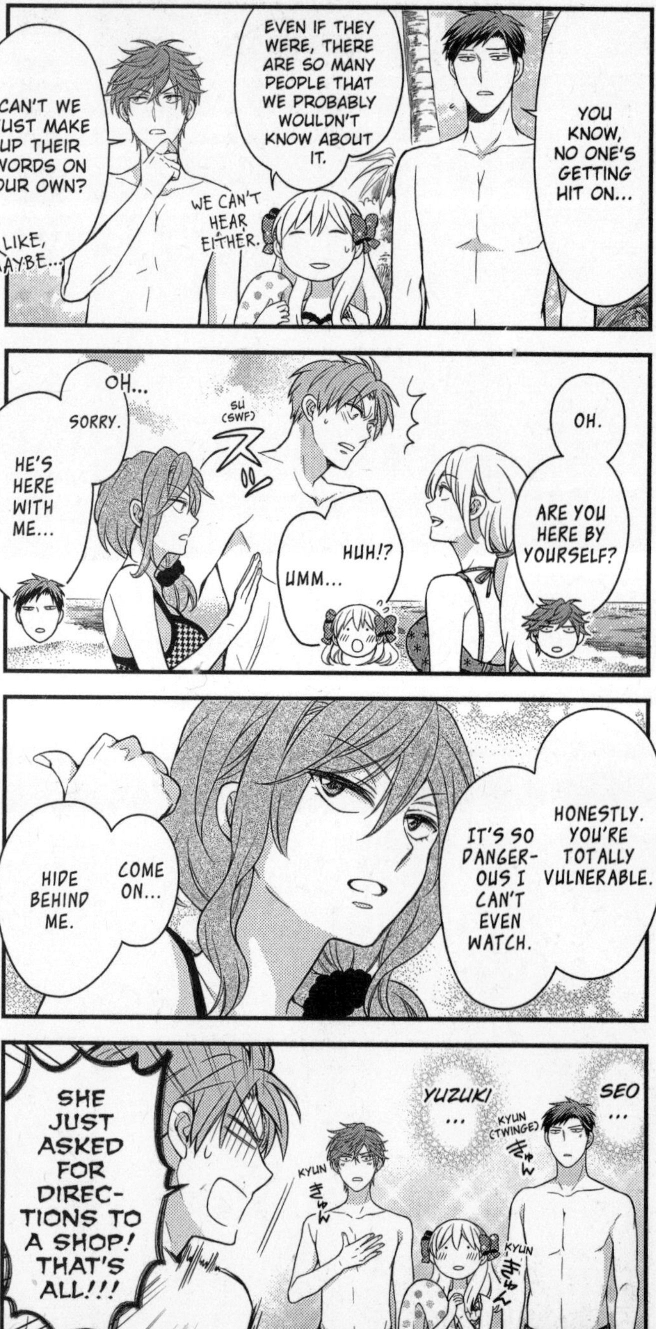

YOU KNOW, NO ONE'S GETTING HIT ON...
EVEN IF THEY WERE, THERE ARE SO MANY PEOPLE THAT WE PROBABLY WOULDN'T KNOW ABOUT IT.
WE CAN'T HEAR EITHER.
CAN'T WE JUST MAKE UP THEIR WORDS ON OUR OWN?
LIKE, MAYBE...
OH.
ARE YOU HERE BY YOURSELF?
HUH!?
UMM...
SU (SWF)
OH...
SORRY.
HE'S HERE WITH ME...
HONESTLY. YOU'RE TOTALLY VULNERABLE.
IT'S SO DANGER-OUS I CAN'T EVEN WATCH.
COME ON...
HIDE BEHIND ME.
SEO ...
KYUN (TWINGE)
きゅん
KYUN
きゅん
YUZUKI ...
KYUN
きゅん
SHE JUST ASKED FOR DIREC-TIONS TO A SHOP! THAT'S ALL!!!

A LITTLE INCIDENT

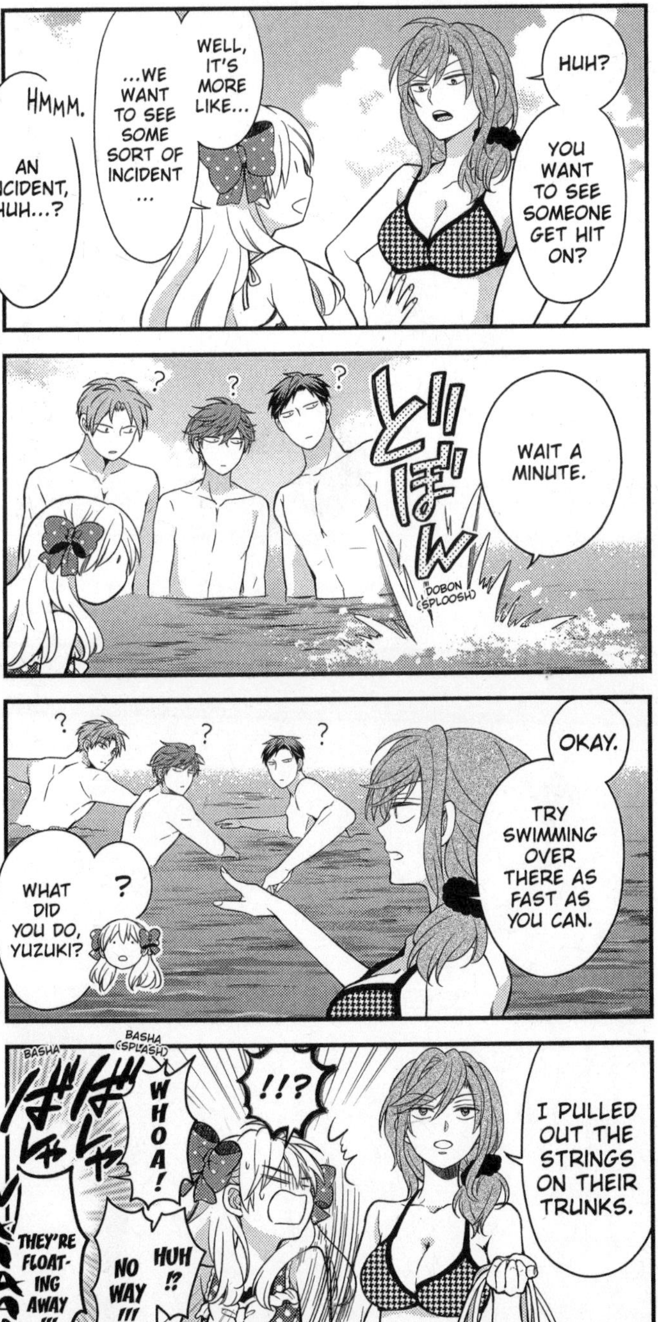
HUH?
YOU WANT TO SEE SOMEONE GET HIT ON?
WELL, IT'S MORE LIKE...
...WE WANT TO SEE SOME SORT OF INCIDENT...
HMMM.
AN INCIDENT, HUH...?
WAIT A MINUTE.
どぼん
DOBON (SPLOOSH)
?
?
?
OKAY.
TRY SWIMMING OVER THERE AS FAST AS YOU CAN.
?
?
?
?
WHAT DID YOU DO, YUZUKI?
I PULLED OUT THE STRINGS ON THEIR TRUNKS.
!!?
HUH!?
NO WAY!!!
BASHA (SPLASH)
ばしゃ
WHOA!
BASHA
ばしゃ
THEY'RE FLOATING AWAY!!!
WAAAAAAAH!

SPREADING PANIC

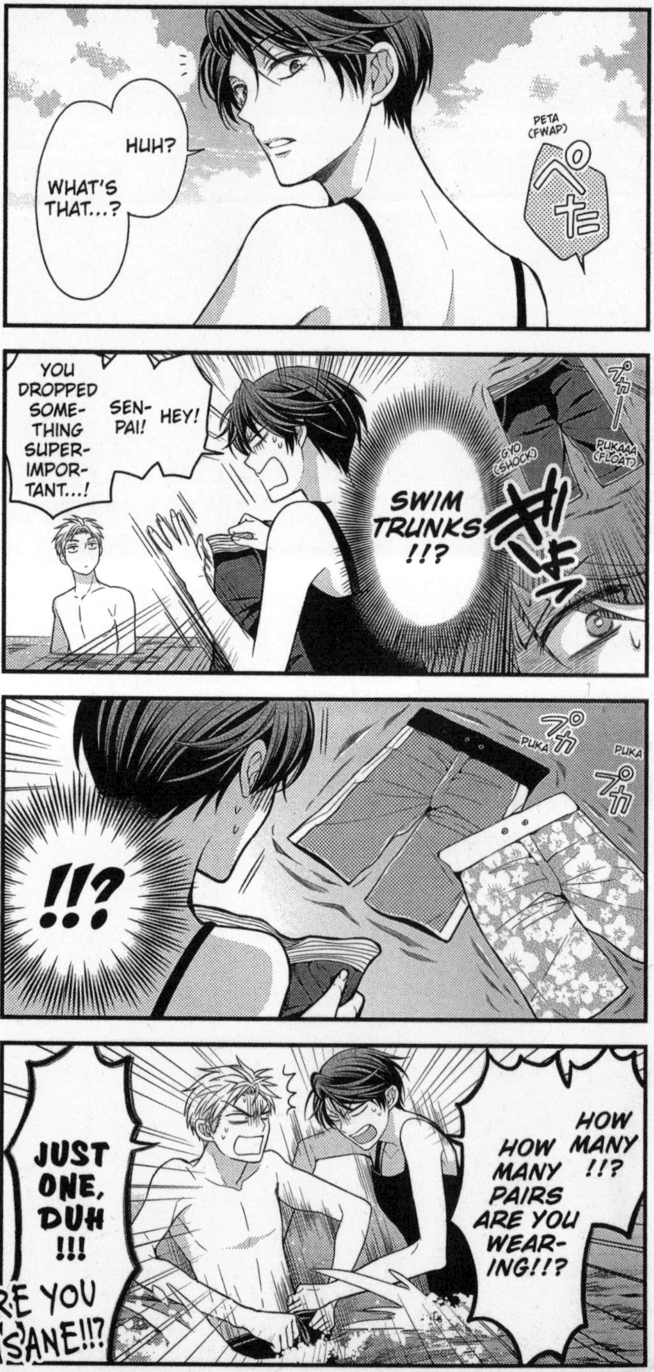
ぺた
PETA (FWAP)
HUH?
WHAT'S THAT...?
ぷかー
PUKAAA (FLOAT)
ぎょっ
GYO (SHOCK)
SWIM TRUNKS!!?
HEY!
SENPAI!
YOU DROPPED SOMETHING SUPER-IMPORTANT...!
ぷか
PUKA
ぷか
PUKA
!!?
HOW MANY!!?
HOW MANY PAIRS ARE YOU WEARING!!?
JUST ONE, DUH!!!
ARE YOU INSANE!!?

EMPATHIZING

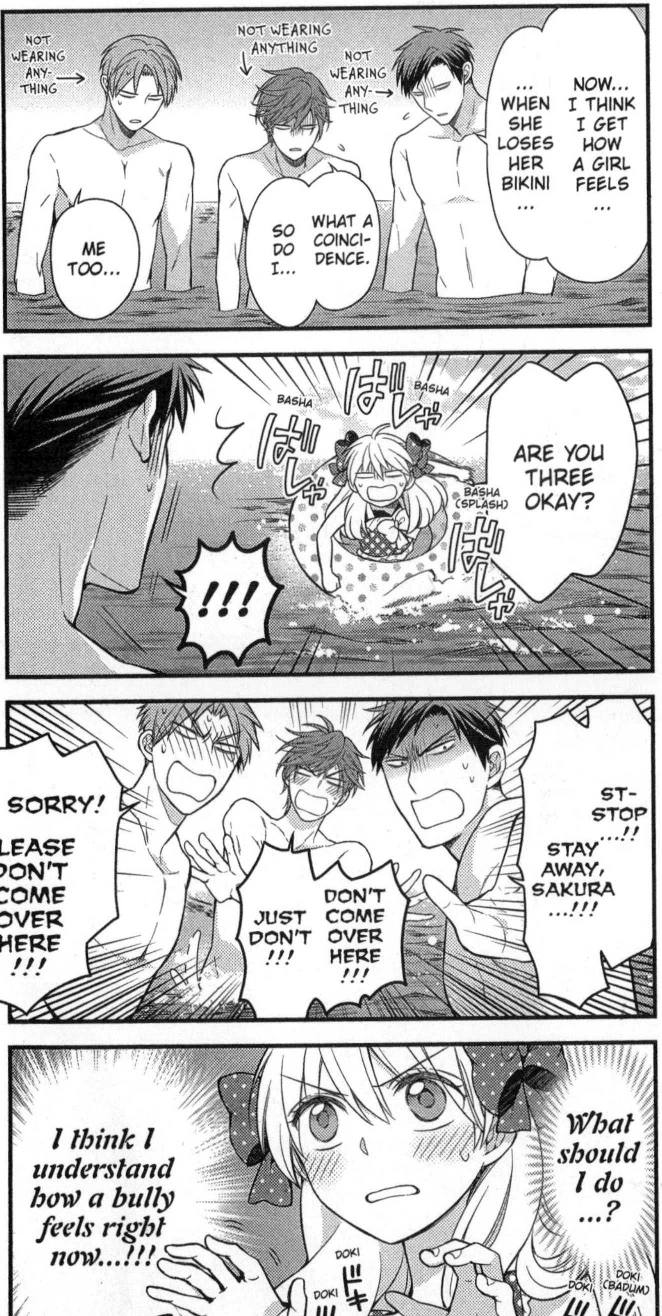
NOW... I THINK I GET HOW A GIRL FEELS...
...WHEN SHE LOSES HER BIKINI...
NOT WEARING ANY-THING
NOT WEARING ANYTHING
NOT WEARING ANY-THING
WHAT A COINCI-DENCE.
SO DO I...
ME TOO...
ARE YOU THREE OKAY?
BASHA
ばしゃ
BASHA (SPLASH)
ばしゃ
BASHA
ばしゃ
!!!
ST-STOP...!!
STAY AWAY, SAKURA...!!!
DON'T COME OVER HERE!!!
JUST DON'T!!!
SORRY!
PLEASE DON'T COME OVER HERE!!!
What should I do...?
DOKI (BADUM)
ドキ
DOKI
ドキ
DOKI
ドキ
DOKI
ドキ
I think I understand how a bully feels right now...!!!
UZU (TWITCH)
うずっ...

THE OCEAN IS DEFINITELY A TROLL

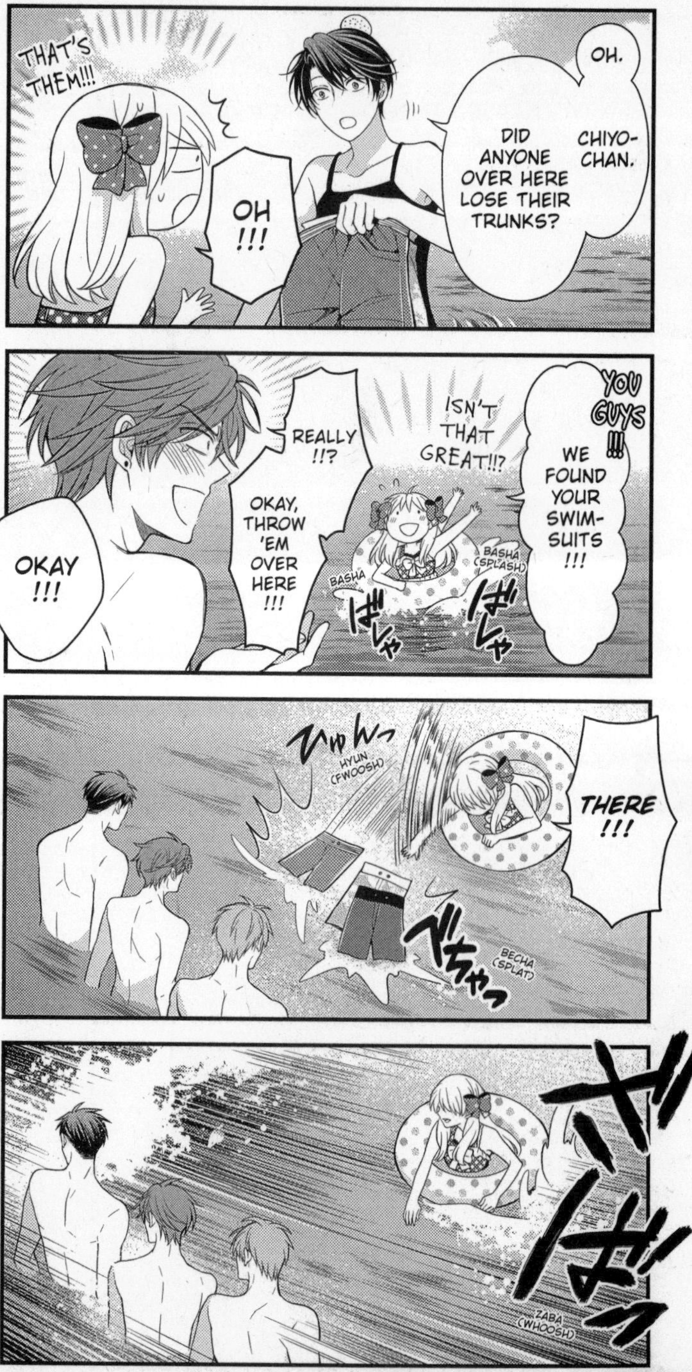
OH.
CHIYO-CHAN.
DID ANYONE OVER HERE LOSE THEIR TRUNKS?
OH !!!
THAT'S THEM!!!
YOU GUYS !!!
WE FOUND YOUR SWIM-SUITS !!!
ISN'T THAT GREAT!!?
ばしゃ
BASHA (SPLASH)
ばしゃ
BASHA
REALLY !!?
OKAY, THROW 'EM OVER HERE !!!
OKAY !!!
THERE !!!
ひゅんっ
HYUN (FWOOSH)
べちゃっ
BECHA (SPLAT)
ざばっ
ZABA (WHOOSH)

A STORY FROM HIS ACTUAL EXPERIENCE

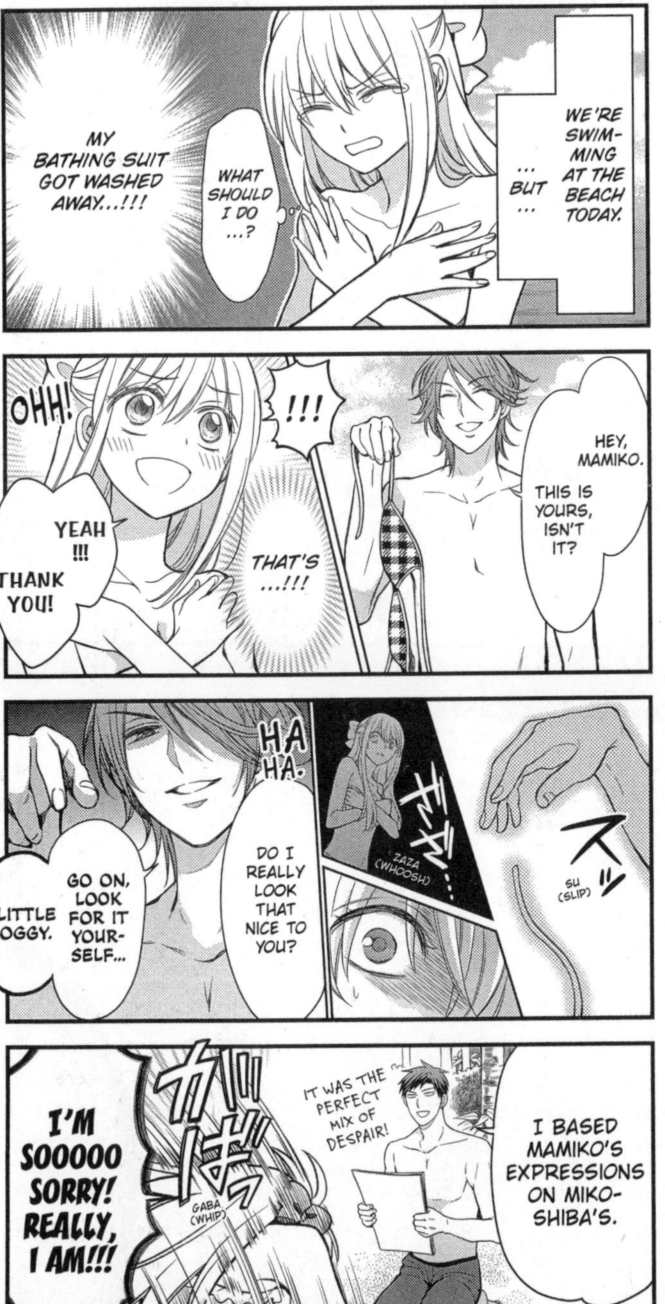

WE'RE SWIMMING AT THE BEACH TODAY.
... BUT ...
WHAT SHOULD I DO ...?
MY BATHING SUIT GOT WASHED AWAY...!!!
HEY, MAMIKO.
THIS IS YOURS, ISN'T IT?
!!!
THAT'S ...!!!
OHH!
YEAH !!! THANK YOU!
SU (SLIP)
ZAZA (WHOOSH)
HA HA.
DO I REALLY LOOK THAT NICE TO YOU?
GO ON, LOOK FOR IT YOURSELF...
...LITTLE DOGGY.
I BASED MAMIKO'S EXPRESSIONS ON MIKO-SHIBA'S.
IT WAS THE PERFECT MIX OF DESPAIR!
GABA (WHIP)
I'M SOOOOO SORRY! REALLY, I AM!!!

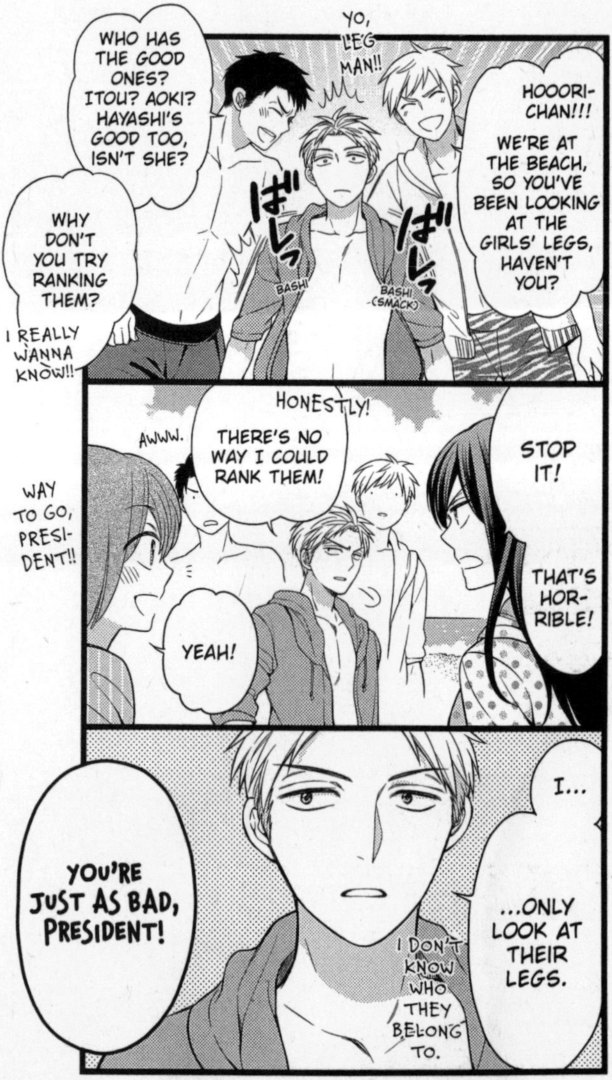
HOOORI-CHAN!!!
WE'RE AT THE BEACH, SO YOU'VE BEEN LOOKING AT THE GIRLS' LEGS, HAVEN'T YOU?
YO, LEG MAN!!
ばしっ
BASHI -(SMACK)
ばしっ
BASHI
WHO HAS THE GOOD ONES? ITOU? AOKI? HAYASHI'S GOOD TOO, ISN'T SHE?
WHY DON'T YOU TRY RANKING THEM?
I REALLY WANNA KNOW!!
STOP IT!
THAT'S HORRIBLE!
HONESTLY!
THERE'S NO WAY I COULD RANK THEM!
AWWW.
YEAH!
WAY TO GO, PRESIDENT!!
I...
...ONLY LOOK AT THEIR LEGS.
I DON'T KNOW WHO THEY BELONG TO.
YOU'RE JUST AS BAD, PRESIDENT!

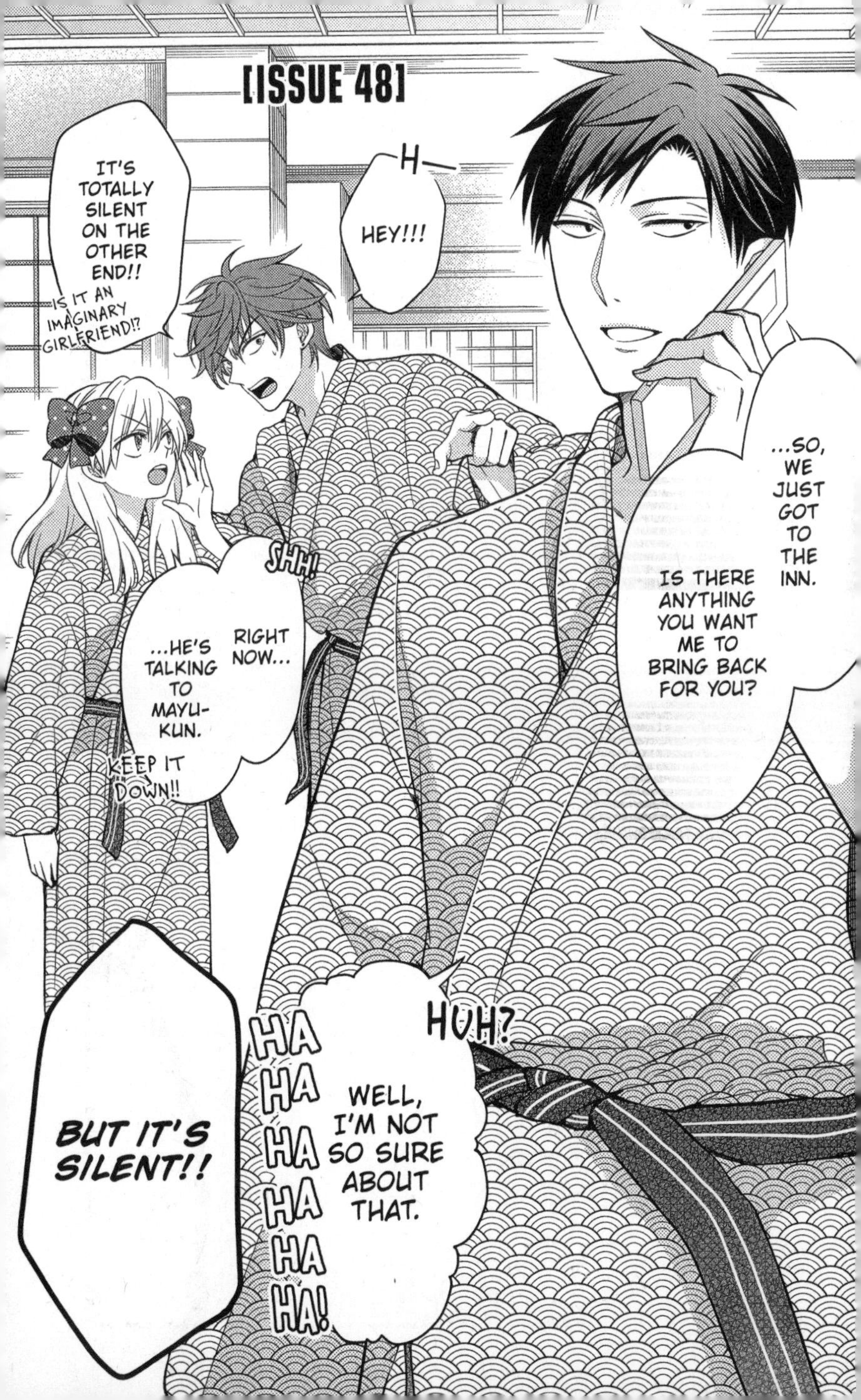
[ISSUE 48]
...SO, WE JUST GOT TO THE INN.
IS THERE ANYTHING YOU WANT ME TO BRING BACK FOR YOU?
H— HEY!!!
IT'S TOTALLY SILENT ON THE OTHER END!!
IS IT AN IMAGINARY GIRLFRIEND!?
SHH!
RIGHT NOW... ...HE'S TALKING TO MAYU-KUN.
KEEP IT DOWN!!
HUH?
WELL, I'M NOT SO SURE ABOUT THAT.
HA HA HA HA HA HA!
BUT IT'S SILENT!!

WHAT ARE YOUR PLANS FOR TONIGHT?

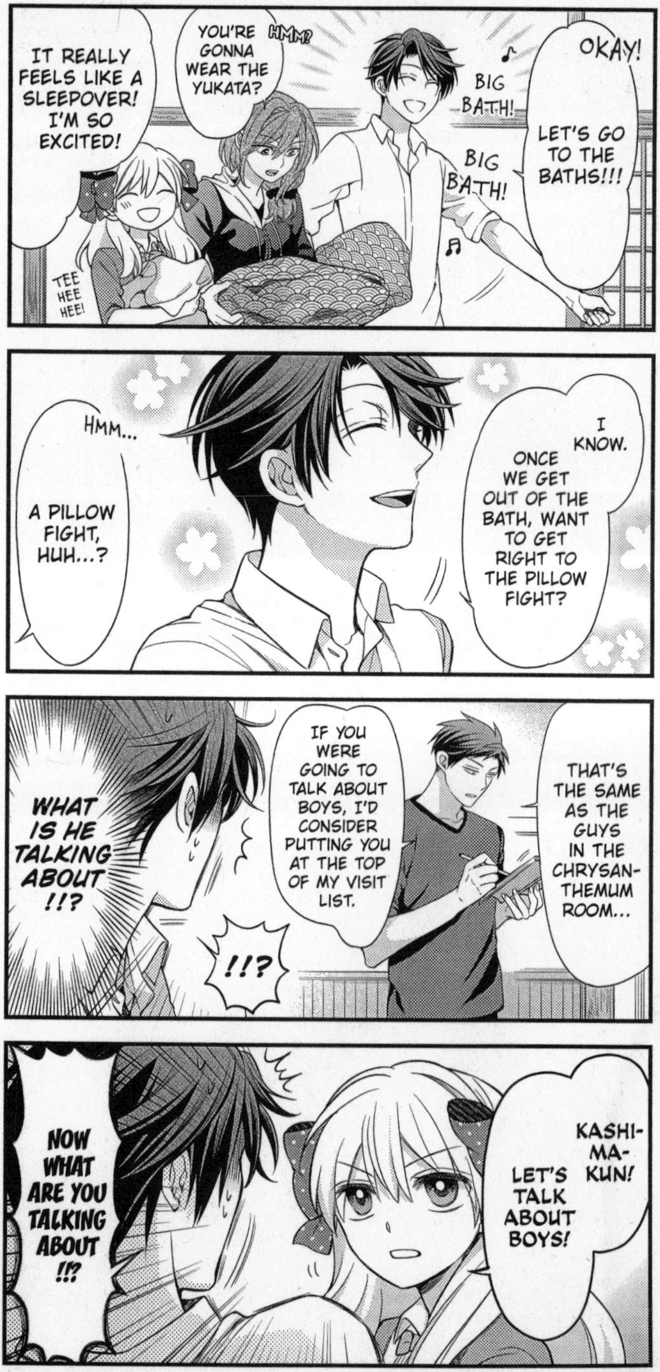
OKAY!
LET'S GO TO THE BATHS!!!
BIG BATH!
BIG BATH!
HMM?
YOU'RE GONNA WEAR THE YUKATA?
IT REALLY FEELS LIKE A SLEEPOVER! I'M SO EXCITED!
TEE HEE HEE!
I KNOW.
ONCE WE GET OUT OF THE BATH, WANT TO GET RIGHT TO THE PILLOW FIGHT?
HMM...
A PILLOW FIGHT, HUH...?
THAT'S THE SAME AS THE GUYS IN THE CHRYSAN-THEMUM ROOM...
IF YOU WERE GOING TO TALK ABOUT BOYS, I'D CONSIDER PUTTING YOU AT THE TOP OF MY VISIT LIST.
!!?
WHAT IS HE TALKING ABOUT !!?
KASHI-MA-KUN!
LET'S TALK ABOUT BOYS!
NOW WHAT ARE YOU TALKING ABOUT !!?

JUST A SINGLE WALL BETWEEN THEM

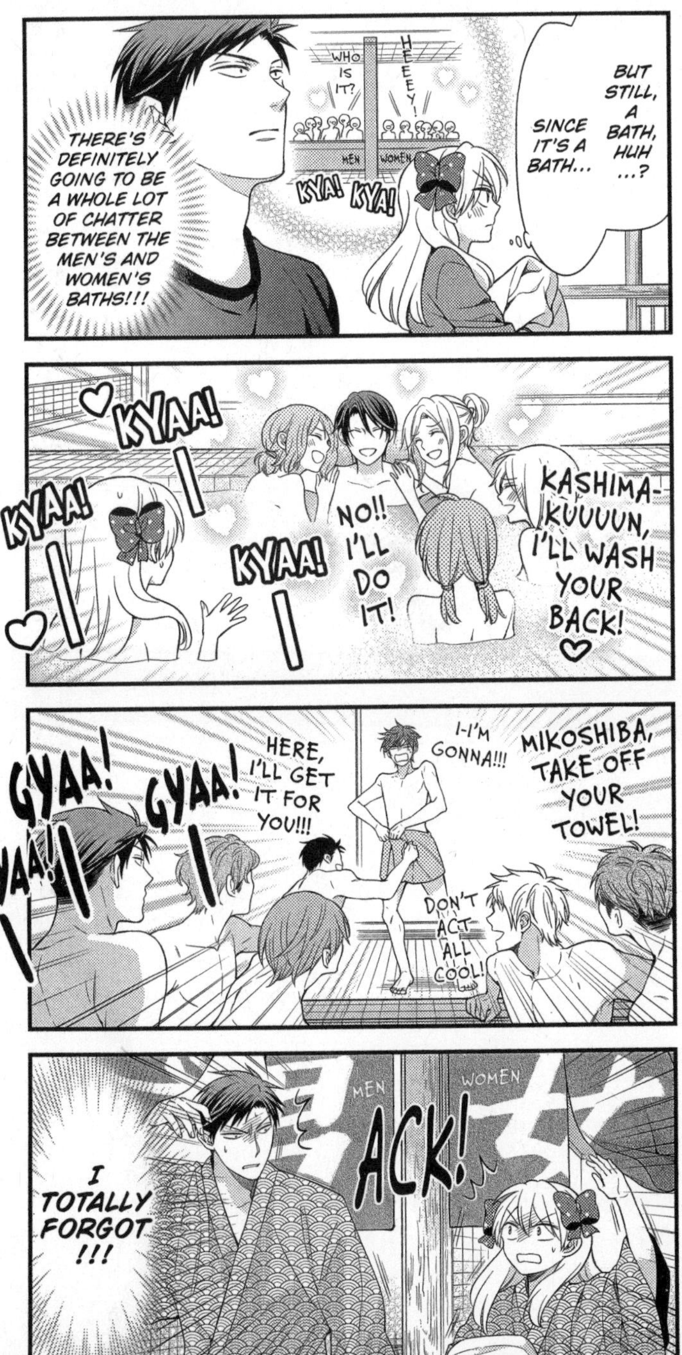

BUT STILL, A BATH, HUH ...?
SINCE IT'S A BATH...
HEEEEY!
WHO IS IT?
WOMEN
MEN
KYA! KYA!
THERE'S DEFINITELY GOING TO BE A WHOLE LOT OF CHATTER BETWEEN THE MEN'S AND WOMEN'S BATHS!!!
KASHIMA-KUUUUN, I'LL WASH YOUR BACK!
KYAA!
NO!! I'LL DO IT!
KYAA!
KYAA!
MIKOSHIBA, TAKE OFF YOUR TOWEL!
I-I'M GONNA!!!
HERE, I'LL GET IT FOR YOU!!!
DON'T ACT ALL COOL!
GYAA!
GYAA!
GYAA!
WOMEN
MEN
ACK!
I TOTALLY FORGOT!!!

EYES AVERTED IN A PASSIONATE GAZE

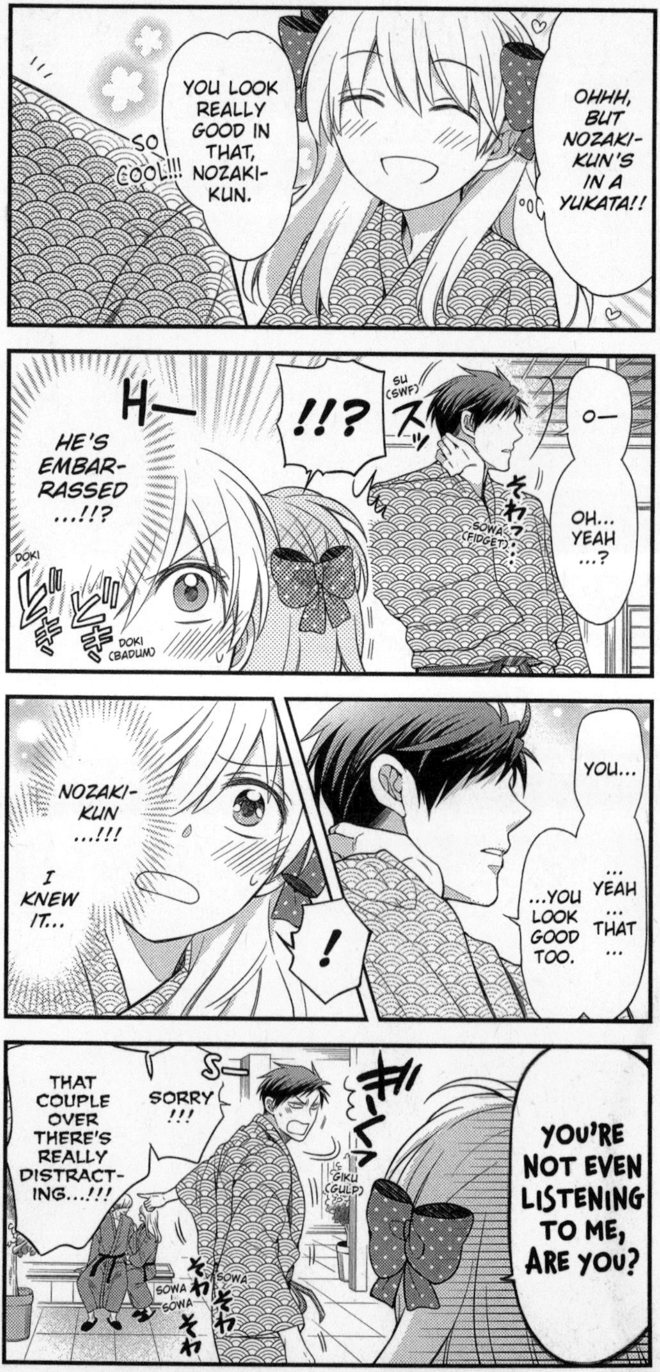
OHHH, BUT NOZAKI-KUN'S IN A YUKATA!!
YOU LOOK REALLY GOOD IN THAT, NOZAKI-KUN.
SO COOL!!!
O— OH... YEAH ...?
SU (SWF)
!!?
SOWA (FIDGET)
H—
HE'S EMBARRASSED ...!!?
DOKI
DOKI (BADUM)
YOU... ...YEAH ...THAT ...
...YOU LOOK GOOD TOO.
!
NOZAKI-KUN ...!!!
I KNEW IT...
YOU'RE NOT EVEN LISTENING TO ME, ARE YOU?
GIKU (GULP)
S— SORRY!!!
THAT COUPLE OVER THERE'S REALLY DISTRACTING...!!!
SOWA
SOWA SOWA

IT'S HARD TO BE A POPULAR GUY!

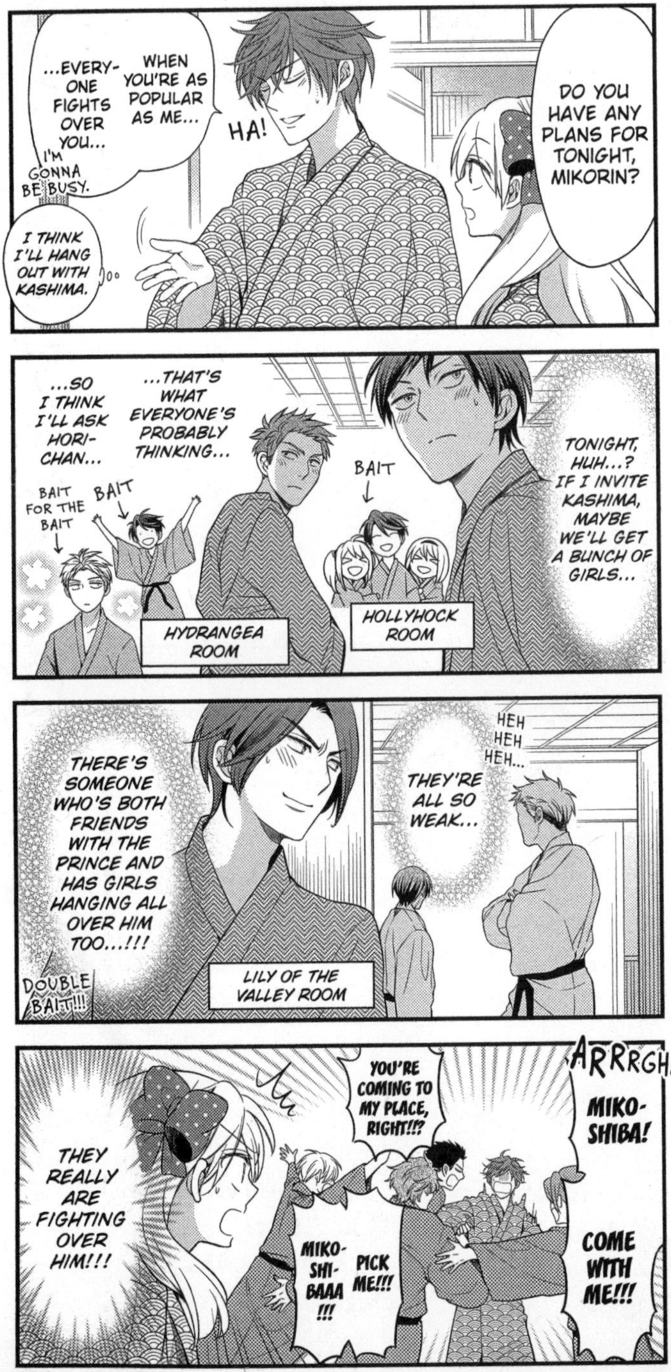
DO YOU HAVE ANY PLANS FOR TONIGHT, MIKORIN?
HA!
WHEN YOU'RE AS POPULAR AS ME...
...EVERYONE FIGHTS OVER YOU...
I'M GONNA BE BUSY.
I THINK I'LL HANG OUT WITH KASHIMA.
TONIGHT, HUH...? IF I INVITE KASHIMA, MAYBE WE'LL GET A BUNCH OF GIRLS...
BAIT
HOLLYHOCK ROOM
...THAT'S WHAT EVERYONE'S PROBABLY THINKING...
...SO I THINK I'LL ASK HORI-CHAN...
BAIT
BAIT FOR THE BAIT
HYDRANGEA ROOM
HEH HEH HEH...
THEY'RE ALL SO WEAK...
THERE'S SOMEONE WHO'S BOTH FRIENDS WITH THE PRINCE AND HAS GIRLS HANGING ALL OVER HIM TOO...!!!
LILY OF THE VALLEY ROOM
DOUBLE BAIT!!!
ARRRGH!
MIKO-SHIBA!
COME WITH ME!!!
YOU'RE COMING TO MY PLACE, RIGHT!!?
PICK ME!!!
MIKO-SHIBAAA!!!
THEY REALLY ARE FIGHTING OVER HIM!!!

PUNISHMENT

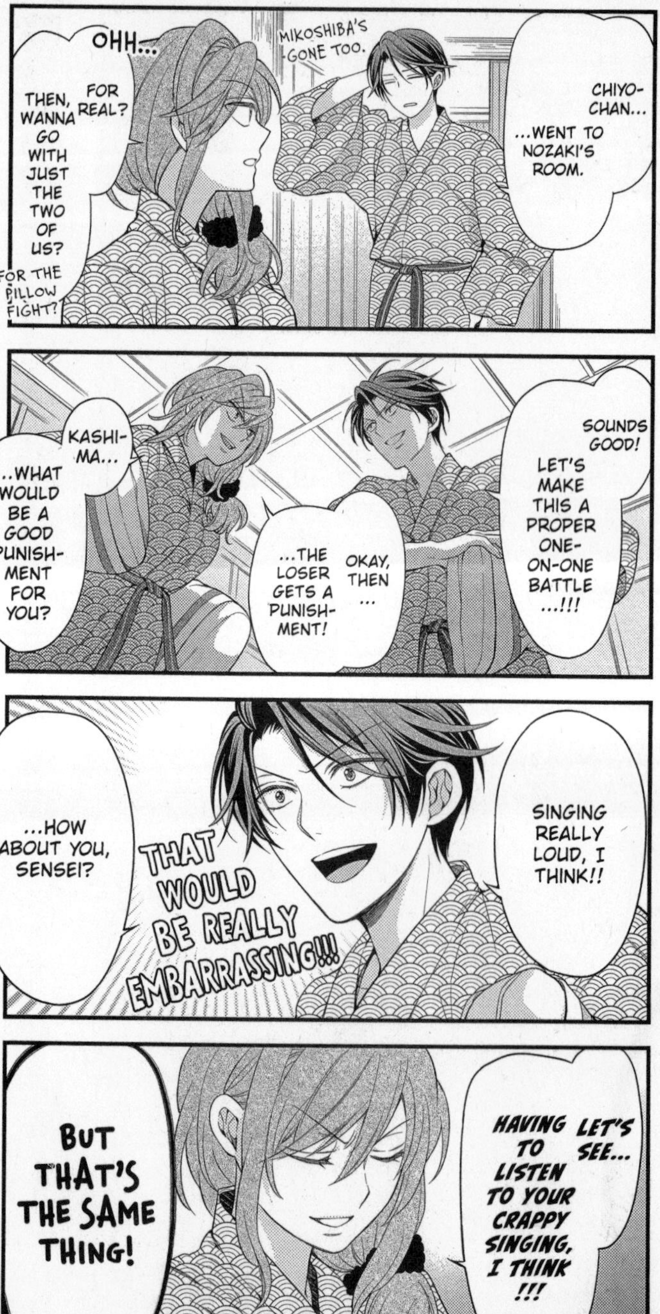
CHIYO-CHAN...
...WENT TO NOZAKI'S ROOM.
MIKOSHIBA'S GONE TOO.
OHH...
FOR REAL?
THEN, WANNA GO WITH JUST THE TWO OF US?
FOR THE PILLOW FIGHT?
SOUNDS GOOD!
LET'S MAKE THIS A PROPER ONE-ON-ONE BATTLE ...!!!
OKAY, THEN ...
...THE LOSER GETS A PUNISHMENT!
KASHIMA...
...WHAT WOULD BE A GOOD PUNISHMENT FOR YOU?
SINGING REALLY LOUD, I THINK!!
THAT WOULD BE REALLY EMBARRASSING!!!
...HOW ABOUT YOU, SENSEI?
LET'S SEE...
HAVING TO LISTEN TO YOUR CRAPPY SINGING, I THINK !!!
BUT THAT'S THE SAME THING!

DOESN'T FEEL RIGHT

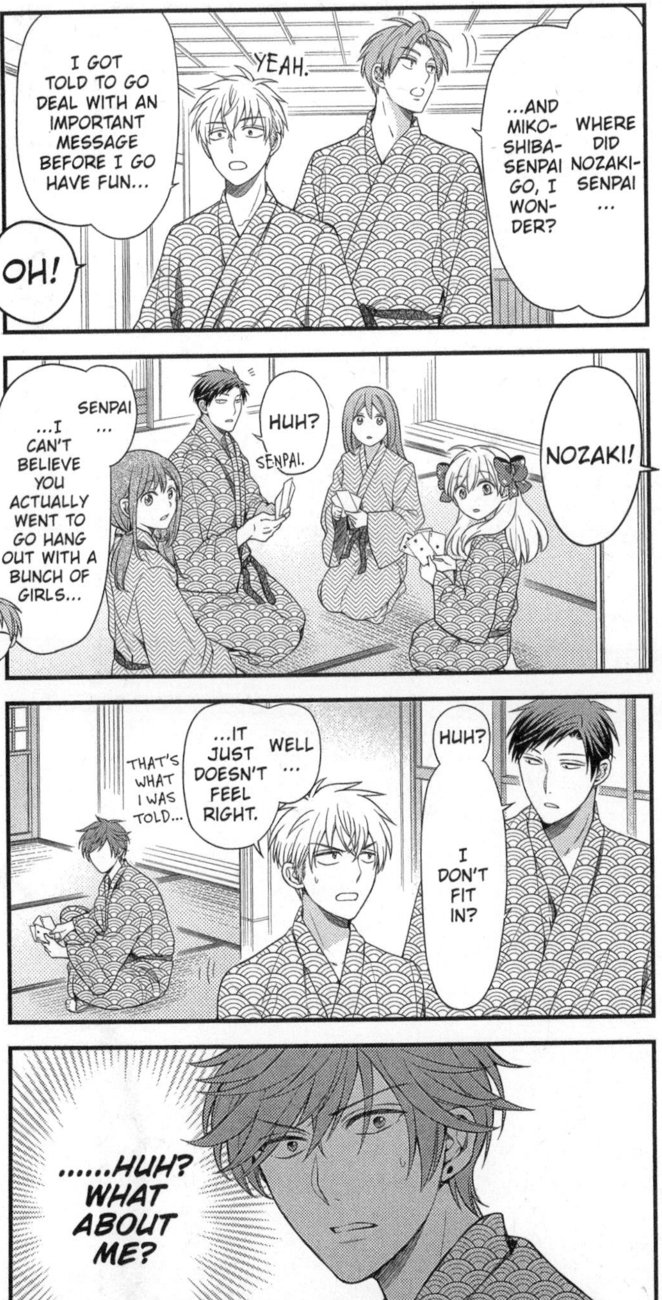
WHERE DID NOZAKI-SENPAI...
...AND MIKOSHIBA-SENPAI GO, I WONDER?
YEAH.
I GOT TOLD TO GO DEAL WITH AN IMPORTANT MESSAGE BEFORE I GO HAVE FUN...
OH!
NOZAKI!
HUH?
SENPAI.
SENPAI...
...I CAN'T BELIEVE YOU ACTUALLY WENT TO GO HANG OUT WITH A BUNCH OF GIRLS...
HUH?
I DON'T FIT IN?
WELL...
...IT JUST DOESN'T FEEL RIGHT.
THAT'S WHAT I WAS TOLD...
......HUH? WHAT ABOUT ME?

SENPAI'S APPROVAL

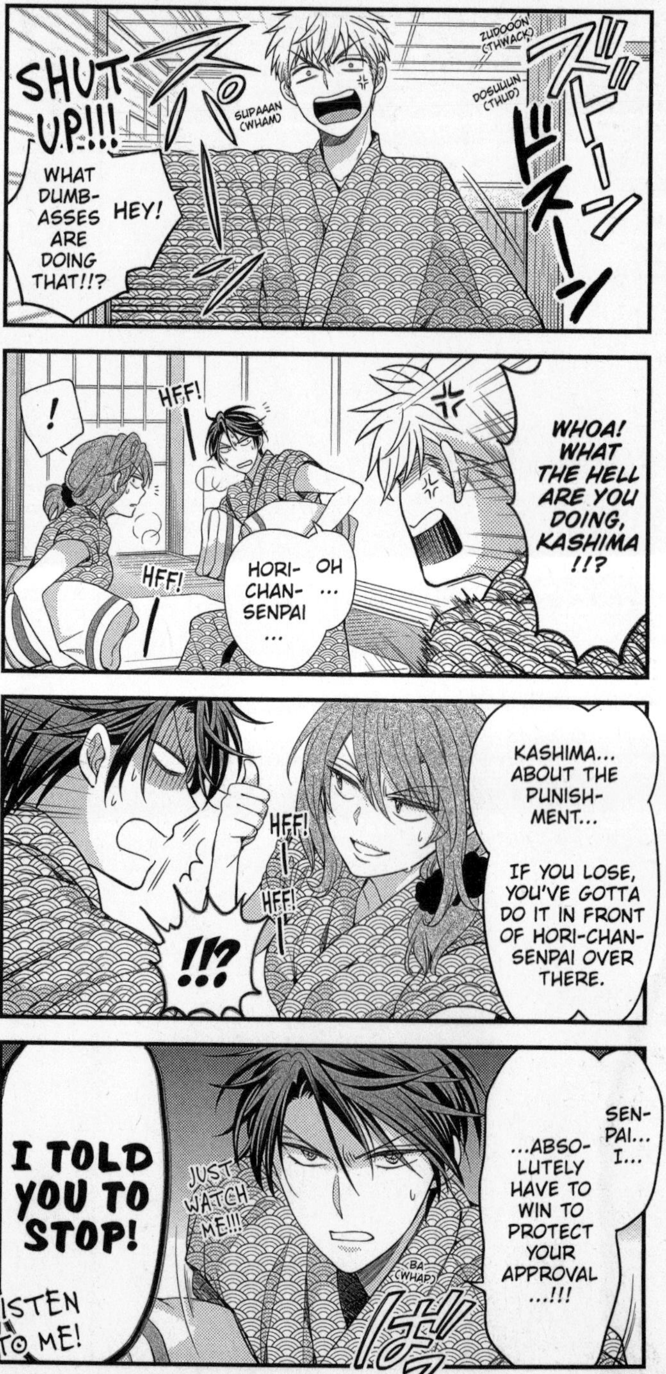
ZUDOOON (THWACK)
DOSUUUN (THUD)
SUPAAAN (WHAM)
HEY!
WHAT DUMB-ASSES ARE DOING THAT!!?
SHUT UP!!!...
WHOA! WHAT THE HELL ARE YOU DOING, KASHIMA!!?
OH...
HORI-CHAN-SENPAI...
HFF!
!
HFF!
KASHIMA... ABOUT THE PUNISH-MENT...
IF YOU LOSE, YOU'VE GOTTA DO IT IN FRONT OF HORI-CHAN-SENPAI OVER THERE.
HFF!
HFF!
!!?
SEN-PAI... I...
...ABSO-LUTELY HAVE TO WIN TO PROTECT YOUR APPROVAL ...!!!
BA (WHAP)
JUST WATCH ME!!!
I TOLD YOU TO STOP!
LISTEN TO ME!

THE DANGER OF GOOFING OFF

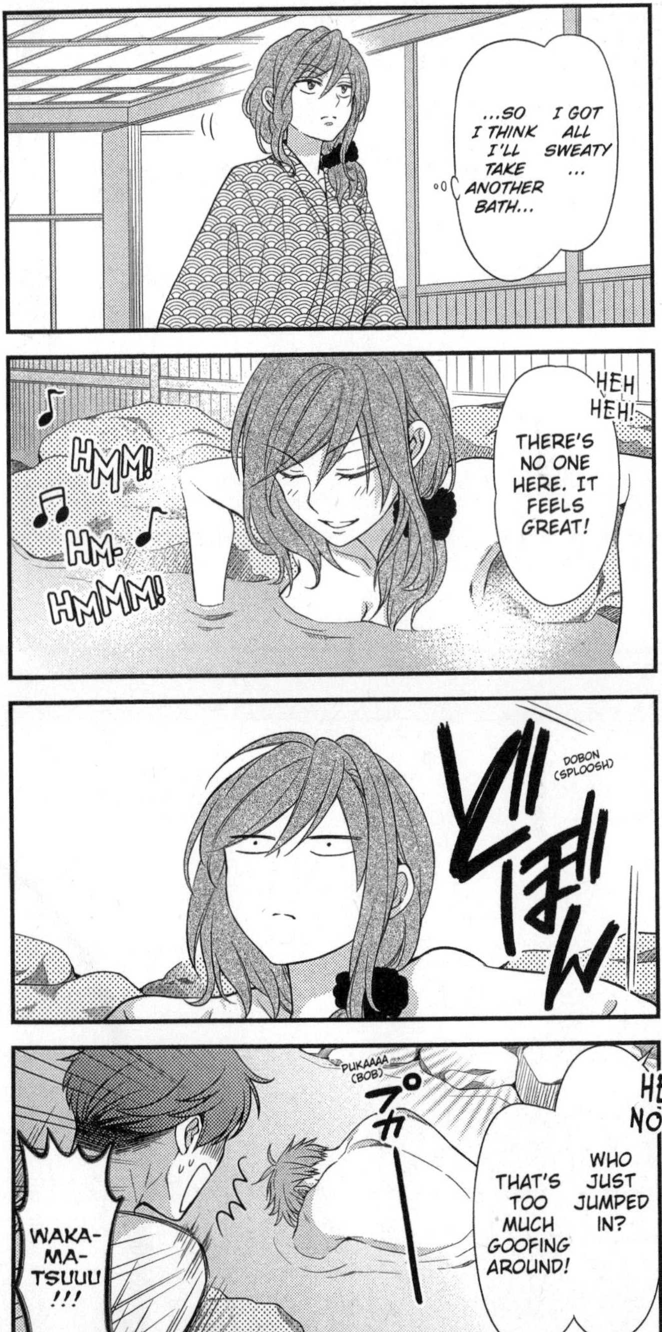
I GOT ALL SWEATY...
...SO I THINK I'LL TAKE ANOTHER BATH...
HEH HEH!
THERE'S NO ONE HERE. IT FEELS GREAT!
HMMM!
HM-HMMMM!
DOBON (SPLOOSH)
HEY NOW!
WHO JUST JUMPED IN?
THAT'S TOO MUCH GOOFING AROUND!
PUKAAAA (BOB)
WAKA-MA-TSUUU!!!

WITH YOUR SONG AND YOUR VOICE

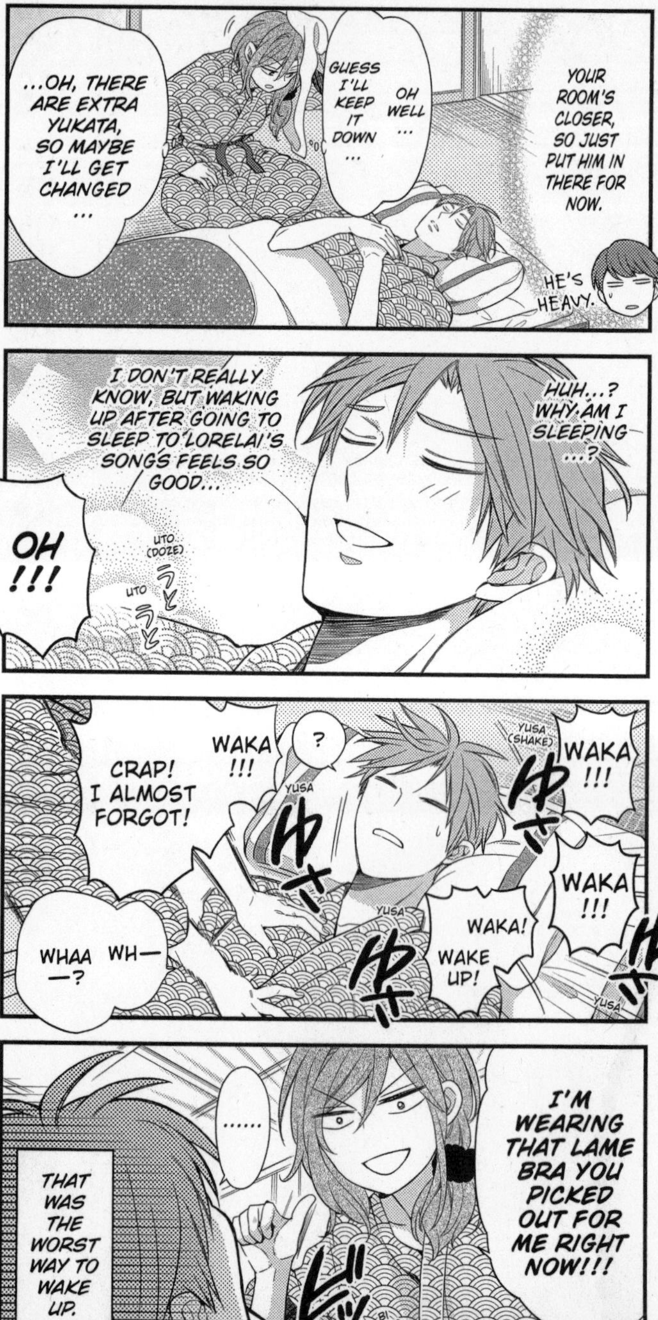
YOUR ROOM'S CLOSER, SO JUST PUT HIM IN THERE FOR NOW.
HE'S HEAVY.
OH WELL...
GUESS I'LL KEEP IT DOWN...
...OH, THERE ARE EXTRA YUKATA, SO MAYBE I'LL GET CHANGED...
HUH...? WHY AM I SLEEPING...?
I DON'T REALLY KNOW, BUT WAKING UP AFTER GOING TO SLEEP TO LORELAI'S SONGS FEELS SO GOOD...
UTO (DOZE)
UTO
OH!!!
YUSA (SHAKE)
WAKA!!!
?
WAKA!!!
CRAP! I ALMOST FORGOT!
YUSA
WAKA!!!
WAKA!
WAKE UP!
YUSA
YUSA
WH—
WHAA—?
I'M WEARING THAT LAME BRA YOU PICKED OUT FOR ME RIGHT NOW!!!
BI (JAB)
......
THAT WAS THE WORST WAY TO WAKE UP.

IS IT GETTING THROUGH?

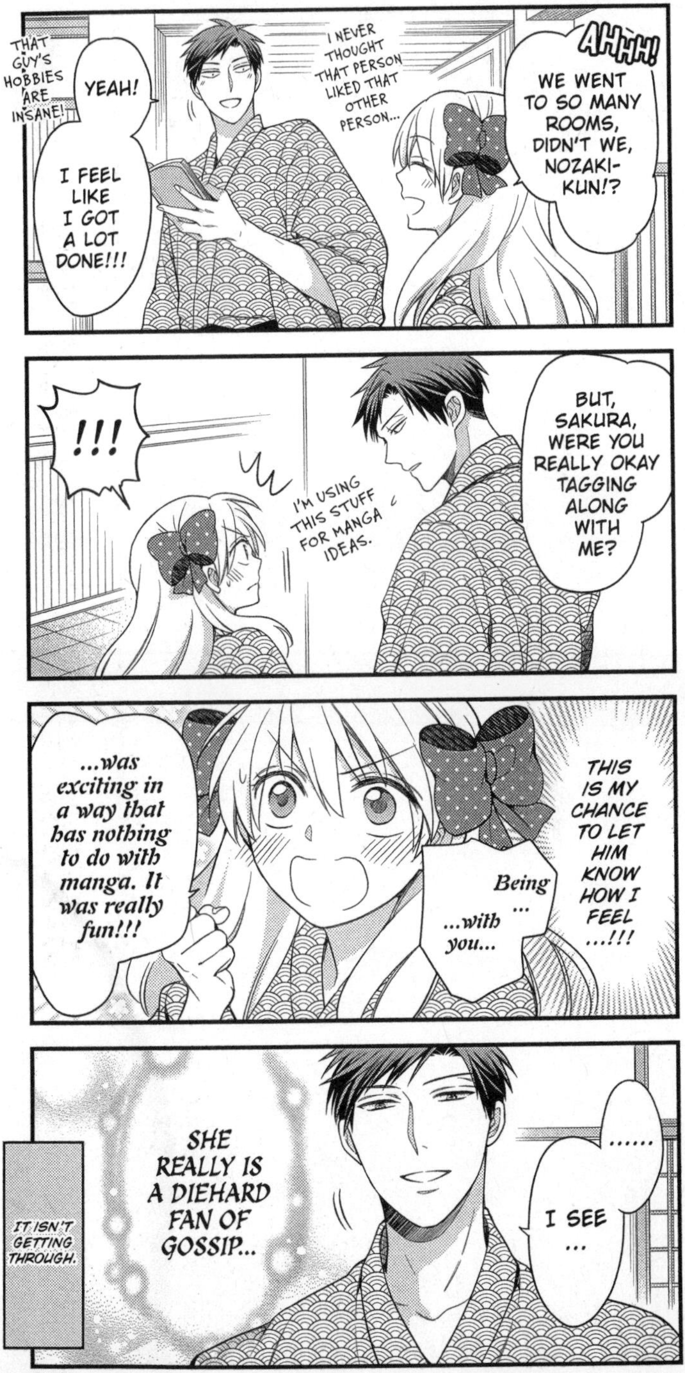
AHHHH!
WE WENT TO SO MANY ROOMS, DIDN'T WE, NOZAKI-KUN!?
I NEVER THOUGHT THAT PERSON LIKED THAT OTHER PERSON...
YEAH!
I FEEL LIKE I GOT A LOT DONE!!!
THAT GUY'S HOBBIES ARE INSANE!
BUT, SAKURA, WERE YOU REALLY OKAY TAGGING ALONG WITH ME?
I'M USING THIS STUFF FOR MANGA IDEAS.
!!!
THIS IS MY CHANCE TO LET HIM KNOW HOW I FEEL ...!!!
Being ... ...with you...
...was exciting in a way that has nothing to do with manga. It was really fun!!!
...... I SEE ...
SHE REALLY IS A DIEHARD FAN OF GOSSIP...
IT ISN'T GETTING THROUGH.

SNEAK, SNEAK... RUMMAGE, RUMMAGE

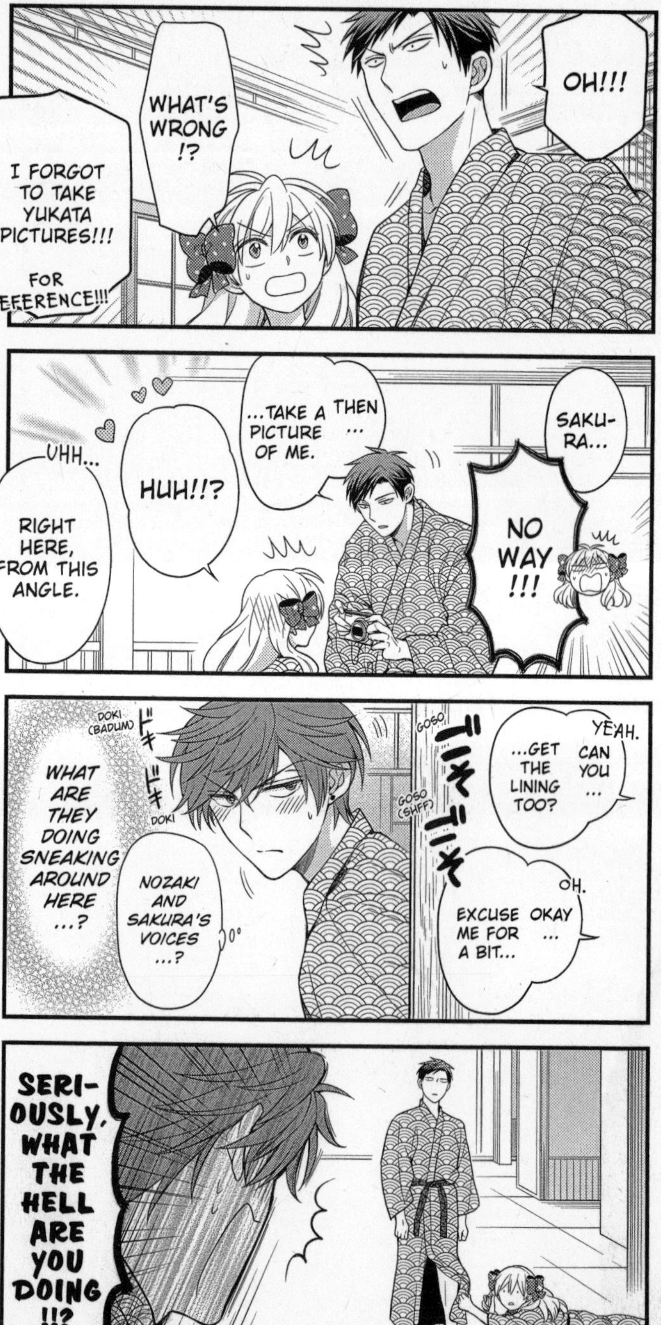
OH!!!
WHAT'S WRONG !?
I FORGOT TO TAKE YUKATA PICTURES!!!
FOR REFERENCE!!!
SAKURA...
NO WAY !!!
THEN ...
...TAKE A PICTURE OF ME.
HUH!!?
UHH...
RIGHT HERE, FROM THIS ANGLE.
YEAH. CAN YOU ...
...GET THE LINING TOO?
OH. OKAY ...
EXCUSE ME FOR A BIT...
GOSO
GOSO (SHFF)
DOKI (BADUM)
DOKI
NOZAKI AND SAKURA'S VOICES ...?
WHAT ARE THEY DOING SNEAKING AROUND HERE ...?
SERIOUSLY, WHAT THE HELL ARE YOU DOING !!?

EVERYONE'S SO CARELESS

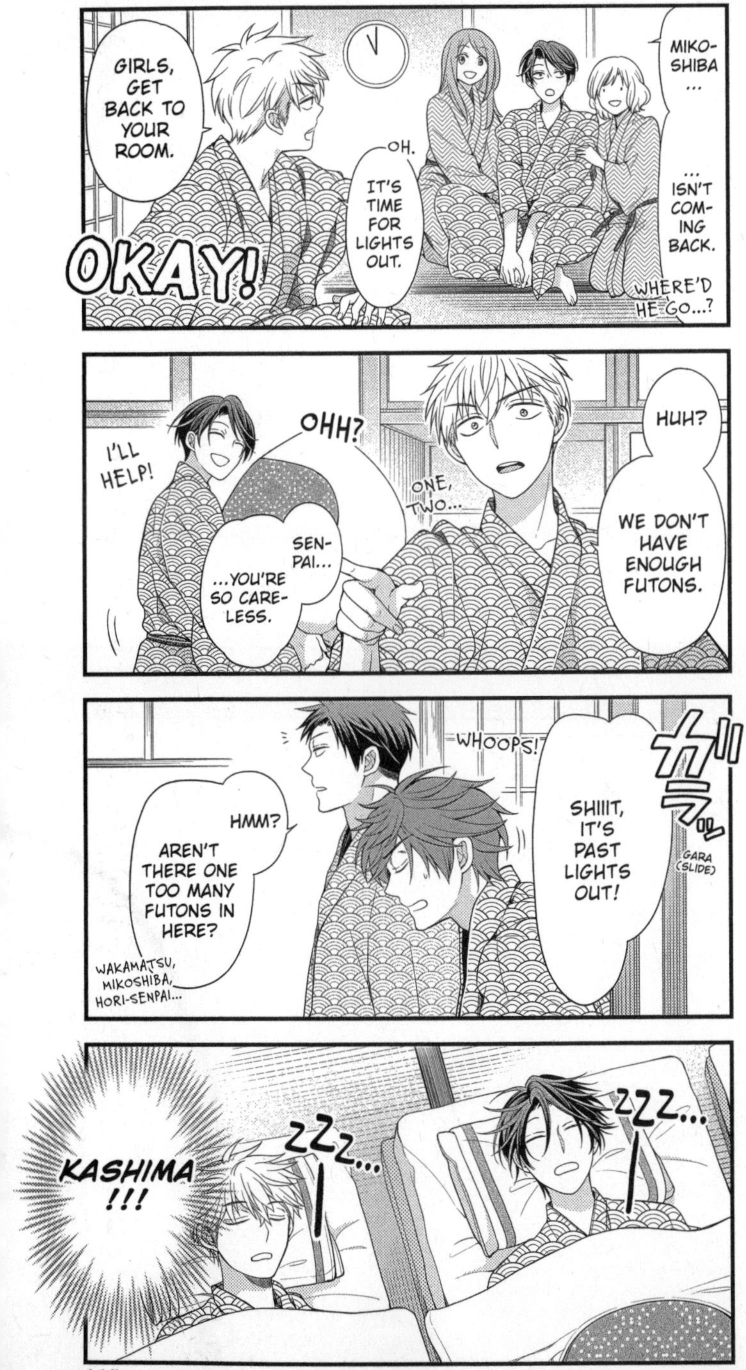

MIKO-SHIBA...
...ISN'T COMING BACK.
WHERE'D HE GO...?
OH. IT'S TIME FOR LIGHTS OUT.
GIRLS, GET BACK TO YOUR ROOM.
OKAY!
HUH?
WE DON'T HAVE ENOUGH FUTONS.
ONE, TWO...
OHH?
SEN-PAI...
...YOU'RE SO CARE-LESS.
I'LL HELP!
ガラッ
GARA (SLIDE)
SHIIIT, IT'S PAST LIGHTS OUT!
WHOOPS!
HMM?
AREN'T THERE ONE TOO MANY FUTONS IN HERE?
WAKAMATSU, MIKOSHIBA, HORI-SENPAI...
ZZZ...
ZZZ...
KASHIMA!!!

SINCE HE JUST WASN'T WAKING UP, THE DRAMA CLUB PLAYED AROUND WITH WAKAMATSU.

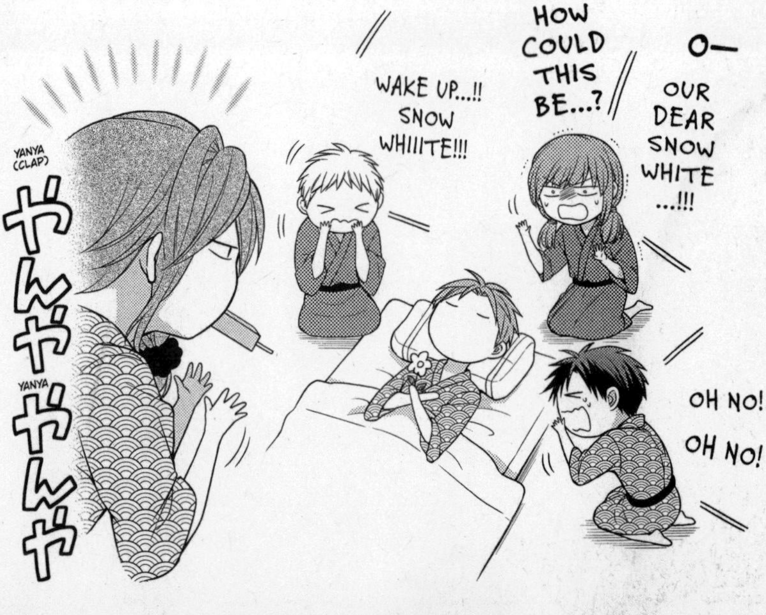
O— OUR DEAR SNOW WHITE ...!!!
HOW COULD THIS BE...?
WAKE UP...!! SNOW WHIIITE!!!
OH NO!
OH NO!
YANYA (CLAP)
やんやんや
YANYA

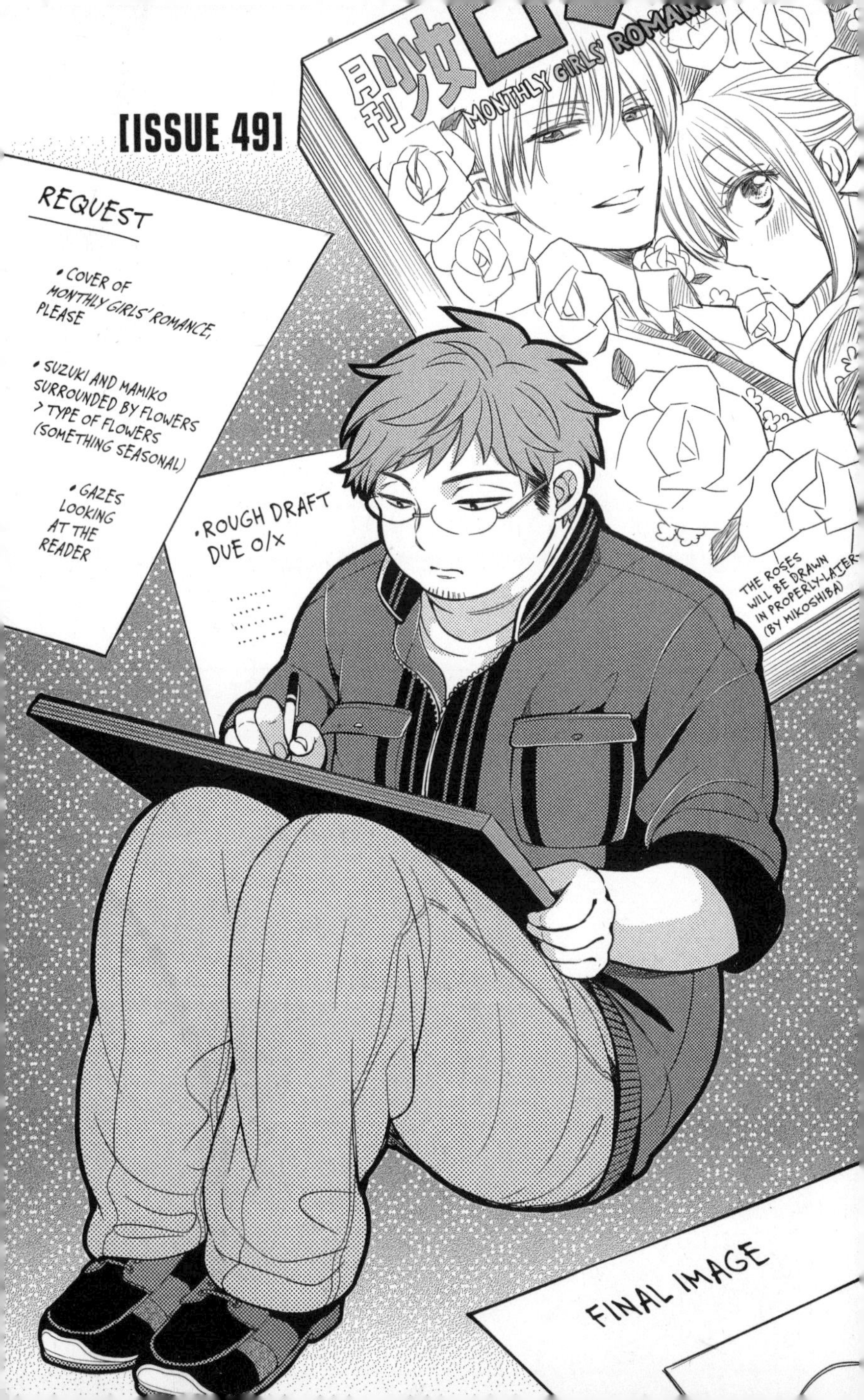
[ISSUE 49]
MONTHLY GIRLS' ROMAN
月刊少女
REQUEST
• COVER OF MONTHLY GIRLS' ROMANCE, PLEASE
• SUZUKI AND MAMIKO SURROUNDED BY FLOWERS > TYPE OF FLOWERS (SOMETHING SEASONAL)
• GAZES LOOKING AT THE READER
• ROUGH DRAFT DUE O/X
THE ROSES WILL BE DRAWN IN PROPERLY LATER (BY MIKOSHIBA)
FINAL IMAGE

IMAGERY FROM OTHER EDITORS

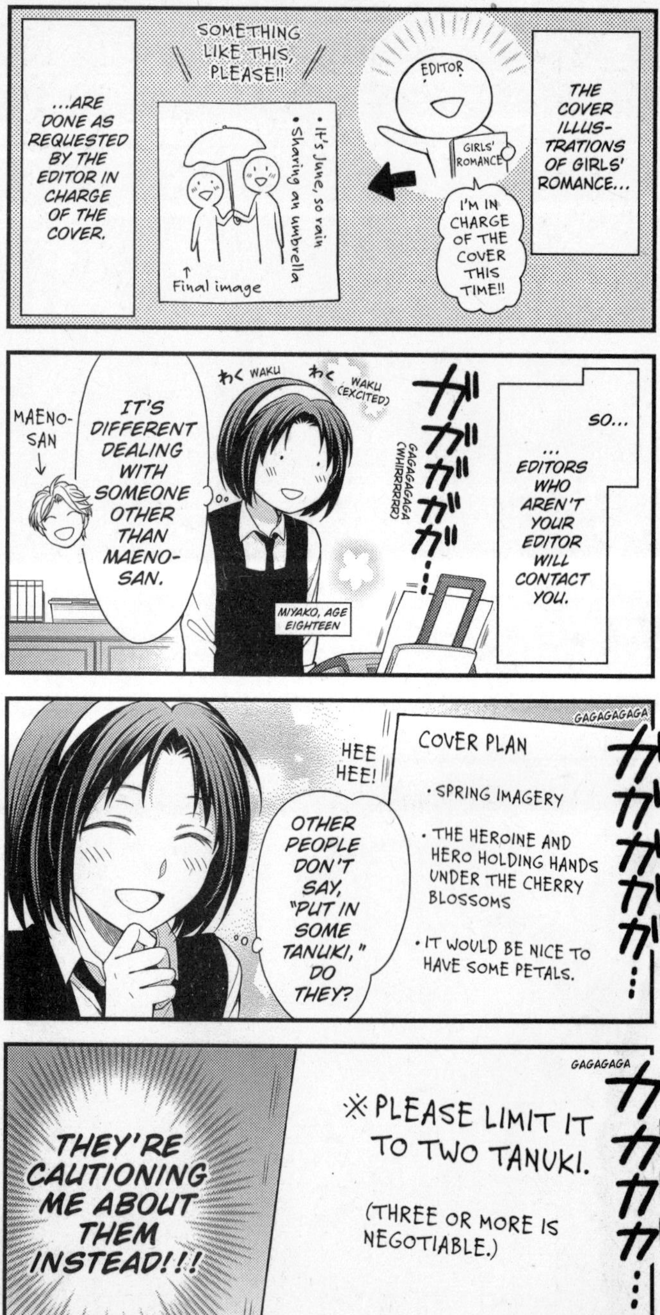
THE COVER ILLUSTRATIONS OF GIRLS' ROMANCE...
EDITOR
GIRLS' ROMANCE
I'M IN CHARGE OF THE COVER THIS TIME!!
SOMETHING LIKE THIS, PLEASE!!
• It's June, so rain
• Sharing an umbrella
Final image
...ARE DONE AS REQUESTED BY THE EDITOR IN CHARGE OF THE COVER.
SO...
...EDITORS WHO AREN'T YOUR EDITOR WILL CONTACT YOU.
ガガガガ…
GAGAGAGAGA (WHIRRRRRR)
わく WAKU わく WAKU (EXCITED)
MIYAKO, AGE EIGHTEEN
IT'S DIFFERENT DEALING WITH SOMEONE OTHER THAN MAENO-SAN.
MAENO-SAN
ガガガガ…
GAGAGAGAGA
COVER PLAN
• SPRING IMAGERY
• THE HEROINE AND HERO HOLDING HANDS UNDER THE CHERRY BLOSSOMS
• IT WOULD BE NICE TO HAVE SOME PETALS.
HEE HEE!
OTHER PEOPLE DON'T SAY, "PUT IN SOME TANUKI," DO THEY?
ガガガガ…
GAGAGAGA
※PLEASE LIMIT IT TO TWO TANUKI.
(THREE OR MORE IS NEGOTIABLE.)
THEY'RE CAUTIONING ME ABOUT THEM INSTEAD!!!

SUPPLEMENTS

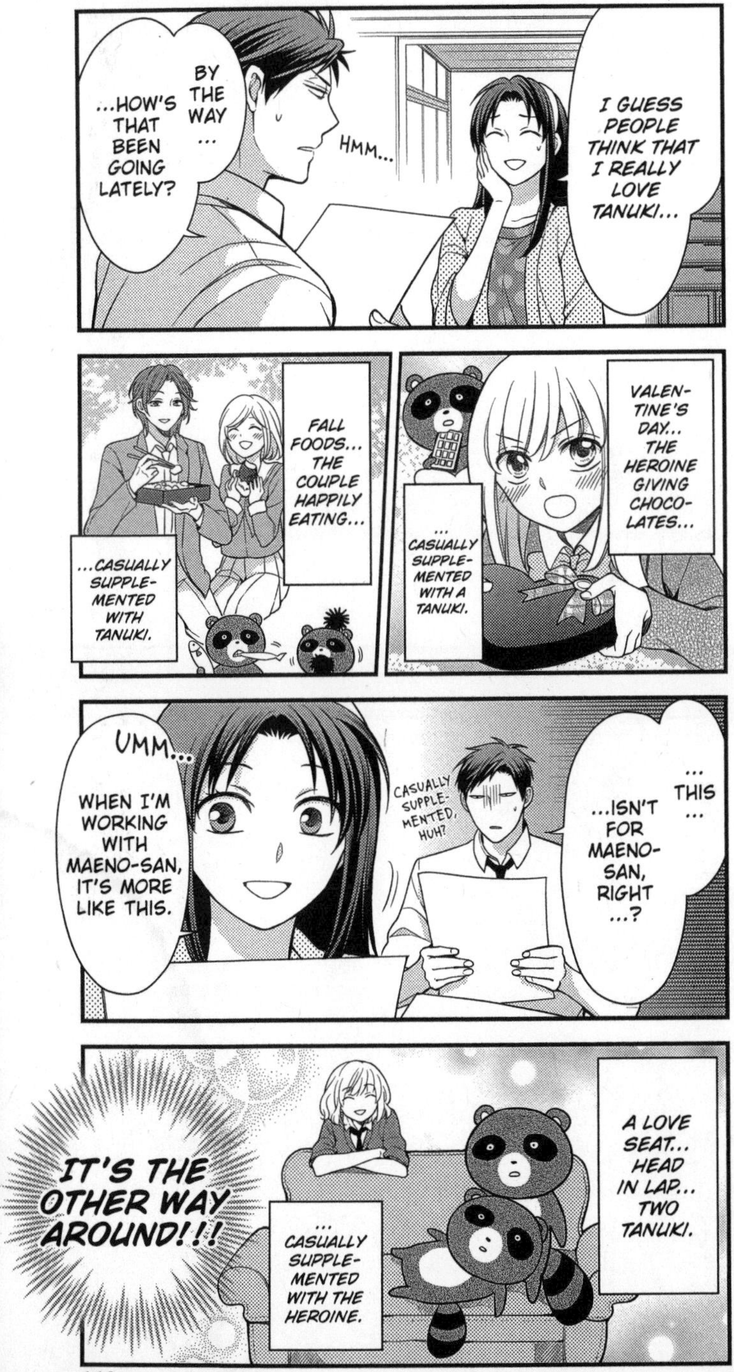
I GUESS PEOPLE THINK THAT I REALLY LOVE TANUKI...
HMM...
BY THE WAY...
...HOW'S THAT BEEN GOING LATELY?
VALEN-TINE'S DAY... THE HEROINE GIVING CHOCO-LATES...
...CASUALLY SUPPLE-MENTED WITH A TANUKI.
FALL FOODS... THE COUPLE HAPPILY EATING...
...CASUALLY SUPPLE-MENTED WITH TANUKI.
... THIS ...
...ISN'T FOR MAENO-SAN, RIGHT ...?
CASUALLY SUPPLE-MENTED, HUH?
UMM...
WHEN I'M WORKING WITH MAENO-SAN, IT'S MORE LIKE THIS.
A LOVE SEAT... HEAD IN LAP... TWO TANUKI.
...CASUALLY SUPPLE-MENTED WITH THE HEROINE.
IT'S THE OTHER WAY AROUND!!!

IN NOZAKI-KUN'S CASE ①

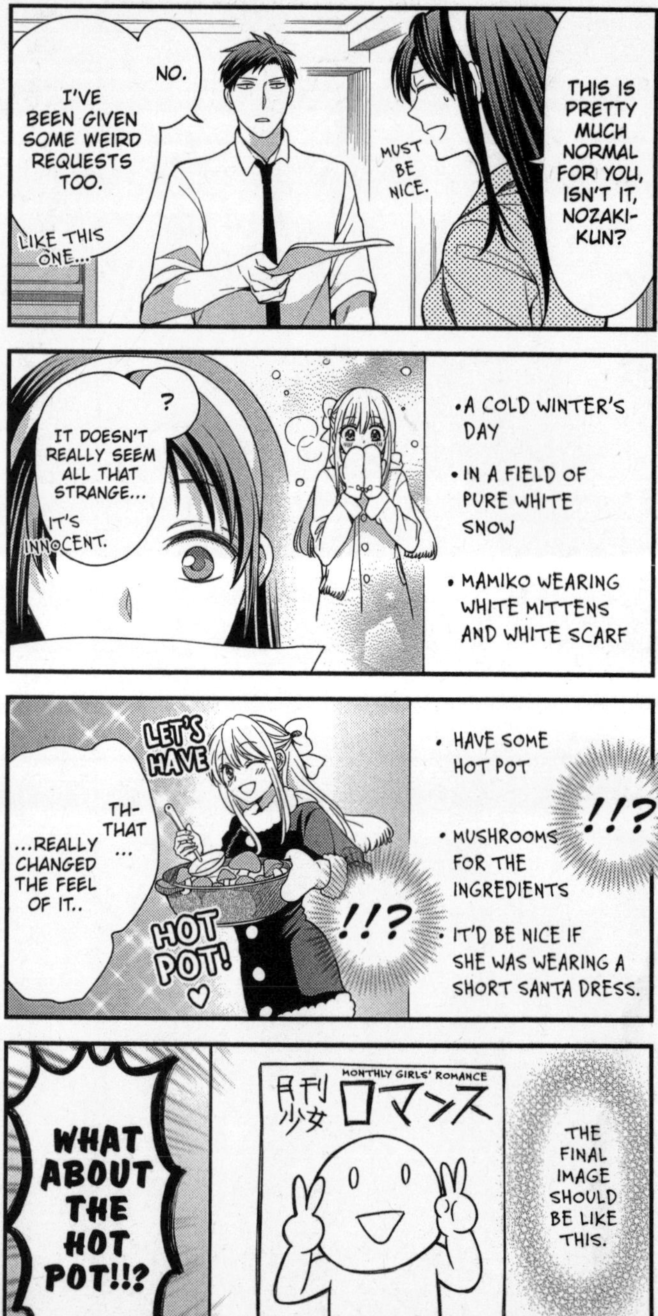
THIS IS PRETTY MUCH NORMAL FOR YOU, ISN'T IT, NOZAKI-KUN?
MUST BE NICE.
NO.
I'VE BEEN GIVEN SOME WEIRD REQUESTS TOO.
LIKE THIS ONE...
•A COLD WINTER'S DAY
•IN A FIELD OF PURE WHITE SNOW
•MAMIKO WEARING WHITE MITTENS AND WHITE SCARF
?
IT DOESN'T REALLY SEEM ALL THAT STRANGE...
IT'S INNOCENT.
•HAVE SOME HOT POT
•MUSHROOMS FOR THE INGREDIENTS
•IT'D BE NICE IF SHE WAS WEARING A SHORT SANTA DRESS.
!!?
!!?
LET'S HAVE HOT POT! ♥
TH-THAT...
...REALLY CHANGED THE FEEL OF IT..
THE FINAL IMAGE SHOULD BE LIKE THIS.
MONTHLY GIRLS' ROMANCE
月刊少女ロマンス
WHAT ABOUT THE HOT POT!!?

IN NOZAKI-KUN'S CASE ②

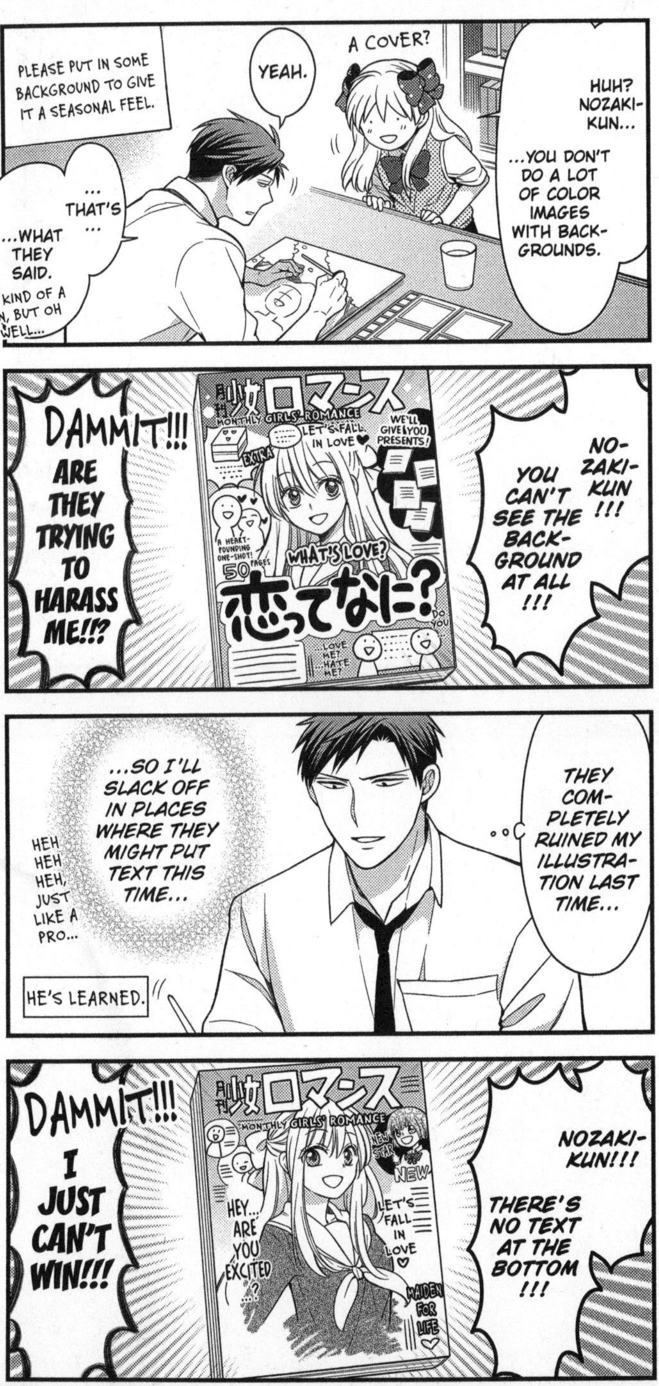
HUH? NOZAKI-KUN... ...YOU DON'T DO A LOT OF COLOR IMAGES WITH BACKGROUNDS.
A COVER?
YEAH.
PLEASE PUT IN SOME BACKGROUND TO GIVE IT A SEASONAL FEEL.
... THAT'S ... ...WHAT THEY SAID.
IT'S KIND OF A PAIN, BUT OH WELL...
NOZAKI-KUN!!! YOU CAN'T SEE THE BACKGROUND AT ALL!!!
月刊少女ロマンス
MONTHLY GIRLS' ROMANCE
WE'LL GIVE YOU PRESENTS!
LET'S FALL IN LOVE
EXTRA
A HEART-POUNDING ONE-SHOT! 50 PAGES
WHAT'S LOVE?
恋ってなに?
DO YOU ...LOVE ME? HATE ME?
DAMMIT!!! ARE THEY TRYING TO HARASS ME!!?
THEY COMPLETELY RUINED MY ILLUSTRATION LAST TIME...
...SO I'LL SLACK OFF IN PLACES WHERE THEY MIGHT PUT TEXT THIS TIME...
HEH HEH HEH, JUST LIKE A PRO...
HE'S LEARNED.
NOZAKI-KUN!!! THERE'S NO TEXT AT THE BOTTOM!!!
月刊少女ロマンス
MONTHLY GIRLS' ROMANCE
NEW STAR
NEW
LET'S FALL IN LOVE
HEY... ARE YOU EXCITED ...?
MAIDEN FOR LIFE
DAMMIT!!! I JUST CAN'T WIN!!!

KEN-SAN'S ILLUSTRATIONS

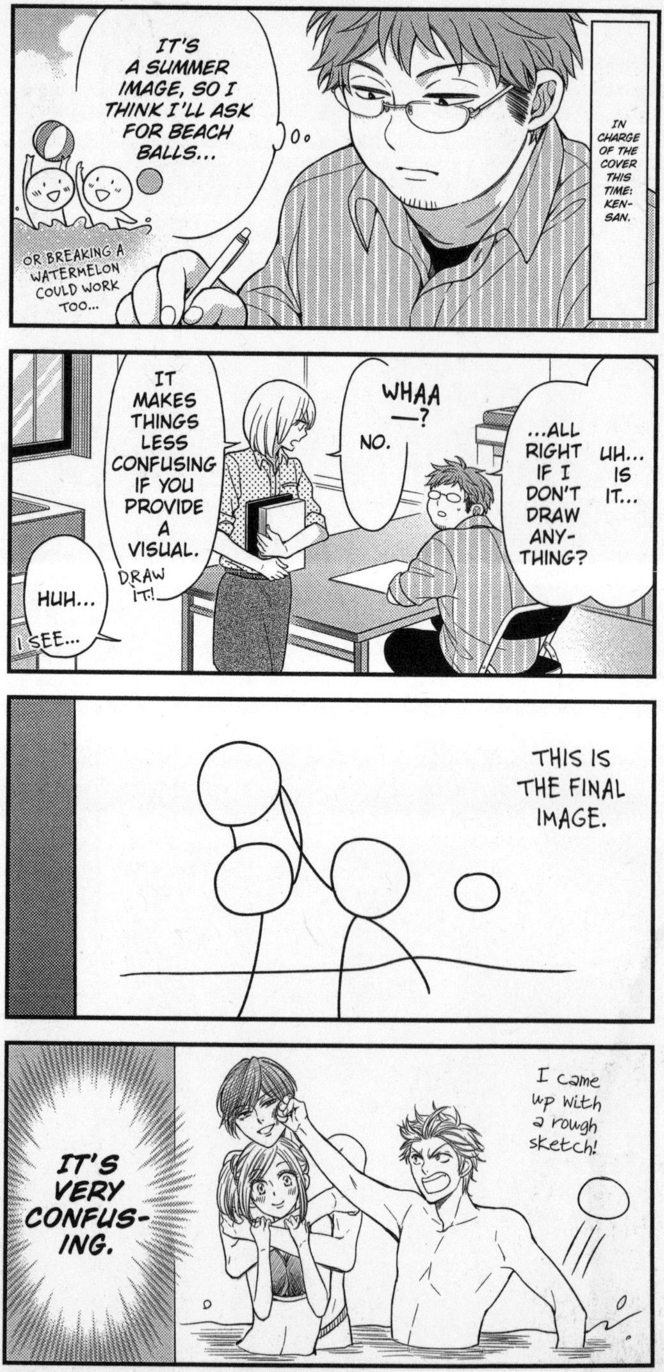
IN CHARGE OF THE COVER THIS TIME: KEN-SAN.
IT'S A SUMMER IMAGE, SO I THINK I'LL ASK FOR BEACH BALLS...
OR BREAKING A WATERMELON COULD WORK TOO...
UH... IS IT...
...ALL RIGHT IF I DON'T DRAW ANYTHING?
WHAA—?
NO.
IT MAKES THINGS LESS CONFUSING IF YOU PROVIDE A VISUAL.
DRAW IT!
HUH...
I SEE...
THIS IS THE FINAL IMAGE.
I came up with a rough sketch!
IT'S VERY CONFUS-ING.

OTHER IDEAS

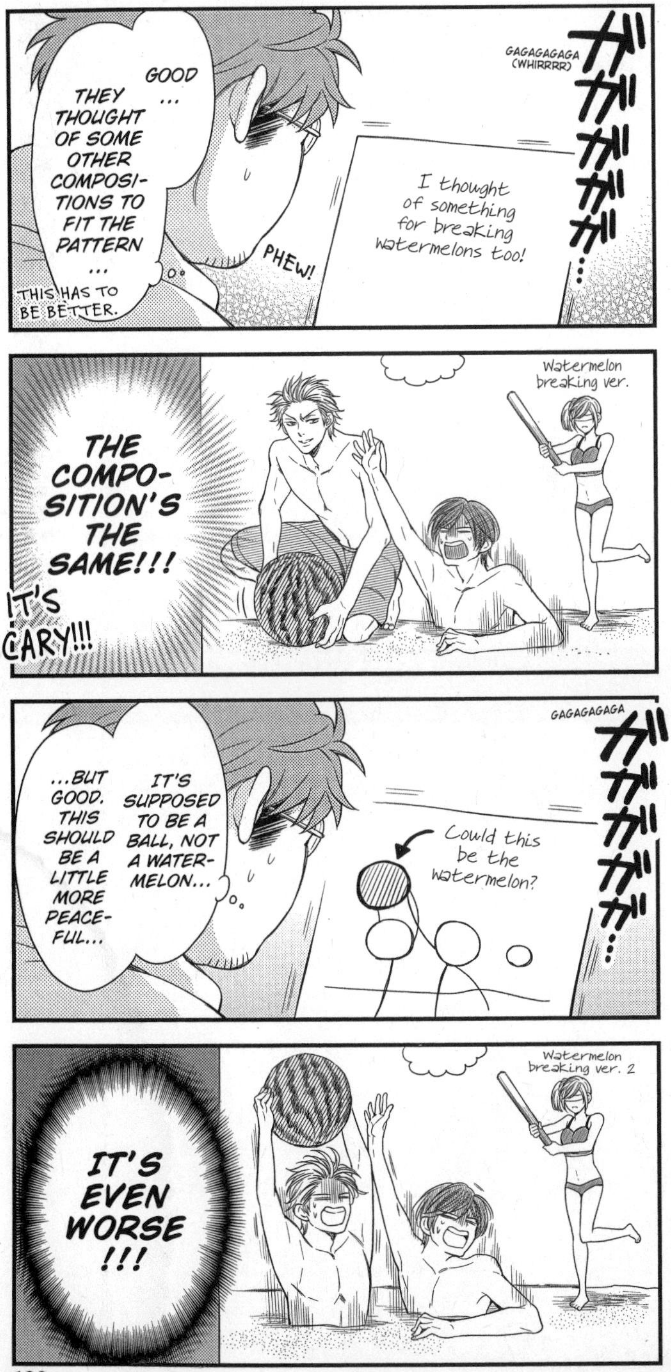
GAGAGAGAGA (WHIRRRR)
I thought of something for breaking watermelons too!
PHEW!
GOOD...
THEY THOUGHT OF SOME OTHER COMPOSI-TIONS TO FIT THE PATTERN...
THIS HAS TO BE BETTER.
Watermelon breaking ver.
THE COMPO-SITION'S THE SAME!!!
IT'S SCARY!!!
GAGAGAGAGA
Could this be the watermelon?
IT'S SUPPOSED TO BE A BALL, NOT A WATER-MELON...
...BUT GOOD. THIS SHOULD BE A LITTLE MORE PEACE-FUL...
Watermelon breaking ver. 2
IT'S EVEN WORSE!!!

MAENO-SENPAI'S ADVICE

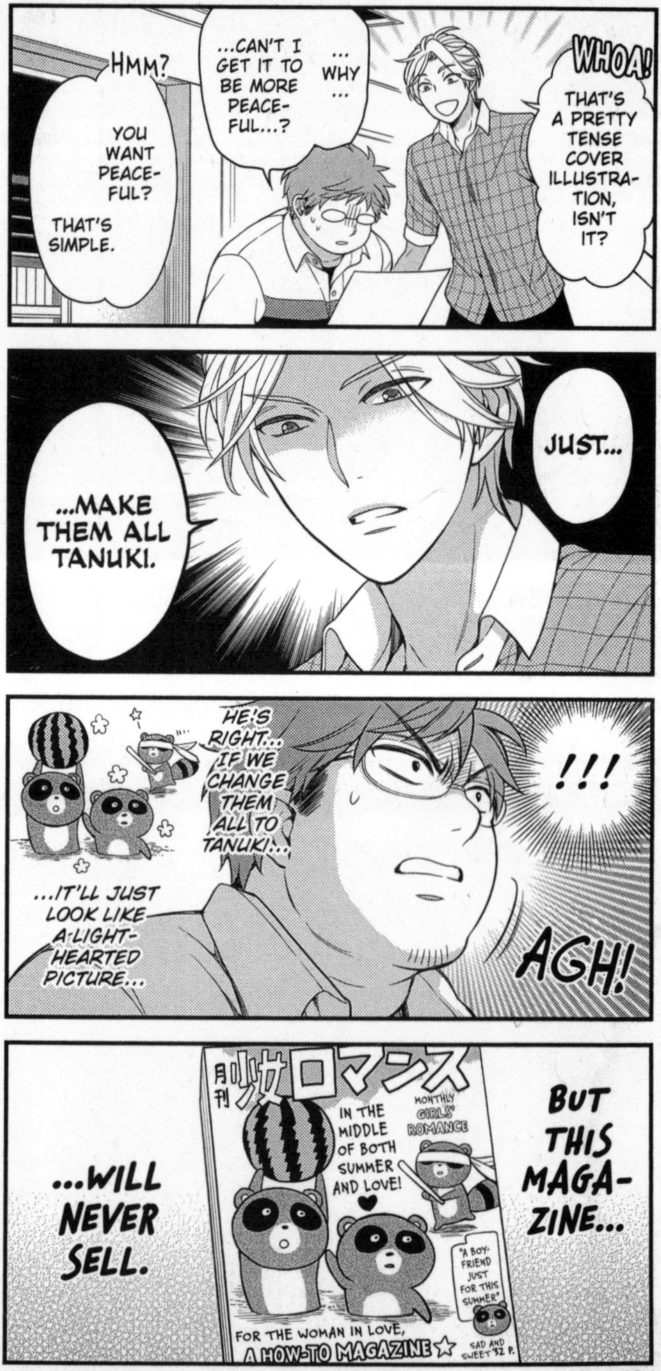

WHOA!
THAT'S A PRETTY TENSE COVER ILLUSTRATION, ISN'T IT?
... WHY ...
...CAN'T I GET IT TO BE MORE PEACEFUL...?
HMM?
YOU WANT PEACEFUL?
THAT'S SIMPLE.
JUST...
...MAKE THEM ALL TANUKI.
!!!
AGH!
HE'S RIGHT... IF WE CHANGE THEM ALL TO TANUKI...
...IT'LL JUST LOOK LIKE A LIGHT-HEARTED PICTURE...
BUT THIS MAGAZINE...
月刊少女ロマンス
MONTHLY GIRLS' ROMANCE
IN THE MIDDLE OF BOTH SUMMER AND LOVE!
"A BOY-FRIEND JUST FOR THIS SUMMER"
SAD AND SWEET 32 P.
FOR THE WOMAN IN LOVE, A HOW-TO MAGAZINE☆
...WILL NEVER SELL.

SHOW ME

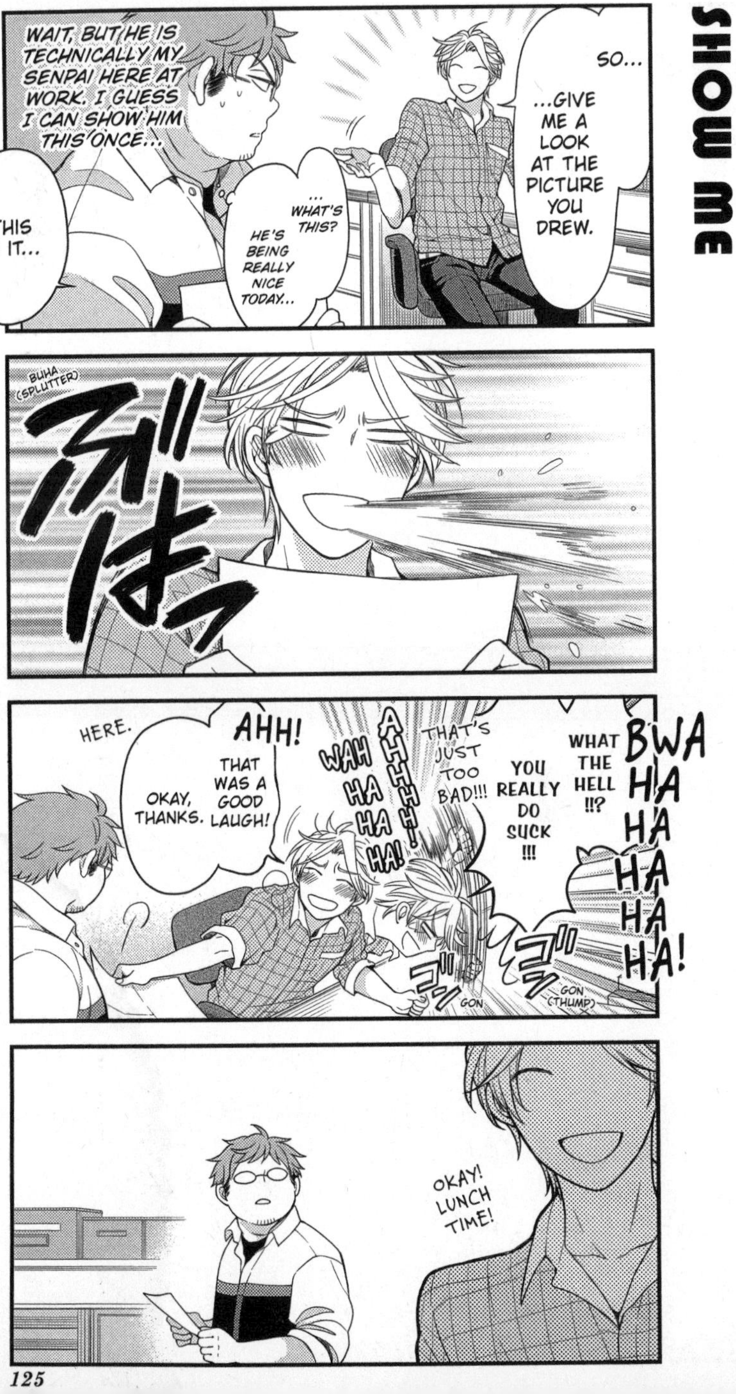
SO...
...GIVE ME A LOOK AT THE PICTURE YOU DREW.
... WHAT'S THIS? HE'S BEING REALLY NICE TODAY...
WAIT, BUT HE IS TECHNICALLY MY SENPAI HERE AT WORK. I GUESS I CAN SHOW HIM THIS ONCE...
THIS IS IT...
ぶはっ
BUHA (SPLUTTER)
BWA HA HA HA HA HA HA!
WHAT THE HELL!!?
YOU REALLY DO SUCK!!!
THAT'S JUST TOO BAD!!!
AHHHHH!
WAH HA HA HA HA!
ゴッ
GON (THUMP)
ゴッ
GON
AHH! THAT WAS A GOOD LAUGH!
OKAY, THANKS.
HERE.
OKAY! LUNCH TIME!

SO I CAN'T SAY ANYTHING

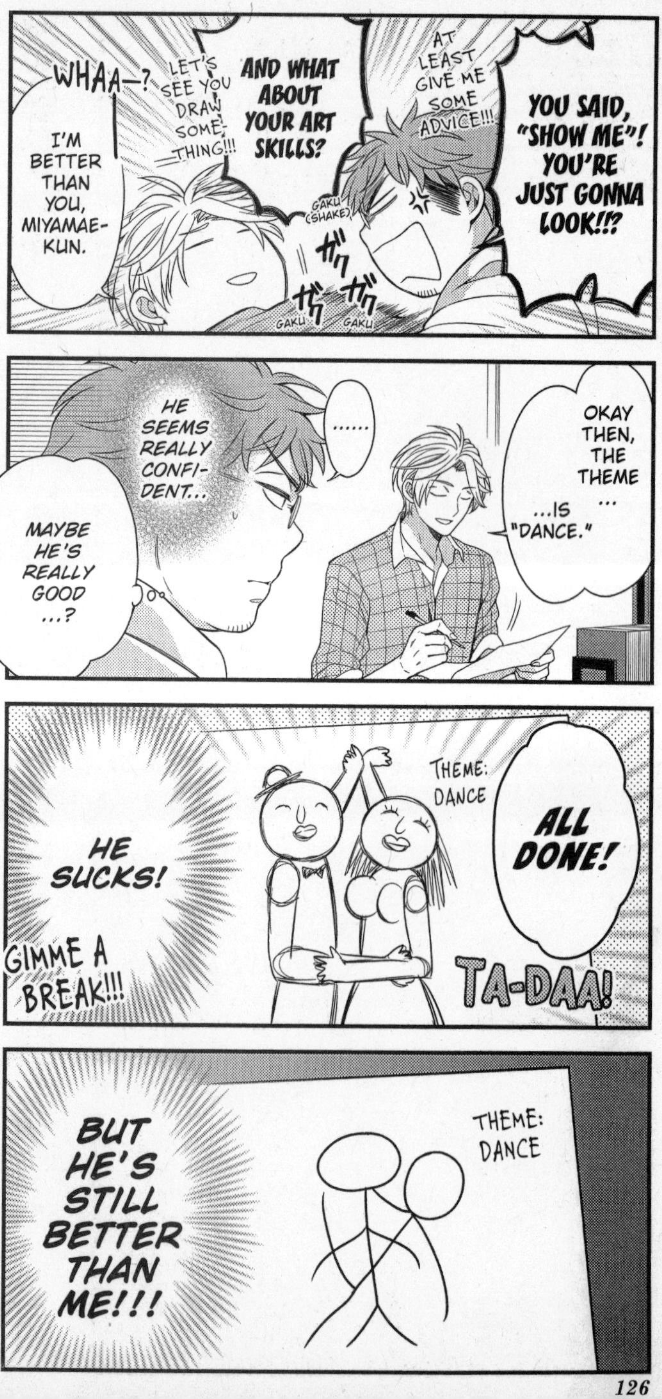
YOU SAID, "SHOW ME"! YOU'RE JUST GONNA LOOK!!?
AT LEAST GIVE ME SOME ADVICE!!!
AND WHAT ABOUT YOUR ART SKILLS?
LET'S SEE YOU DRAW SOMETHING!!!
WHAA—?
I'M BETTER THAN YOU, MIYAMAE-KUN.
GAKU (SHAKE)
GAKU
GAKU
OKAY THEN, THE THEME... ...IS "DANCE."
......
HE SEEMS REALLY CONFIDENT...
MAYBE HE'S REALLY GOOD...?
ALL DONE!
TA-DAA!
THEME: DANCE
HE SUCKS!
GIMME A BREAK!!!
THEME: DANCE
BUT HE'S STILL BETTER THAN ME!!!

THINGS THAT CHANGE AND THINGS THAT DON'T

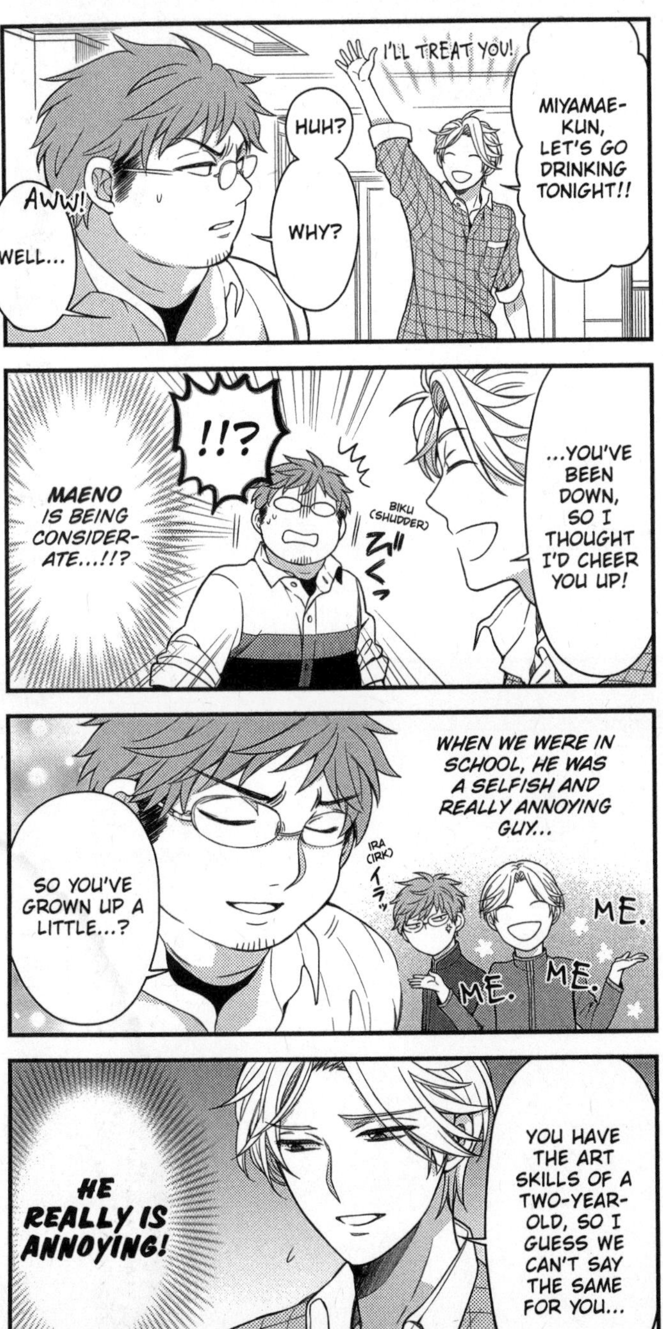
MIYAMAE-KUN, LET'S GO DRINKING TONIGHT!!
I'LL TREAT YOU!
HUH?
WHY?
AWW!
WELL...
...YOU'VE BEEN DOWN, SO I THOUGHT I'D CHEER YOU UP!
!!?
BIKU (SHUDDER)
MAENO IS BEING CONSIDER-ATE...!!?
WHEN WE WERE IN SCHOOL, HE WAS A SELFISH AND REALLY ANNOYING GUY...
ME.
ME.
ME.
IRA (IRK)
SO YOU'VE GROWN UP A LITTLE...?
YOU HAVE THE ART SKILLS OF A TWO-YEAR-OLD, SO I GUESS WE CAN'T SAY THE SAME FOR YOU...
HE REALLY IS ANNOYING!

THE RESULTS OF HIS HARD WORK

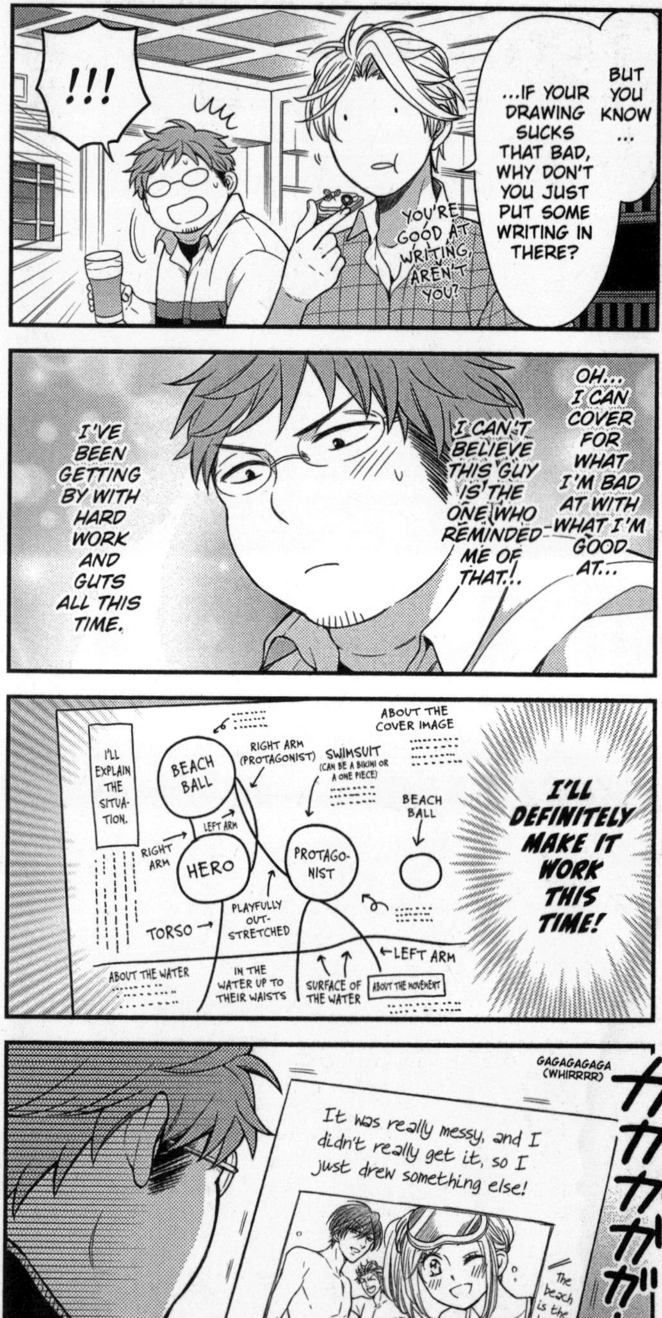

BUT YOU KNOW...
...IF YOUR DRAWING SUCKS THAT BAD, WHY DON'T YOU JUST PUT SOME WRITING IN THERE?
YOU'RE GOOD AT WRITING, AREN'T YOU?
!!!
OH... I CAN COVER FOR WHAT I'M BAD AT WITH WHAT I'M GOOD AT...
I CAN'T BELIEVE THIS GUY IS THE ONE WHO REMINDED ME OF THAT...!
I'VE BEEN GETTING BY WITH HARD WORK AND GUTS ALL THIS TIME.
I'LL DEFINITELY MAKE IT WORK THIS TIME!
ABOUT THE COVER IMAGE
SWIMSUIT (CAN BE A BIKINI OR A ONE PIECE)
BEACH BALL
RIGHT ARM (PROTAGONIST)
BEACH BALL
I'LL EXPLAIN THE SITUA-TION.
LEFT ARM
RIGHT ARM
HERO
PROTAGO-NIST
PLAYFULLY OUT-STRETCHED
TORSO
LEFT ARM
ABOUT THE WATER
IN THE WATER UP TO THEIR WAISTS
SURFACE OF THE WATER
ABOUT THE MOVEMENT
GAGAGAGAGA (WHIRRRR)
ガガガガガ…
It was really messy, and I didn't really get it, so I just drew something else!
The beach is the best!

HUMBLE WITH ALL HIS MIGHT

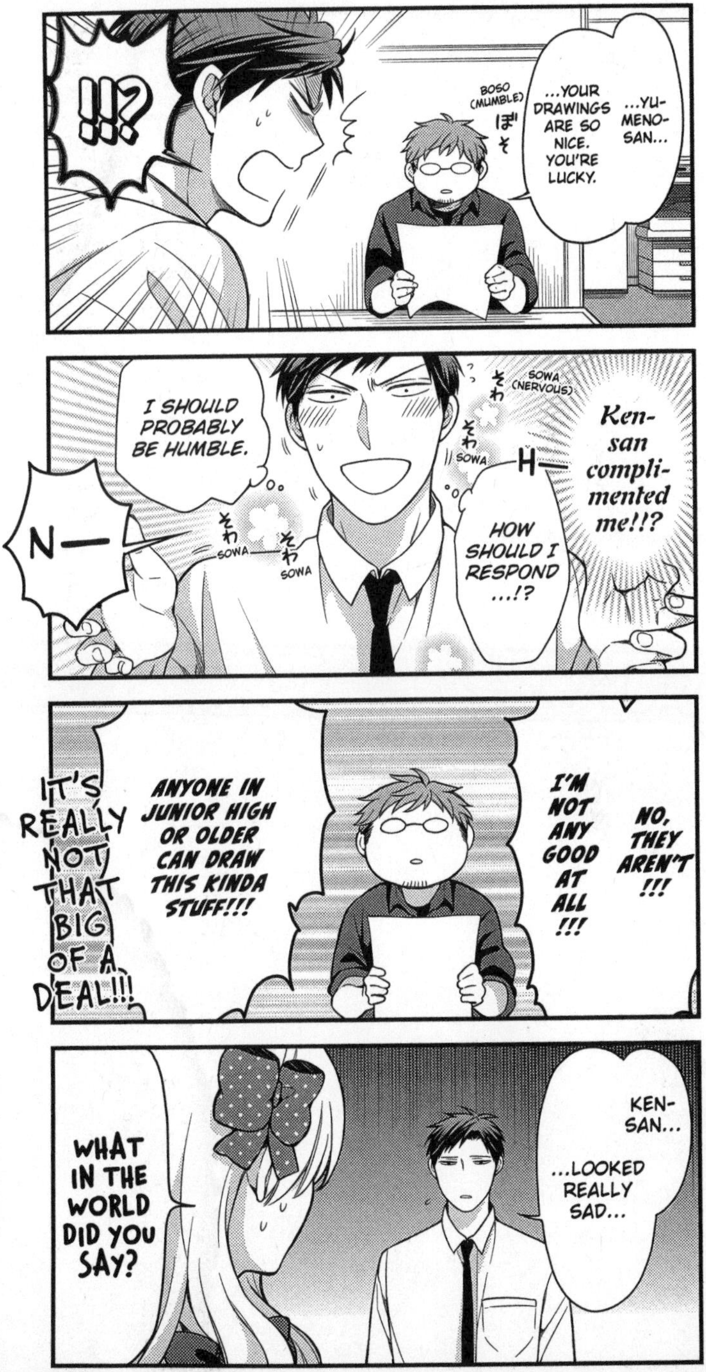
...YU-MENO-SAN...
...YOUR DRAWINGS ARE SO NICE. YOU'RE LUCKY.
BOSO (MUMBLE) ぼそ
!!?
Ken-san complimented me!!?
H—
HOW SHOULD I RESPOND ...!?
そわ SOWA (NERVOUS)
そわ SOWA
I SHOULD PROBABLY BE HUMBLE.
そわ SOWA
そわ SOWA
N—
NO, THEY AREN'T !!!
I'M NOT ANY GOOD AT ALL !!!
ANYONE IN JUNIOR HIGH OR OLDER CAN DRAW THIS KINDA STUFF!!!
IT'S REALLY NOT THAT BIG OF A DEAL!!!
KEN-SAN...
...LOOKED REALLY SAD...
WHAT IN THE WORLD DID YOU SAY?

[How to make a magazine cover]

Making a cover is... **Request from an editor** → **Draw** → **Design**

The designer is in charge.

This is the general flow of things, but there are various ways to do it depending on the magazine! This time we'll show you a few of those!

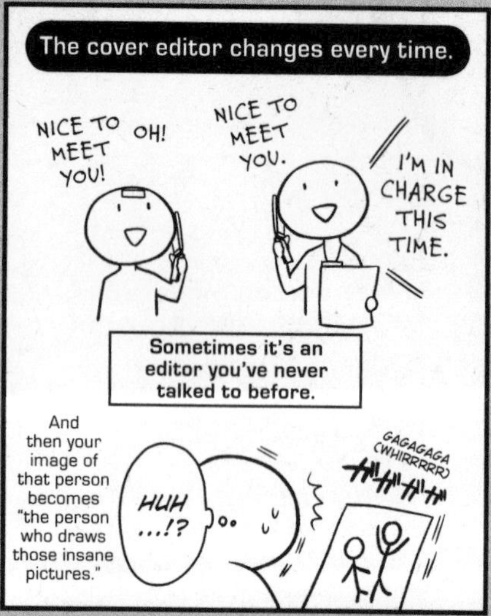
The cover editor changes every time.
I'M IN CHARGE THIS TIME.
NICE TO MEET YOU.
OH!
NICE TO MEET YOU!
Sometimes it's an editor you've never talked to before.
GAGAGAGA (WHIRRRRR)
HUH ...!?
And then your image of that person becomes "the person who draws those insane pictures."

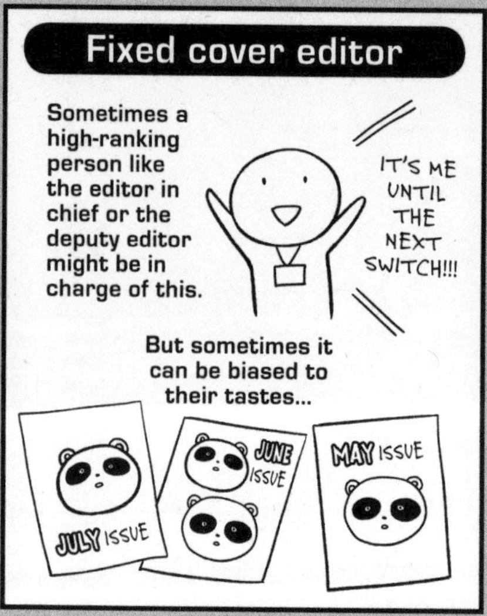
Fixed cover editor
IT'S ME UNTIL THE NEXT SWITCH!!!
Sometimes a high-ranking person like the editor in chief or the deputy editor might be in charge of this.
But sometimes it can be biased to their tastes...
MAY ISSUE
JUNE ISSUE
JULY ISSUE

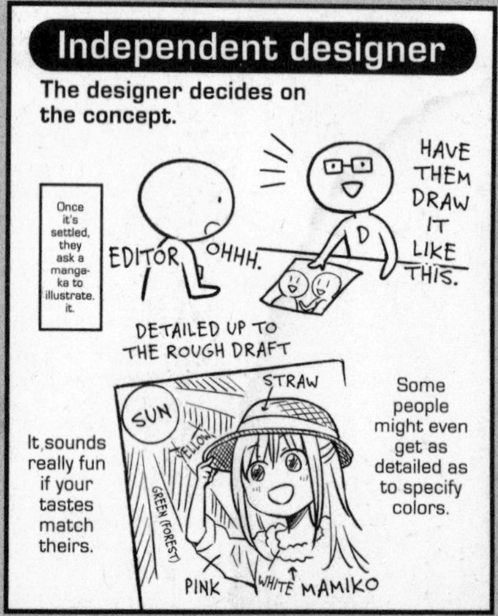
Independent designer
The designer decides on the concept.
HAVE THEM DRAW IT LIKE THIS.
OHHH.
EDITOR
D
Once it's settled, they ask a manga-ka to illustrate. it.
DETAILED UP TO THE ROUGH DRAFT
Some people might even get as detailed as to specify colors.
STRAW
SUN
YELLOW
GREEN (FOREST)
PINK
WHITE
MAMIKO
It sounds really fun if your tastes match theirs.

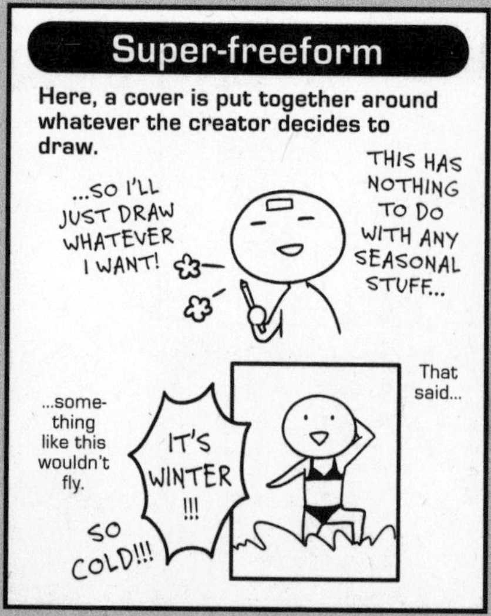
Super-freeform
Here, a cover is put together around whatever the creator decides to draw.
THIS HAS NOTHING TO DO WITH ANY SEASONAL STUFF...
...SO I'LL JUST DRAW WHATEVER I WANT!
That said...
IT'S WINTER !!!
SO COLD!!!
...some-thing like this wouldn't fly.

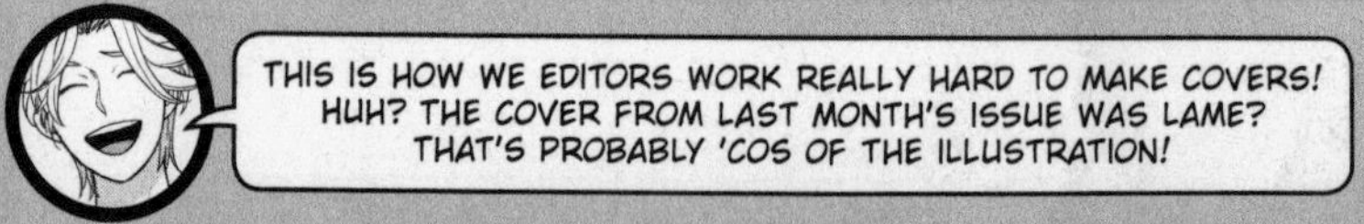
THIS IS HOW WE EDITORS WORK REALLY HARD TO MAKE COVERS!
HUH? THE COVER FROM LAST MONTH'S ISSUE WAS LAME?
THAT'S PROBABLY 'COS OF THE ILLUSTRATION!

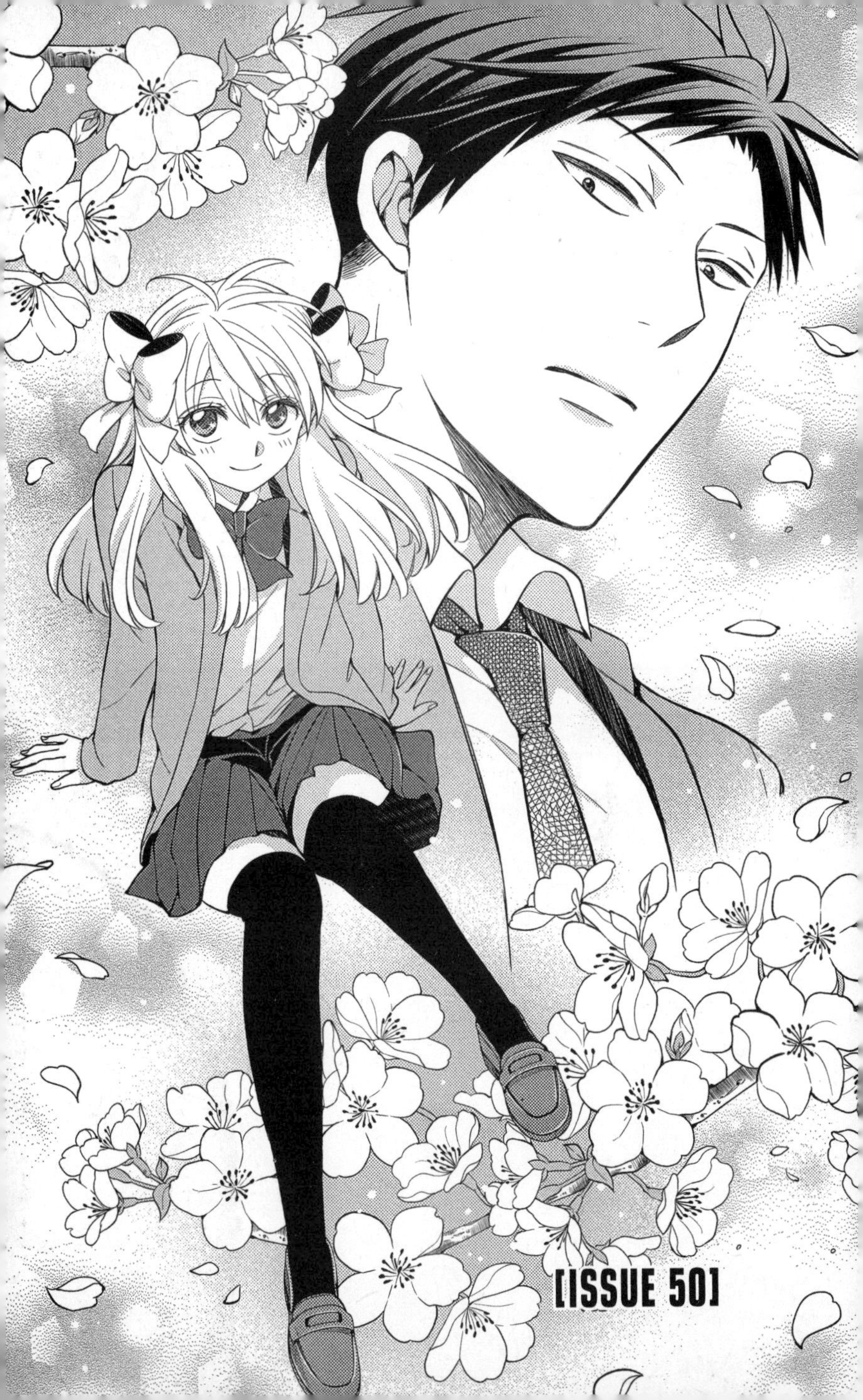
[ISSUE 50]

LET'S TALK ABOUT HIM

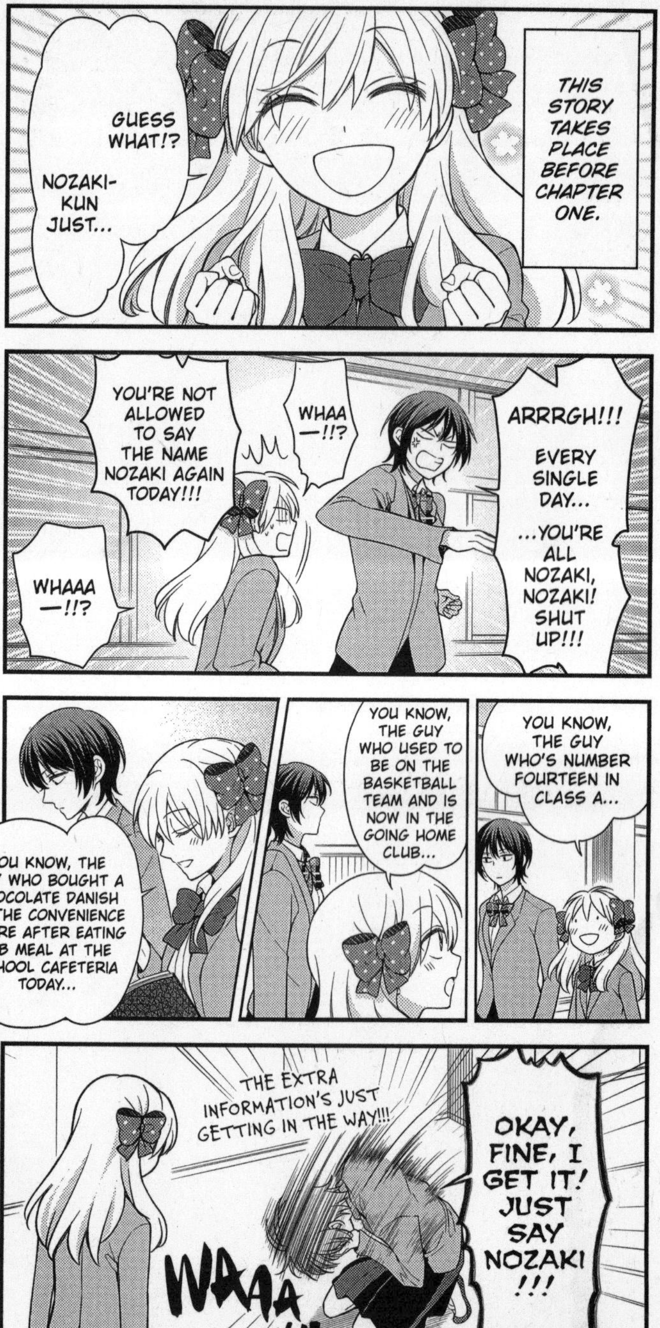
THIS STORY TAKES PLACE BEFORE CHAPTER ONE.
GUESS WHAT!?
NOZAKI-KUN JUST...
ARRRGH!!!
EVERY SINGLE DAY...
...YOU'RE ALL NOZAKI, NOZAKI! SHUT UP!!!
WHAA—!!?
YOU'RE NOT ALLOWED TO SAY THE NAME NOZAKI AGAIN TODAY!!!
WHAAA—!!?
YOU KNOW, THE GUY WHO'S NUMBER FOURTEEN IN CLASS A...
YOU KNOW, THE GUY WHO USED TO BE ON THE BASKETBALL TEAM AND IS NOW IN THE GOING HOME CLUB...
YOU KNOW, THE GUY WHO BOUGHT A CHOCOLATE DANISH AT THE CONVENIENCE STORE AFTER EATING A B MEAL AT THE SCHOOL CAFETERIA TODAY...
OKAY, FINE, I GET IT! JUST SAY NOZAKI!!!
THE EXTRA INFORMATION'S JUST GETTING IN THE WAY!!!
WAAAAH!

NOZAKI QUIZ

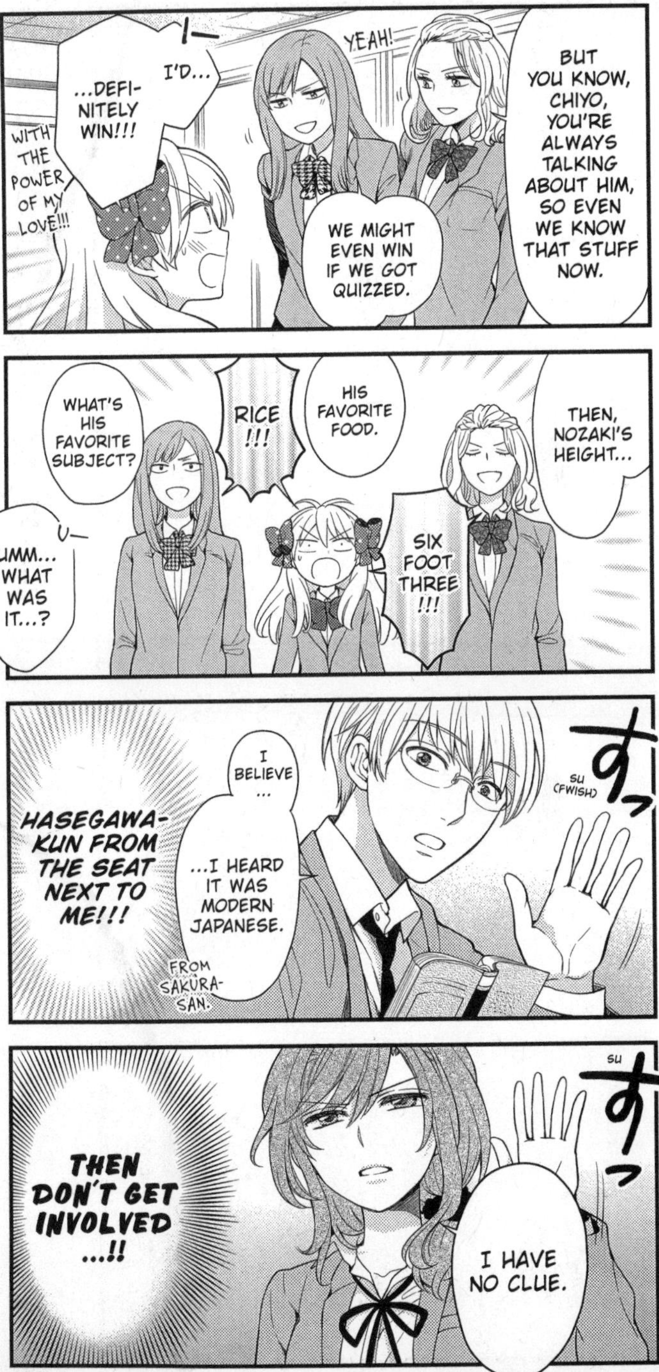
BUT YOU KNOW, CHIYO, YOU'RE ALWAYS TALKING ABOUT HIM, SO EVEN WE KNOW THAT STUFF NOW.
YEAH!
WE MIGHT EVEN WIN IF WE GOT QUIZZED.
I—
I'D...
...DEFI-NITELY WIN!!!
WITH THE POWER OF MY LOVE!!!
THEN, NOZAKI'S HEIGHT...
SIX FOOT THREE !!!
HIS FAVORITE FOOD.
RICE !!!
WHAT'S HIS FAVORITE SUBJECT?
U—
UMM... WHAT WAS IT...?
すっ
SU (FWISH)
I BELIEVE ...
...I HEARD IT WAS MODERN JAPANESE.
FROM SAKURA-SAN.
HASEGAWA-KUN FROM THE SEAT NEXT TO ME!!!
すっ
SU
I HAVE NO CLUE.
THEN DON'T GET INVOLVED ...!!

STEPPING IT UP

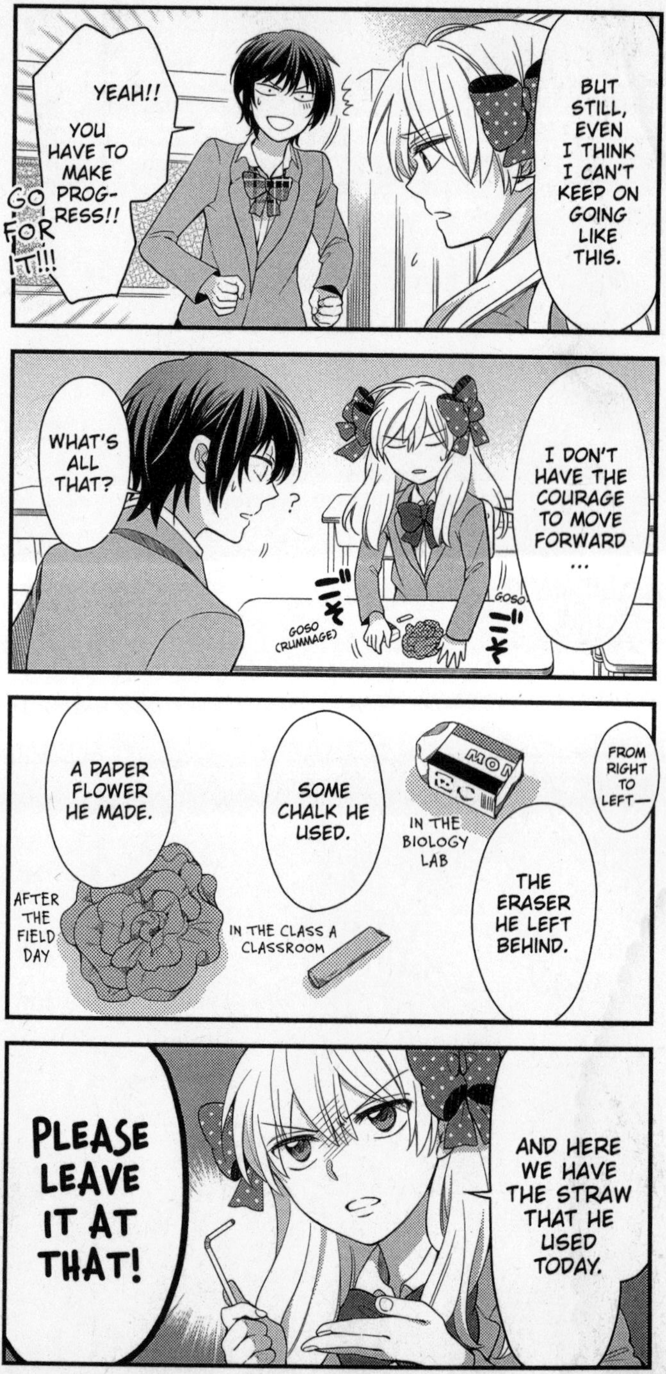
BUT STILL, EVEN I THINK I CAN'T KEEP ON GOING LIKE THIS.
YEAH!!
YOU HAVE TO MAKE PROG-RESS!!
GO FOR IT!!!
I DON'T HAVE THE COURAGE TO MOVE FORWARD...
GOSO
GOSO (RUMMAGE)
WHAT'S ALL THAT?
FROM RIGHT TO LEFT—
THE ERASER HE LEFT BEHIND.
IN THE BIOLOGY LAB
SOME CHALK HE USED.
IN THE CLASS A CLASSROOM
A PAPER FLOWER HE MADE.
AFTER THE FIELD DAY
AND HERE WE HAVE THE STRAW THAT HE USED TODAY.
PLEASE LEAVE IT AT THAT!

A VIEW YOU CAN'T LOOK AWAY FROM

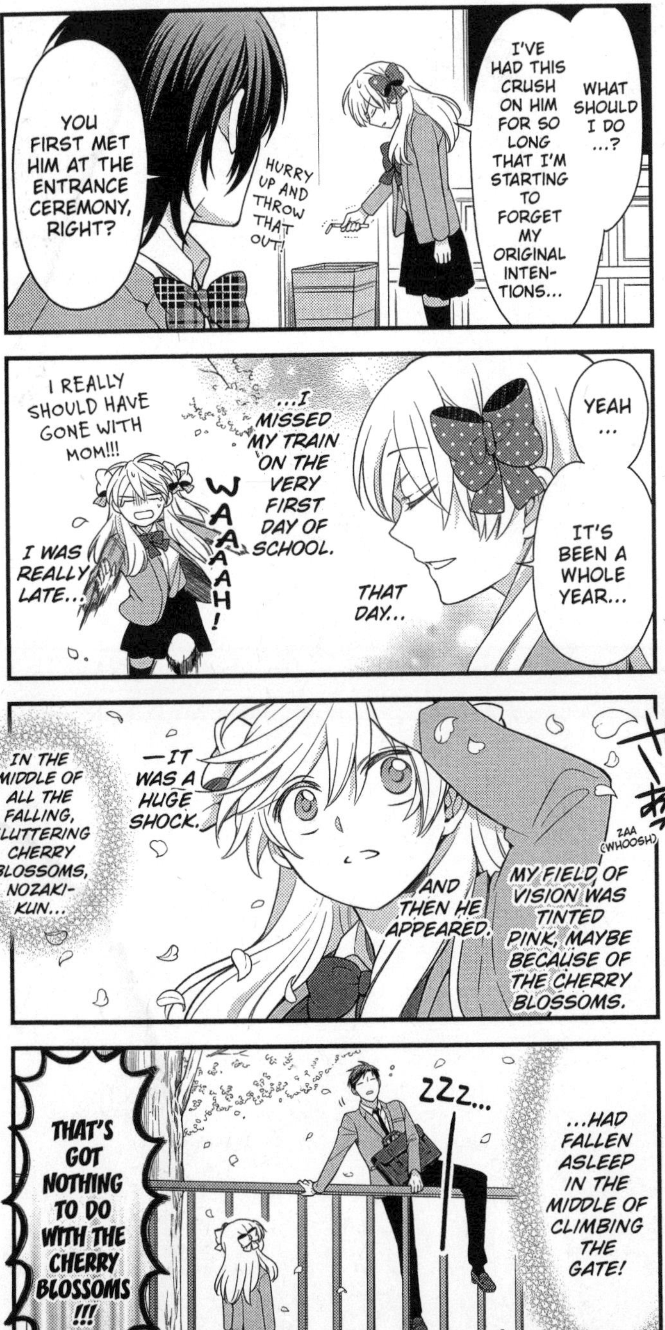
I'VE HAD THIS CRUSH ON HIM FOR SO LONG THAT I'M STARTING TO FORGET MY ORIGINAL INTEN-TIONS...
WHAT SHOULD I DO ...?
HURRY UP AND THROW THAT OUT!
YOU FIRST MET HIM AT THE ENTRANCE CEREMONY, RIGHT?
YEAH ...
IT'S BEEN A WHOLE YEAR...
THAT DAY...
...I MISSED MY TRAIN ON THE VERY FIRST DAY OF SCHOOL.
WAAAAAH!
I REALLY SHOULD HAVE GONE WITH MOM!!!
I WAS REALLY LATE...
ZAA (WHOOSH)
MY FIELD OF VISION WAS TINTED PINK, MAYBE BECAUSE OF THE CHERRY BLOSSOMS.
AND THEN HE APPEARED.
—IT WAS A HUGE SHOCK.
IN THE MIDDLE OF ALL THE FALLING, FLUTTERING CHERRY BLOSSOMS, NOZAKI-KUN...
...HAD FALLEN ASLEEP IN THE MIDDLE OF CLIMBING THE GATE!
ZZZ...
THAT'S GOT NOTHING TO DO WITH THE CHERRY BLOSSOMS!!!

HOLDING THEM IN BOTH ARMS

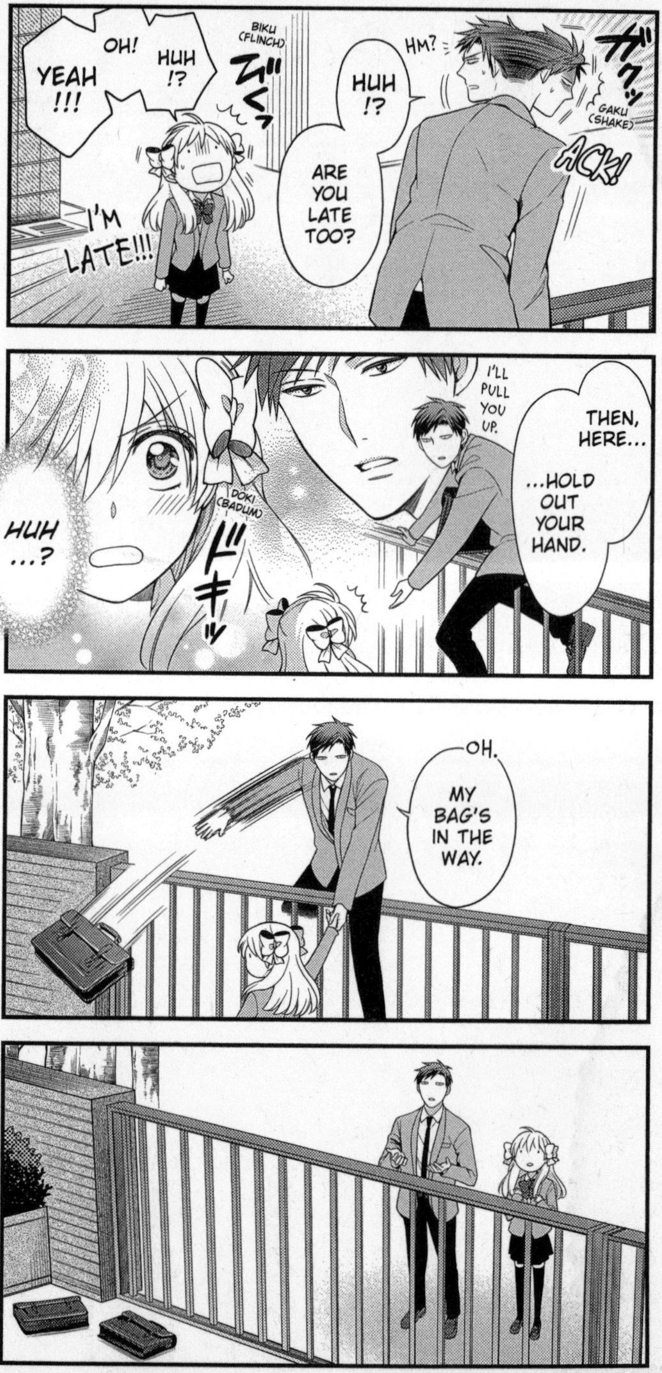
ガクッ
GAKU (SHAKE)
ACK!
HM?
HUH !?
ARE YOU LATE TOO?
BIKU (FLINCH)
びくっ
HUH !?
OH!
YEAH !!!
I'M LATE!!!
I'LL PULL YOU UP.
THEN, HERE...
...HOLD OUT YOUR HAND.
DOKI (BADUM)
ドキッ
HUH ...?
OH.
MY BAG'S IN THE WAY.

MESSED-UP ORDER

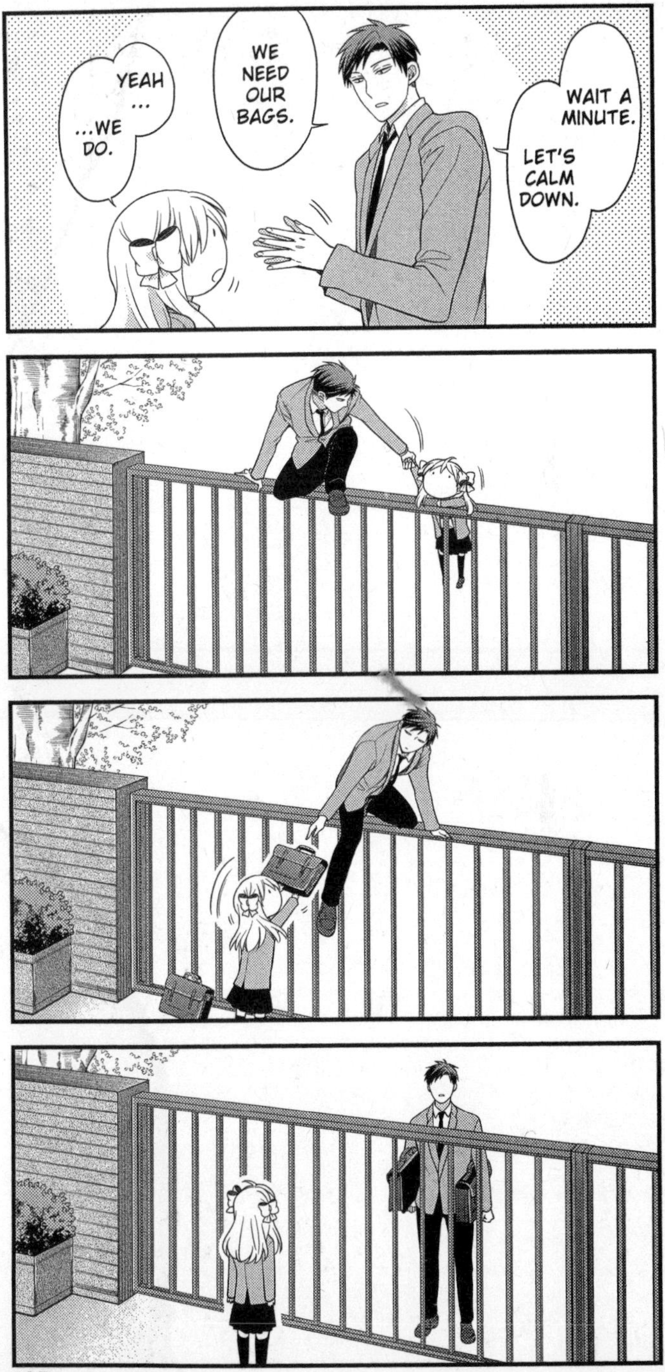
WAIT A MINUTE.
LET'S CALM DOWN.
WE NEED OUR BAGS.
YEAH... ...WE DO.

GO BACK TO THE START

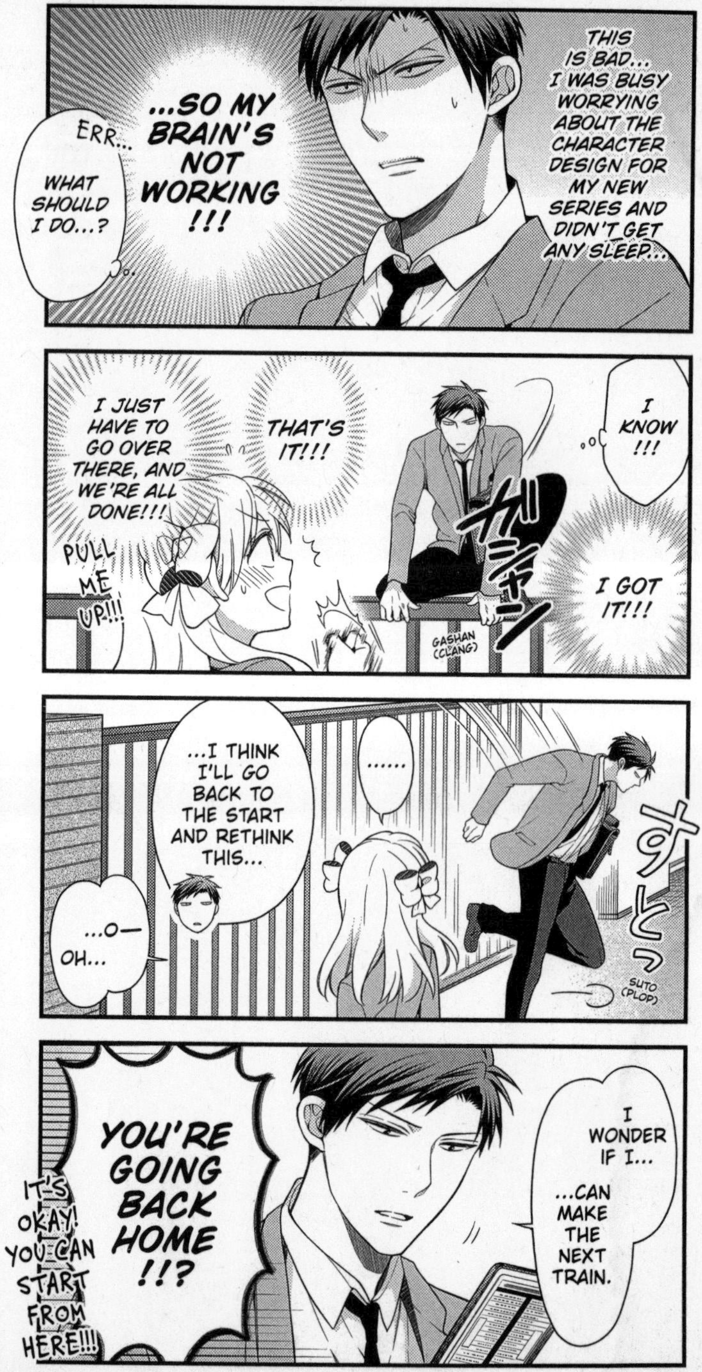

THIS IS BAD... I WAS BUSY WORRYING ABOUT THE CHARACTER DESIGN FOR MY NEW SERIES AND DIDN'T GET ANY SLEEP...
...SO MY BRAIN'S NOT WORKING!!!
ERR...
WHAT SHOULD I DO...?
I KNOW!!!
I GOT IT!!!
GASHAN (CLANG)
THAT'S IT!!!
I JUST HAVE TO GO OVER THERE, AND WE'RE ALL DONE!!!
PULL ME UP!!!
SUTO (PLOP)
......
...I THINK I'LL GO BACK TO THE START AND RETHINK THIS...
...O—OH...
I WONDER IF I...
...CAN MAKE THE NEXT TRAIN.
YOU'RE GOING BACK HOME!!?
IT'S OKAY! YOU CAN START FROM HERE!!!

A DANGEROUS PRINCE

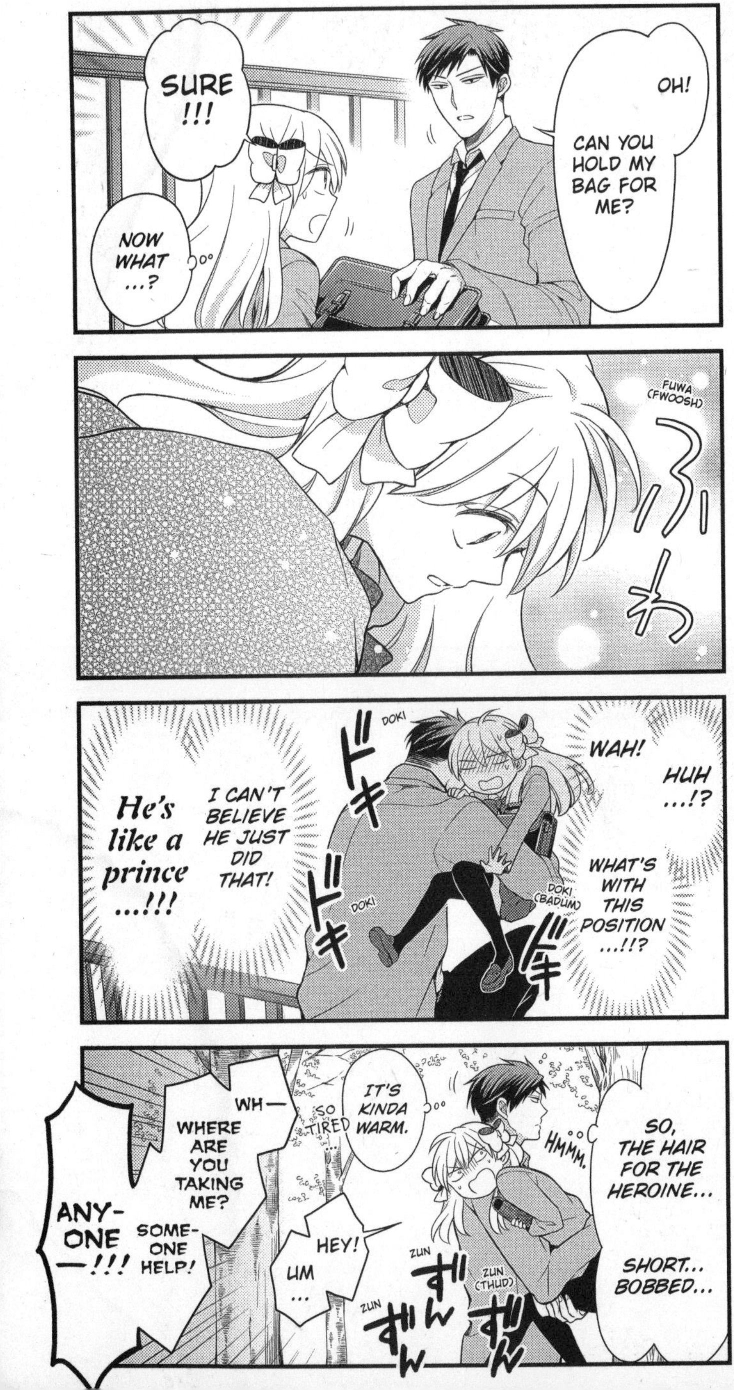
OH!
CAN YOU HOLD MY BAG FOR ME?
SURE!!!
NOW WHAT...?
FUWA (FWOOSH)
ふわ
WAH!
HUH...!?
WHAT'S WITH THIS POSITION...!!?
DOKI (BADUM)
ドキ
DOKI
ドキ
DOKI
ドキ
I CAN'T BELIEVE HE JUST DID THAT!
He's like a prince...!!!
SO, THE HAIR FOR THE HEROINE...
SHORT... BOBBED...
HMMM.
ZUN (THUD)
ずん
ZUN
ずん
ZUN
ずん
IT'S KINDA WARM.
SO TIRED...
HEY!
UM...
WH— WHERE ARE YOU TAKING ME?
SOME-ONE HELP!
ANY-ONE—!!!

FRIGHTENING NOZAKI-KUN

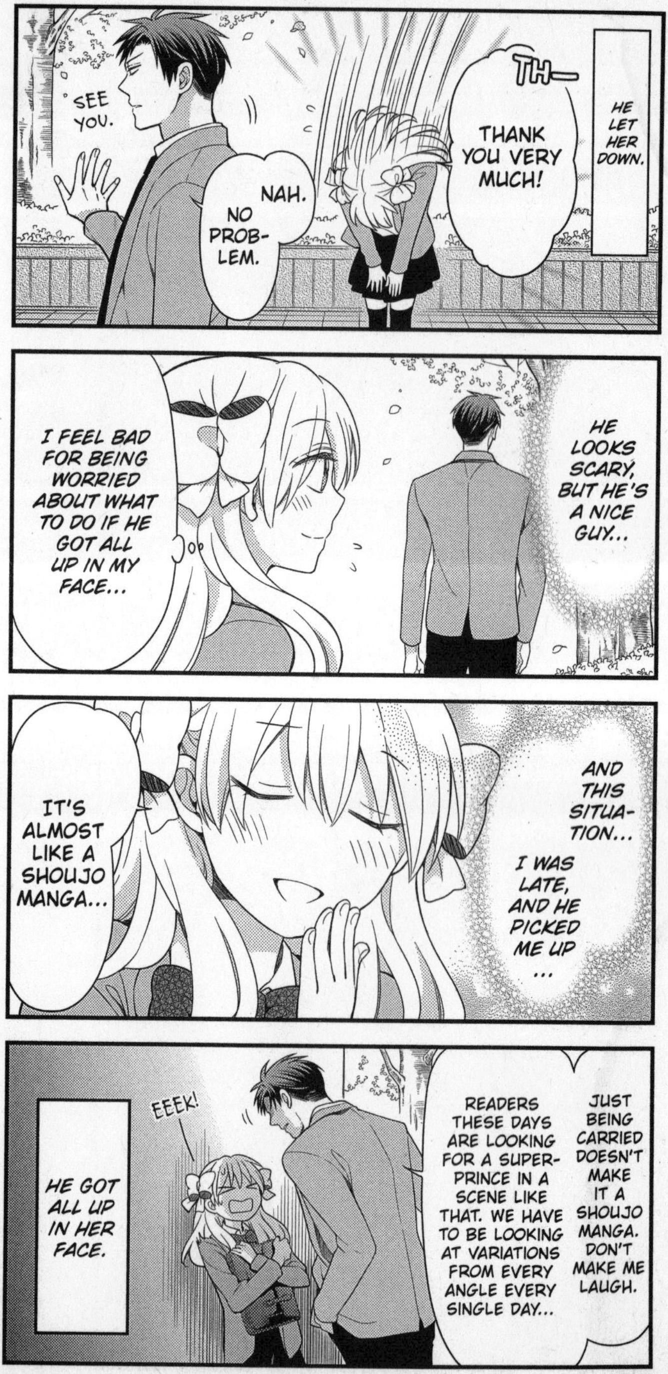
HE LET HER DOWN.
TH— THANK YOU VERY MUCH!
NAH. NO PROB-LEM.
SEE YOU.
HE LOOKS SCARY, BUT HE'S A NICE GUY...
I FEEL BAD FOR BEING WORRIED ABOUT WHAT TO DO IF HE GOT ALL UP IN MY FACE...
AND THIS SITUA-TION...
I WAS LATE, AND HE PICKED ME UP ...
IT'S ALMOST LIKE A SHOUJO MANGA...
JUST BEING CARRIED DOESN'T MAKE IT A SHOUJO MANGA. DON'T MAKE ME LAUGH.
READERS THESE DAYS ARE LOOKING FOR A SUPER-PRINCE IN A SCENE LIKE THAT. WE HAVE TO BE LOOKING AT VARIATIONS FROM EVERY ANGLE EVERY SINGLE DAY...
EEEK!
HE GOT ALL UP IN HER FACE.

THE REASON'S EXACTLY THE SAME

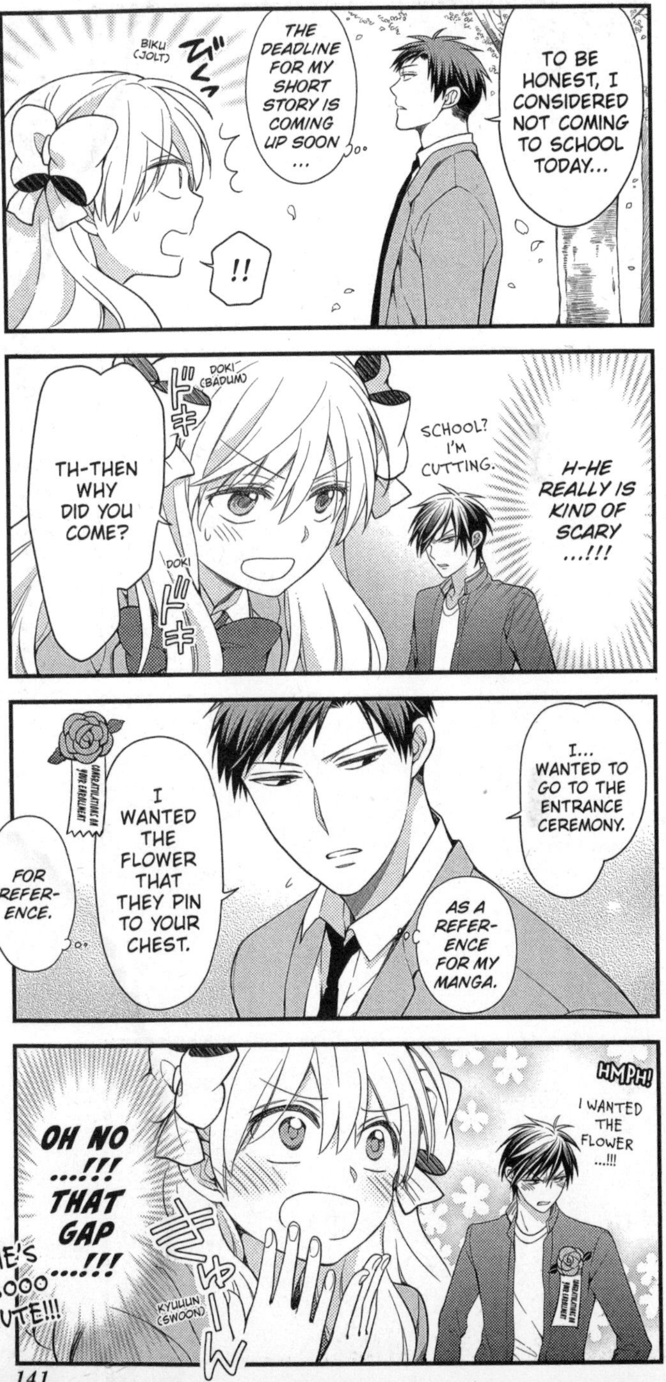
TO BE HONEST, I CONSIDERED NOT COMING TO SCHOOL TODAY...
THE DEADLINE FOR MY SHORT STORY IS COMING UP SOON ...
BIKU (JOLT)
!!
H-HE REALLY IS KIND OF SCARY ...!!!
SCHOOL? I'M CUTTING.
DOKI (BADUM)
TH-THEN WHY DID YOU COME?
DOKI
I... WANTED TO GO TO THE ENTRANCE CEREMONY.
AS A REFERENCE FOR MY MANGA.
I WANTED THE FLOWER THAT THEY PIN TO YOUR CHEST.
CONGRATULATIONS ON YOUR ENROLLMENT
FOR REFERENCE.
HMPH!
I WANTED THE FLOWER ...!!!
OH NO !!! ....!?! THAT GAP ....!!!
KYUUUN (SWOON)
HE'S SOOO CUTE!!!

IT'S ALL A BLUR

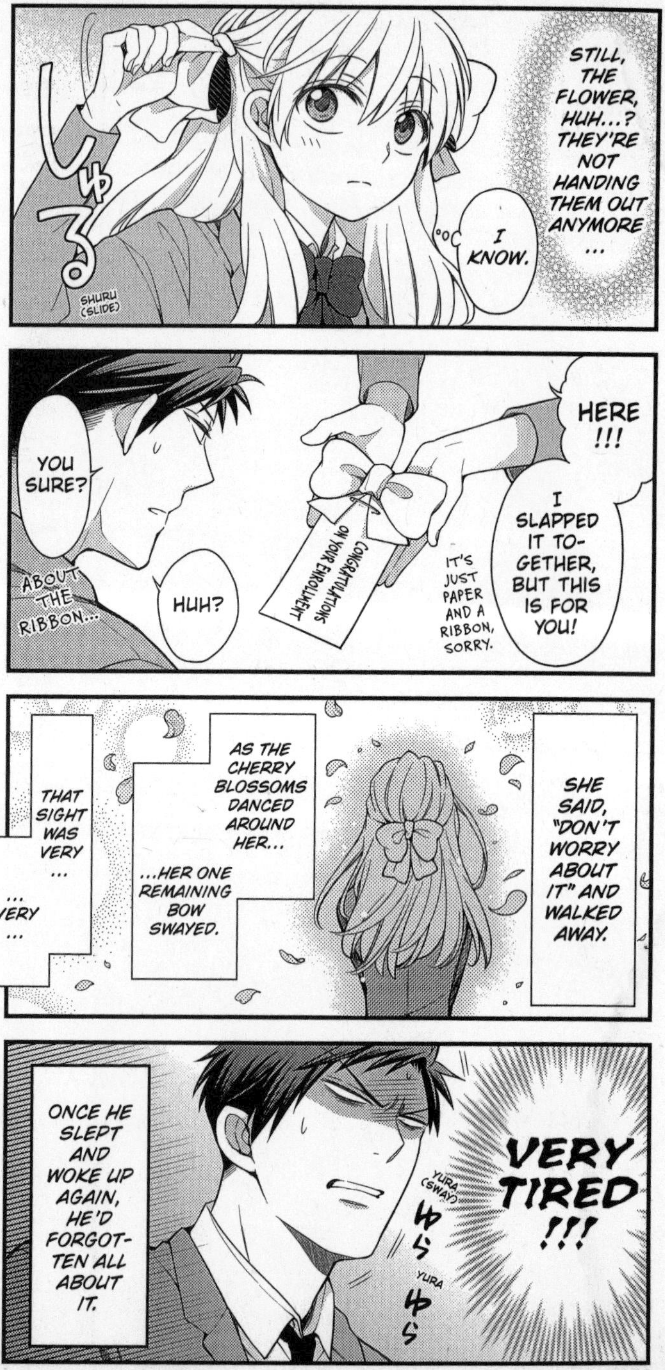
STILL, THE FLOWER, HUH...? THEY'RE NOT HANDING THEM OUT ANYMORE...
I KNOW.
しゅる
SHURU (SLIDE)
HERE!!!
I SLAPPED IT TO-GETHER, BUT THIS IS FOR YOU!
IT'S JUST PAPER AND A RIBBON, SORRY.
CONGRATULATIONS ON YOUR ENROLLMENT
HUH?
YOU SURE?
ABOUT THE RIBBON...
SHE SAID, "DON'T WORRY ABOUT IT" AND WALKED AWAY.
AS THE CHERRY BLOSSOMS DANCED AROUND HER...
...HER ONE REMAINING BOW SWAYED.
THAT SIGHT WAS VERY...
...VERY...
VERY TIRED!!!
YURA (SWAY)
ゆら
YURA
ゆら
ONCE HE SLEPT AND WOKE UP AGAIN, HE'D FORGOT-TEN ALL ABOUT IT.

THE INFLUENCE OF THAT DAY

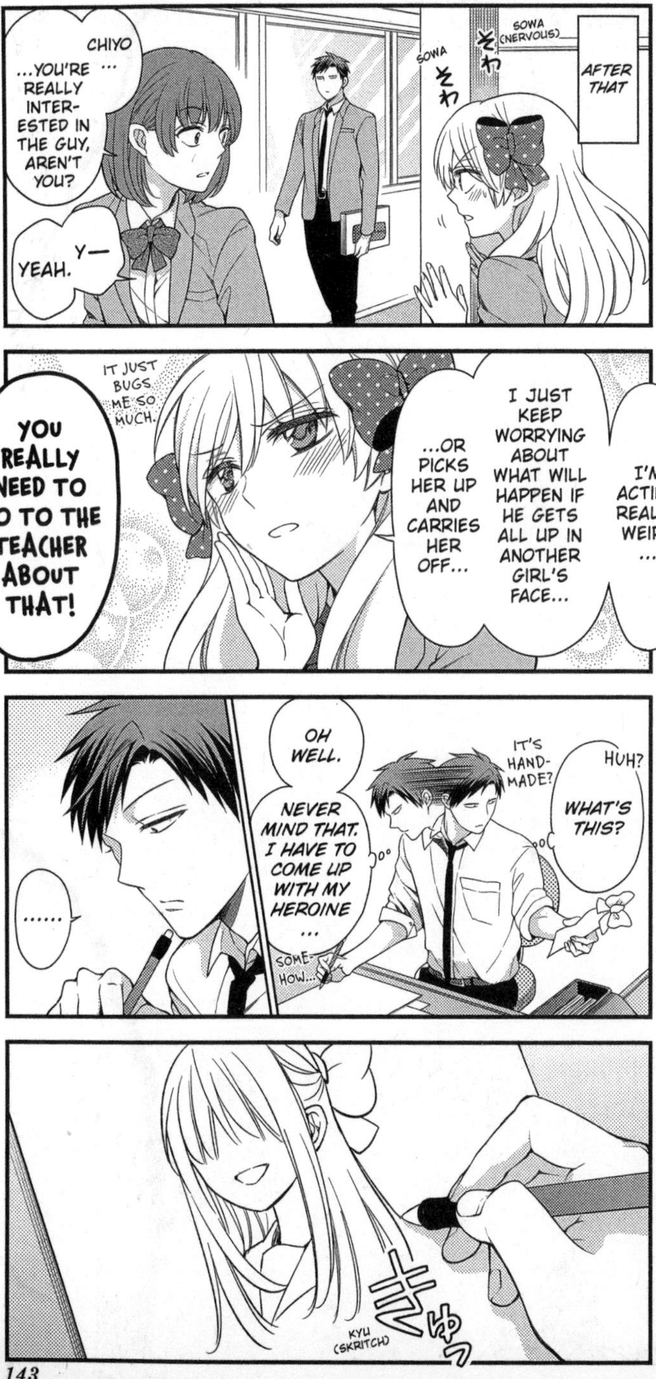
AFTER THAT
SOWA (NERVOUS)
SOWA
CHIYO …YOU'RE REALLY INTERESTED IN THE GUY, AREN'T YOU?
Y— YEAH.
I'M ACTING REALLY WEIRD …
I JUST KEEP WORRYING ABOUT WHAT WILL HAPPEN IF HE GETS ALL UP IN ANOTHER GIRL'S FACE…
…OR PICKS HER UP AND CARRIES HER OFF…
IT JUST BUGS ME SO MUCH.
YOU REALLY NEED TO GO TO THE TEACHER ABOUT THAT!
HUH?
WHAT'S THIS?
IT'S HAND-MADE?
OH WELL.
NEVER MIND THAT. I HAVE TO COME UP WITH MY HEROINE …
SOME-HOW…
……
KYU (SKRITCH)

SHE SAW REALITY

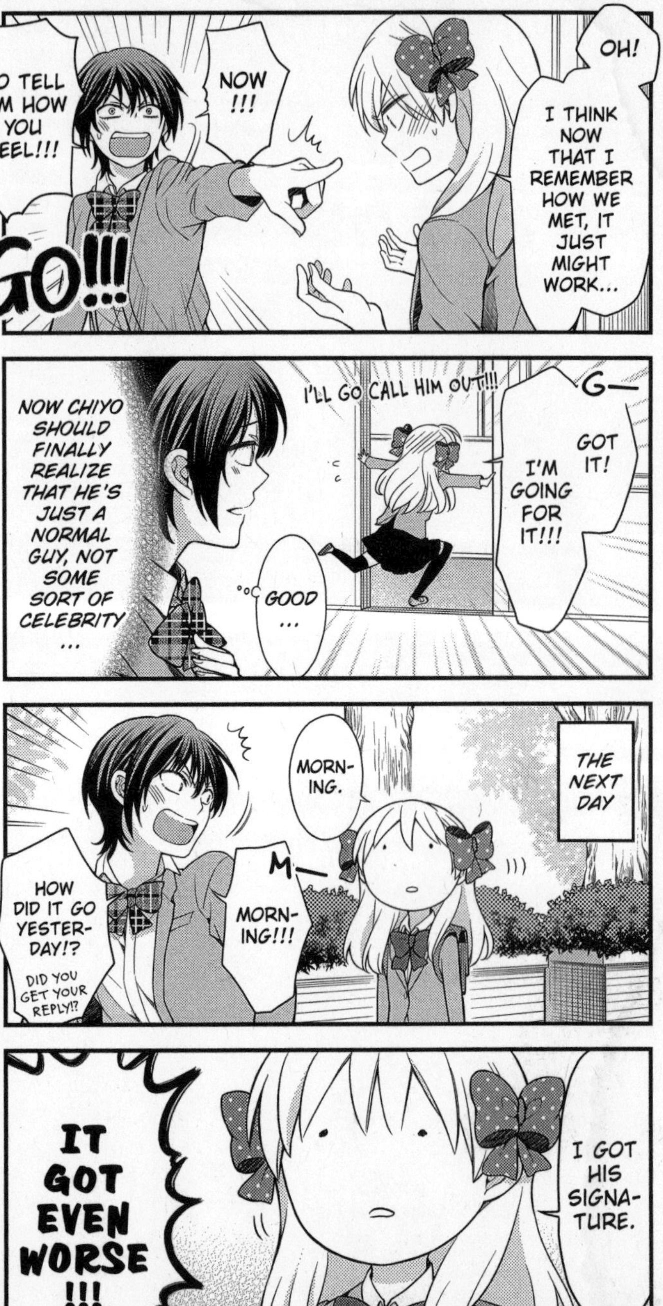
OH!
I THINK NOW THAT I REMEMBER HOW WE MET, IT JUST MIGHT WORK...
NOW!!!
GO TELL HIM HOW YOU FEEL!!!
GO!!!
G—
GOT IT!
I'M GOING FOR IT!!!
I'LL GO CALL HIM OUT!!!
GOOD...
NOW CHIYO SHOULD FINALLY REALIZE THAT HE'S JUST A NORMAL GUY, NOT SOME SORT OF CELEBRITY...
THE NEXT DAY
MORN-ING.
M—
MORN-ING!!!
HOW DID IT GO YESTER-DAY!?
DID YOU GET YOUR REPLY!?
I GOT HIS SIGNA-TURE.
IT GOT EVEN WORSE!!!

MONTHLY GIRLS' NOZAKI-KUN 5 END

SUBSEQUENT PROGRESS

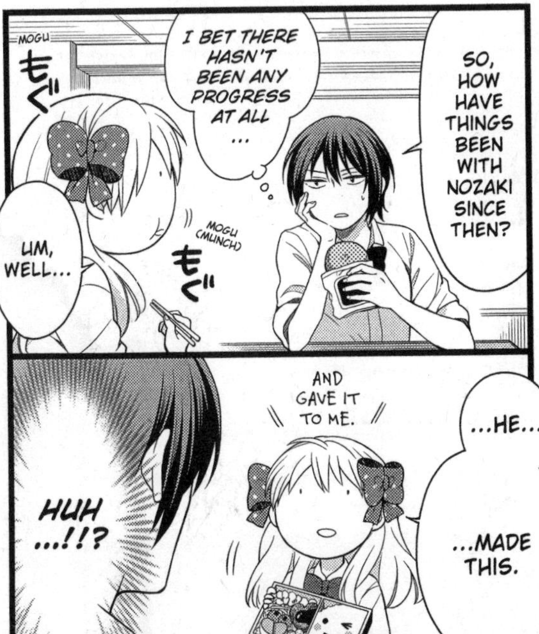
SO, HOW HAVE THINGS BEEN WITH NOZAKI SINCE THEN?
I BET THERE HASN'T BEEN ANY PROGRESS AT ALL ...
MOGU (MUNCH)
もぐ
MOGU
もぐ
UM, WELL...
...HE...
...MADE THIS.
AND GAVE IT TO ME.
HUH ...!!?

MONTHLY GIRLS' NOZAKI-KUN

Izumi Tsubaki

Translation: Leighann Harvey
Lettering: Lys Blakeslee

GEKKAN SHOJO NOZAKI KUN Volume 5 © 2014 Izumi Tsubaki / SQUARE ENIX CO., LTD. First published in Japan in 2014 by SQUARE ENIX CO., LTD. English translation rights arranged with SQUARE ENIX CO., LTD. and Yen Press, LLC through Tuttle-Mori Agency, Inc.

English translation © 2016 by SQUARE ENIX CO., LTD.

Yen Press

Library of Congress Control Number: 2015952610

ISBN: 978-0-316-39161-0 (paperback)

10 9 8 7 6 5 4 3 2 1

BVG

Printed in the United States of America